BULL IN
THE RING

JOE CASTELLANO

BULL IN THE RING

FOOTBALL AND FAITH

REFUGE IN A TROUBLED TIME

JALA
PUBLISHING

Bull in the Ring
Football and Faith – Refuge in a Troubled Time

Published by JALA Publishing
Publishing division of JALA Enterprises LLC
5520 Telegraph Road
Suite 202
St. Louis, MO 63129

Book and Cover Design:
Mark Arnold, andarnold.com
Andrew Arnold, Production

Additional copies:
www.Amazon.com
www.BullintheRingSTL.com
Selected bookstores

Paperback ISBN: 978-0-9992477-0-9

© 2017 by JALA Enterprises LLC

// Dedication

This book is a salute to the late Pat "Del" Bannister
and all my St. Louis U. High teammates and classmates,
all vital to the story but too numerous to describe;
to our coaches and teachers; and to the Jesuits,
whose selfless devotion to the academic, spiritual and athletic
development of their students prepared me for life.
I wrote this story for them.

Finally, I dedicate this to my family,
especially my late parents Jimmy and Leona,
my siblings, my kids and—
most especially—to my wife Lyn,
whose patience, encouragement, great judgment,
and love continue to inspire me.

// Acknowledgements

The dramatic story of the 1970 St. Louis University High School football season stayed dormant deep within me for the years I worked, first as a sportswriter, then as a businessman for almost four decades. When my career as a beer company executive ended in 2008, I had the time I would need to retreat into this story.

I am grateful that two dozen witnesses to the story—teammates, opponents, coaches, teachers, classmates, friends and alumni—were willing to sit with me and recall the joy, the angst, the pain of the experience we shared. I am especially grateful to teammates Tim Fleming and Tim Kellett for their sharp memories and insights, as they read several drafts and offered invaluable contributions. I would not have proceeded without a nod from Rev. Jack Warner, S.J., the Jesuit priest who was my first and best writing coach, who said this story was worth telling. A lifelong friend, Jack provided much needed and appreciated manuscript mending along the way.

I am also grateful to Rob Rains, Bob Costas, Henry Jones, David Laughlin, Mike Jones, Rob Wilson, Jack Dougherty, Frank Pawloski, Mike Weinberg, Tom Nolan, Tom Townsend, and Christopher Kellett for their encouragement and guidance.

I was fortunate to have the historical record provided by the 8-millimeter game films Coach Paul Martel used to critique our performances; a multitude of newspaper clippings from the era, with special thanks to the *St. Louis Post-Dispatch* and *St. Louis Globe-Democrat*; a recording of the 1970 Halloween Night SLUH-Althoff game done by WIBV Radio in Belleville, Illinois; and the memories and photos in the St. Louis U. High Class of 1971 yearbook.

// Contents

Foreword   *XIII*

Prologue   *1*

PART I: A TROUBLED TIME

1   Covering Everything *9*

2   Going to State *12*

3   Change the World *17*

4   The "Black Robes" *19*

5   A Season Ruined *23*

6   Union of North and South *28*

7   Crazy Joe *33*

8   "Part of a Greater Organism" *38*

9   "He Was My Hero" *42*

10 Thoughts of the War *44*

11 Getting Involved *46*

12 Black in America *50*

13 "Whites Live Yet Blacks Die!" *55*

14 "How Does It Feel To Be A Nigger Lover?" *57*

15 The Roy Rogers Hotel in Springfield *59*

16 "They Always Tried To Reach High" *60*

17 "Will You Be a Championship Team?" *63*

18 "Keep Refilling the Glasses" *68*

19 "We Were Invincible" 73

20 "You Got the Time?" 77

21 "When Are We Going To Have Our Meeting?" 79

22 A Price Way Too Steep 82

23 One Lap Short 83

24 "Has Anybody Here Seen My Old Friend Ed?" 86

25 "Think About Your Ring" 91

PART II: REFUGE

26 "Around Here We Shower *After* Practice" 97

27 50½ Players on the Roster 100

28 Captain Jim Castellano 103

29 "Talk about Embarrassing Moments" 104

30 "Did You Sell Your House Yet?" 106

31 "Blocking Is Generally Weak" 108

32 "I Didn't Know Where It Came From" 114

33 "Whaddaya Gonna Do?" 121

34 Bring on the State Champions! 124

35 "Joe, What Do I Need To Know?" 131

36 "Babe, If It Was Up To Me, You Would Have Played" 136

37 Thorough and Convincing 140

38 Dominant 148

39 A Training Table Delicacy 154

40 Inspiring a Lasting Commitment to Service 156

41 Divine Intervention 162

42 Homecoming 168

43 Dream Game 173

44 A Sense of Community 176

45 In Trouble 179

46 Driven Hard into History 182

47 "Whatever You Do, Don't Run the Ball" 187

48 Give It To Ziegler 191

Photos

PART III: TO STATE AND BEYOND

49   We're Not Finished Yet *201*

50   It's Up To Us *203*

51   Bring on the Sophomore *205*

52   "We Knew They Ran a Lot" *211*

53   Here We Go Again *215*

54   Back in the Game *216*

55   A Strange Confidence *220*

56   Momentum *221*

57   It Was Our Time *223*

58   "You're Ziegler, Aren't You?" *228*

59   "We Won It with You Guys" *230*

60   Great Men of Influence *232*

61   More Football *241*

62   Beyond Football *245*

63   "I Didn't Get the Chance To Say Good-Bye" *251*

64   "An Island of Purpose" *253*

65   A September to December to Remember *259*

66   "She Understands" *265*

Endnotes *269*

About the Author

// *Foreword*

DAVID SHAW HAS REFERRED TO Stanford University football as "intellectual brutality." He played there as a wide receiver in the early 1990s, then went on to succeed Jim Harbaugh as head coach in 2011. "Intellectual brutality" is a strong way to say it, but I think that is awesome. You think of Stanford football, you think of smart guys who line up against you and play relentlessly.

I like to think of St. Louis U. High like that. Coach Paul Martel always scheduled the biggest, strongest, toughest teams in the area. We were not afraid to play anybody. I really liked that about our school. Those teams always knew that when they played us,

Henry Jones and Coach Paul Martel

they were going to be playing a smart, well-coached team, that was going to be physical and tough, and came to play. I think "intellectual brutality" is a pretty good saying, and I'd like to associate that with SLUH football.

Joe Castellano has captured the spirit of St. Louis U. High football in this compelling story about the 1970 Junior Billiken season. It is inspiring to read his account of how kids from so many different backgrounds came together for a common purpose, especially as they were confronted by the turmoil and tragedy of the times. The story brought to my mind the wonderful time I had in high school, playing the game for the pure joy of it, and making lifelong friends through experiences well beyond the football field. Bull in the Ring is Joe's story of his experience at St. Louis U. High, but it is a universal story that should appeal to anyone.

His insightful description of the head coach we shared, 15 seasons apart, was so revealing. Coach Martel could be tough, but his coaching genius had us well prepared for every opponent, and he cared about developing us as men beyond football.

In reading this story, I was reminded once again of just how difficult it is to win the ultimate championship. We came up a little short of winning a state title when I was there, but I do not remember one bad day. It was just so much fun playing ball at SLUH. I am grateful to Coaches Martel and Gary Kornfeld, and all my coaches, teammates and classmates for helping to make it such a great experience. It helped me in my career, to instill in me a love for football, and to have the personal success I enjoyed.

—*Henry Jones*

Note: *After graduating from St. Louis U. High in 1986, Henry Jones became an All-American at the University of Illinois. In 1991, he was a first-round draft choice of the NFL's Buffalo Bills, where he became an All-Pro safety and played on three Super Bowl teams. Among the wide receivers he defended were Jerry Rice, Michael Irvin, Mark Duper, Mark Clayton, and Marvin Harrison.*

// *Prologue*

December 2013

PAT BANNISTER'S HEAD stretched slightly to the right; his frail, 61-year-old body lay motionless in the railed bed at Barnes Hospital. His eyes were closed, and it is unclear whether or not he was aware I was there, on Christmas Eve 2013. Cancer had metastasized, and in its relentless march to end his life, it had invaded his brain. I had to get there fast, to tell this man I had known like a brother for more than 55 years that I loved him.

Just hours earlier, to test his acuity, Pat's attending physician had asked him to name the President. "You mean of 'The U High?'" Pat had replied.

His answer said as much about what Pat Bannister had come to value, as it did about the sharpness of his faculties. By "the U High," he meant St. Louis University High School, or SLUH, the institution in the central west end of the City of St. Louis from which he and I had graduated in 1971. Four years prior, at age 14, I had endeavored to gain admission to St. Louis U. High because my older brother Jim was a student there, and because Pat Bannister was going to go there, just as his three older brothers and his father had gone there before us. Pat and I became men together at that school. We created bonds with classmates that have endured for our lifetimes.

I had known Pat since we were five-year-olds in kindergarten at the Epiphany of Our Lord Catholic grade school in south St. Louis, in a quiet neighborhood unthreatened by violence, wealth or pretension. Common in the Epiphany parish were large families, five children or more, with mothers who stayed home to tend to the children and fathers who worked in small businesses, the trade unions, or civil service. Mike Shannon came from one of those families, and went on to more than five decades with the St. Louis Cardinals, the first as a championship player; the last four as a beloved broadcaster. Francis Slay came from one of those families, and went on to become the longest-serving Mayor in the history of the City of St. Louis. Pat Bannister was the sixth of the seven children of Irene and Del Bannister, a proud Irishman who served as the City of St. Louis Collector of Revenue in the 1950s. Pat and I became friends in 1958, fast and forever, and spent the next 13 years going to school together every day.

After separating to attend different colleges, he first at Rockhurst in Kansas City then later at St. Louis University, I at Northwestern in Evanston, Illinois, we reunited to share a rent-subsidized apartment in St. Louis for a couple years in the mid-1970s.

In the first grade, when given the opportunity to add a Christian name to commemorate the Catholic sacrament of Confirmation, the two of us conspired to entwine our best friendship forever. Thus, he became Patrick Michael *Joseph* Bannister, and I became Joseph Patrick *Michael* Castellano. At seven years old, we were true friends indeed.

In the summer between second and third grade, Pat and I and other kids from Epiphany took a bus to swimming lessons at a forlorn city public facility on South Broadway called Downs Pool. I recall cutting the bottoms of my feet on the rough, chipped concrete surface at the bottom of that pool. For us, though, this was a beloved luxury, and a chance for relief from the oppressive St. Louis summer. The sound of Freddy "Boom Boom" Cannon blaring the pop hit *Palisades Park*[1] over the pool's creaky sound system, the sharp smell of chlorine and grilled meat, the adventure of an experience beyond the boundaries of our neighborhood … that memory of youthful innocence remains a sweet one.

I do not recall feeling particularly underprivileged, though I guess I envied the kids whose parents gave them money to buy a hamburger or hot dog after swimming lessons. I felt entrepreneurial, not ashamed, as I quenched my hunger by lapping up some of the condiment table's free mustard that I had squirted directly into my hand. A tasty treat. In fact, an objective observer likely would have declared that version of me incapable of shame, had he witnessed an incident after one particular day at swimming lessons.

Pat Bannister had a family commitment that day and was dismissed early when his Dad arrived to pick him up. Later, the lesson over and Pat long gone, I opened the small locker we shared, prepared to change from my swimming trunks into my dry clothes, and was troubled by what I saw: Pat's underwear briefs, a different brand and at least one size larger than mine. No sign of my own. Quickly concluding Pat mistakenly had taken my underwear, and without for one minute even considering the option of traveling home "commando," I simply put on Pat's briefs, then the rest of my clothes, and headed for the bus for the ride home. Later, we made the exchange of undergarments, after our mothers dutifully laundered them. Well, yes, now it sounds creepy, but those were not sensibilities I had developed as an eight-year-old boy. Thankfully, our mothers never spoke of the incident.

In the fifth grade, we had a dedicated teacher who introduced us to the concept of pursuing our *Castles in Spain*, something Henry David Thoreau and others have referred to, over the years, as having grand dreams. Mrs.

Theresa Mitchell challenged us to write an essay describing our dreams for the future. On lined graph paper in handsome cursive penmanship, dated February 26, 1964, the 11-year-old Pat Bannister had declared his ambition to some day become President of the United States.

> *I hope that the future holds for me a life of politics. First I want to become a lawyer, then a judge, then Governor of Missouri, then a Senator from the State of Missouri. Then, if it is God's will, the President of the United States. I am so hopeful and sure that I will win the election, that next week I will start writing my Inaugural Address.*

I thought of that essay as I watched Pat's earthly life slipping away. I thought of our lives together, of ambitions realized, of others altered or unfulfilled. I thought of how much the world had changed since we first became aware of it in the mid-1950s. And of how much it had stayed the same. I touched Pat's arm, and encouraged him to get well so we could go out and get a beer together. Just like always. I realized later I said that for me, much more than for him.

The next day, as the world's Christians celebrated Christmas and much of the world took the day off from work, I went back to Barnes Hospital. Quietly, I said good-bye to my lifelong friend. He died the next day.

I reflect now on how it was that Pat Bannister evolved in 50 years from wanting to be President of the United States, to concluding his life more focused on the high school he had attended. There was something special about that school, about that time in our lives, about that time in history, that embedded in our skins, our hearts, our souls. While significant U.S. and world history were being made at a seemingly unprecedented pace, my St. Louis U. High classmates and I were holding on for dear life … spooked by some of that history; largely unaware of most of it. We were just kids, like all kids looking for their place.

Infused with the hubris of teenage boys, for whom the development of our bodies far outpaced that of our minds, self-awareness or judgment, we traveled fearlessly forward on our journey through adolescence. Encouraged to feel privileged by virtue of our acceptance into St. Louis U. High, the prestigious all-boys academy that annually was able to select from an aspiring group of applicants from among the community's eighth graders, we expected that life held something special for us.

Dick Keefe was a teacher and administrator at St. Louis U. High for 43 years. He started at the school the same year my classmates and I started, in the late summer of 1967, and has retained a fondness for our class. He recalled that our school theater group staged the musical, *The Fantasticks*[2] , during our senior year. "That play was a metaphor for your class," he said. Written by Tom Jones and Harvey Schmidt, the innovative musical debuted in May of 1960 at the Sullivan Street Playhouse in Greenwich Village, and ran there for 42 years. Jack Warner, a young teacher and Jesuit scholastic in training to be a priest, directed the production at SLUH during the fall of 1970, while my teammates and I were beating our brains out on the football field. Early in Act I, Luisa sings:

I'm sixteen years old,
And every day something happens to me.
Oh! Oh! Oh!
I hug myself till my arms turn blue,
Then I close my eyes and I cry and cry
Till the tears come down
And I taste them. Ah!
I love to taste my tears!
I am special!
I am special!
Please, God, please! Don't – let – me – be – normal!

Holy crap, it's hard to accept that we could have been that insufferably self-indulgent. That number was not what prompted Keefe to cite the musical as a metaphor for our class, but SLUH boys throughout the years probably have earned our reputation for having an elevated opinion of ourselves. Early in his career, the young Keefe had been advised by a veteran school administrator: "The students that come to St. Louis U. High pretty much all come in with a strong self-image." Keefe recalls the advice that followed that understatement: "You have to deal with that."

Still, for our particular class, the Class of 1971, whatever confidence we started with would be battered by a relentless assault of obstacles, seemingly one after another, as we pursued the fulfillment of our expectations. As in *The Fantasticks*, our story featured friction between the generations and the erosion of youthful innocence. These were the themes Keefe had in mind when he made the connection.

This is the story of how this group of young men navigated a course that whipsawed us between the treacherous and frivolous, how we sought both relevance and fun in a rapidly changing world, and how we ultimately stumbled onto a most unlikely achievement in the autumn of 1970. Inclined to think we were on our own, we pulled together like an abandoned *Lord of the Flies* experiment gone well, and found ourselves competing for a football championship few thought we were capable of winning, or that we deserved.

The journey to that achievement, likely much more than the result itself, would affect many of those young men for the rest of their lives.

PART I

A TROUBLED TIME

1// *Covering Everything*

November 1970

THE WORDS KEPT COMING, wafting over a deliberate monotone most likely designed to convey a tone of seriousness the topic did not quite deserve. "The bus will take us straight to the hotel," said Coach Paul Martel. "There, we will be dropped off, and we will check into our rooms."

Bob Thibaut, a team captain who was finishing his third season under the coach's leadership, rolled his eyes, knowing too well what was in store for us over the next few minutes.

It was unclear on that frosty Thanksgiving Day morning in the late fall of 1970, and has remained largely unclear decades later, why Coach Martel regarded it necessary to recite the logistics of our travel plans to Columbia, Missouri, for the state championship football game, in such agonizing detail, right then and there on the miserable school practice field, as 50 members of the St. Louis University High School Junior Billikens team focused mostly on potential remedies for frostbite.

"We will have lights out at 10 p.m. In the morning, it will be a bacon and eggs situation."

A "bacon and eggs situation"?! Coach was making breakfast sound like a strategic military operation.

I caught the eye of Tim Kellett, our starting offensive left tackle, and we strained to keep from laughing. Thibaut, Kellett and I had spent the previous summer getting paid to deliver rented tables, chairs and party supplies to St. Louis County public high schools and the homes of wealthy St. Louis families who lived in mansions in our community's toniest neighborhoods. During those suffocating tropical days we mostly laughed, and did not think much of our chances for a state football title.

No team in St. Louis U. High history had ever played a football game during the last week in November. Therefore, it was likely that no team in school history had ever been asked to endure a practice in the frigid, windy conditions of the "lower field," as a St. Louis autumn was feebly yielding to the roar of the coming winter.

"OK, men, let's huddle up over here," Coach Martel had called out, and we were thankful we had survived the last full practice of the 1970 season.

Soon, we knew, we would peel off for the last time the stained, remarkably durable practice football trousers we had worn on about 80 of the previous 110 days. For most of us, the stains from mud, sweat, blood, and God knows what other human effluence survived the mere six or eight encounters with a washing machine during the season. These pants, which compressed the legs and posteriors of the young men who had worn them from August 15 through the end of November, likely could have taken the field on their own, empty of human flesh, and given some of the lesser teams on the SLUH schedule a competitive game. It would be good to shed these stinking pants for the last time.

Of course, Coach Paul Martel had details to convey. "You should pack a toothbrush and toothpaste," he went on.

Cripes, it was freezing. As several players had done, our star linebacker and running back Bill Ziegler had covered the ear holes of his helmet with athletic adhesive tape, to block the blasting wind from entering. Some of us improvised to turn blue fingers back to their normal color. As the starting center, I would need fully functional fingers to grip the football for snaps to the quarterback. I cupped them in front of my mouth, and emptied my lungs of hot air, and that seemed to help. Dan Calacci, whose hands were perhaps the most important on the team, jammed them down the front of his pants. Our quarterback, Calacci had to have full use of his palms and digits if we were to stand a chance in the championship game against the bigger, faster, favored, undefeated Kansas City Center High Yellowjackets.

Most of us bounced up and down, hoping our extremities would get the message that we were still faintly alive. At least Errol Patterson, our star receiver and defensive back, was prepared for the cold weather—he was snug in the long underwear he had procured and worn in our triumphant state tournament semifinal game the previous Saturday. Fortunately, for reasons we were to find out much later, he already had decided *against* wearing them in the championship game on the upcoming Saturday afternoon.

It was at a different one of these post-practice gatherings that the legend of Paul Martel had grown a somewhat rare humorous tributary. While engaged in one of his customary soliloquies about one arcane football concept or another, Coach Martel absent-mindedly put his embered pipe into his pocket. A moment or two later, as smoke began to emerge from near his hip, he scrambled to extinguish the thing as members of the team looked on in awe. On this particular day, I suppose, we would have welcomed a little flame of our own down there.

After nearly 25 minutes of the kind of attention to detail that made Paul Martel the successful mastermind of high school football that he surely was, with the players mostly numb, Coach Martel turned to Ebbie Dunn, his lone assistant coach.

"Coach Dunn, you have anything to add?"

Ebbie Dunn, an Irishman whose substantial girth certainly gave him an advantage in staving off the cold but whose red face had shaded toward a crimson not often seen on a human being, was as cold as the rest of us. I clearly recall a tiny mucus bubble dangling from the tip of his nose, a snotsicle petrified like a stalactite from the frigid air. Often an advocate for the underdog, Coach Dunn delivered a remarkable understatement, a perfect line that clearly answered the question, but doubled to offer us oppressed victims a comic respite that I swear was needed to thaw us enough so we could commence trudging in to our locker room.

"No, Coach," Ebbie said, holding onto a dramatic pause for the perfect length of time. "I think you covered just about everything."

It was good to see Pat Bannister laugh at that. My neighbor and my closest friend since we first sat near each other in kindergarten in 1958, Bannister had not frozen to death, as I had feared.

2// *Going to State*

THE IDEA OF A PLAYOFF for the state high school football championship in Missouri was still something of a novelty in November of 1970. After decades without a means to declare an *official* state champion, the Missouri State High School Activities Association had inaugurated a post-season playoff tournament two seasons earlier. Of hundreds of high schools in the state, 16 would play beyond their regular seasons to compete for four state titles, one in each of four classifications based on the size of their student enrollment. McCluer High, a large public school in Ferguson, Missouri, one of the northern suburbs of St. Louis, had won the first two state titles in the Class 4A division, which was for the schools with the largest student enrollments.

Bursting at the seams with more than 4,000 post-World War II "baby boomers," many from blue-collar families who made their living in the big industrial plants that churned out automobiles, airplane engines and other rugged products that helped build a strong American middle class in the middle part of the 20th century, McCluer High seemed a fitting champion. One of those students was Michael McDonald, who entered with the Class of 1970 but left before graduation to pursue a career in music. He would earn fame as a vocalist, first for Steely Dan, then for the Doobie Brothers. It would be another year before the Ferguson-Florissant School District opened a second high school, McCluer North, to relieve the pressure of so many students on one campus.

To qualify for the state tournament, a school had to have competed, and won, against enough successful teams to generate sufficient "strength of schedule" points. When we defeated Riverview Gardens, like McCluer a team of tough young men from the Suburban North Conference in St. Louis, and completed a 9-1 regular season, we were a bit surprised to learn we had qualified for the playoff tournament, along with three other teams in the "large schools" division: Center High and Oak Park from Kansas City, and, in a strange twist, Riverview Gardens, the team we had just defeated to end the regular season and the team we would face again the very next Saturday in the state semifinals.

Why were we surprised? Well, St. Louis University High certainly had a rich tradition in sports, and the school had enjoyed many seasons of football excellence. However, SLUH's first loyalties were to academic excellence and the spiritual formation of its students. My senior year curriculum included Calculus, History of Western Civilization, Russian language, Physics, Advanced English, and Philosophy. By earning at least a "B" grade in the first three, I would be able to skip those classes in college, saving a full year of undergraduate work and the associated tuition costs. It was rigorous academic fare, but typical. Football players were not offered cupcake classes. Further, most of our players never played organized football until the day they stepped onto the SLUH practice field as freshmen, and on that day most of the players were meeting their classmates and teammates for the first time, since the school drew its students from the entire metropolitan St. Louis area—from more than 100 different grade schools. And with fewer than 900 students, SLUH was among the smallest of the schools competing in the Class 4A for large schools ... even compensating for the reasonable practice of doubling our enrollment number because we were a one-gender school.

Also, our team speed was just average and our size well below average, with the estimable Fred Daues, our starting defensive right tackle, the only player weighing more than 200 pounds. Remarkably, we gasped to the championship game having beaten our last four opponents by an average of just 4.5 points. Not exactly a fearsome juggernaut.

Finally, our class and team were infected with a collection of smart asses, Baby Boomers forming our identity as a generation which sort of believed the world had begun only a few years before we came along to enjoy it. During our junior year, our class was summoned to the gym for a special assembly, for which the school's Vice President for Academics had devised a scheme obviously designed to embarrass us.

"There are five students in the freshmen class in danger of failing classes this quarter," he started, fully in command of the room. "In the sophomore and senior classes, there are 10."

Pat Bannister and I had gone to the assembly together, and he sensed what was next. "Here it comes," Pat said. By this time, I should point out, Pat had become "Del" Bannister, the nickname we hung on him in honor of his father, Delbert Leo Bannister. By this time, his friends and even his family members called him Del. Del had a sense about things like this assembly, and he seemed to delight in what was coming next. The VP in charge did not disappoint us.

"Now, the junior class," he began, as he held up a printout on the prehistoric computer paper used at the time, the folded pleats of which he allowed to unfold dramatically downward, clearly conveying an unusually long list of names. Instead of hanging our heads in shame, as he might have anticipated or desired, we spontaneously rose and applauded, giving our academic indifference a standing ovation.

"I was probably on that list," recalled Phil Schaefer, a very good student who a few months later would be voted by our classmates as Treasurer of the Student Council for our senior year. "In families, there often is a dynamic in which there is one weak link, one problem child. I felt we probably were that class, though we weren't necessarily trying to be. I don't think the class ahead of, or the class behind us, pushed the edge the way our class did. I'm not sure why that was, or even if it's true, but that's the way it seemed to me. We were that class."

In *The Fantasticks*[3], the fathers Hucklebee and Bellomy lament the contrariness of the younger generation. Huck and Bell sing:

Dog's got to bark, a mule's got to bray.
Soldiers must fight and preachers must pray.
And children, I guess, must get their own way
The minute that you say no.

Why did the kids put beans in their ears?
No one can hear with beans in their ears.
After a while the reason appears.
They did it cause we said no.

With a seed of self-absorption, we the students at St. Louis U. High were nurtured to think for ourselves by the Jesuits, as the men of the Society of Jesus religious order are known. Indeed, many members of the football team had a vigorous disdain for authority of any kind, free spirits and free thinkers who were in open rebellion against established institutions, adults in general, and their parents in particular. Independent thinking is vital to a free society, of course, but it is not generally an asset for the sport of football, an endeavor in which teams exhibiting compliance, discipline, and synchronization of action generally prevail.

In many ways, our football experience reflected the tension of the anti-establishment battle being waged in the larger American society at the time. Many of us, infused with youthful rebellion, were frustrated by an authoritarian regime of adults on whom we were so dependent. We relied on the trappings their system had provided us, yet we desperately wanted to change that system and create our own way. The football field was an odd battleground for this generational fight, perhaps, but it did give us something concrete on which to forge our brotherhood and unity.

Our wonderment at the notion of St. Louis U. High in a football state championship game seems to have been borne out by subsequent history, as in the more than four decades since our serendipitous stroll into the state finals, only one other SLUH team ever made it that far. Those Junior Billikens lost their big game, 10-7, to Jefferson City High in 1991.

While I cannot say *all* my teammates were joyous that the finish line for the arduous football season had just been extended, meaning up to two more weeks of practice, most of us were excited at the opportunity for legacy. Del Bannister's three older brothers went through St. Louis U. High in the 1950s, during the seemingly worry-free Eisenhower years. To them, high school football was an important ritual, and through their influence Del had become imbued with the spirit of it all. Brainwashed, I guess one could say. His enthusiasm surely had influenced me. "Can you believe we're going to State?" he said to me. We had developed a reasonable sense of history, and we had a feeling this could be something very special. After all, we knew we were living in an interesting, volatile time, and it seemed somewhat fitting that we had been given the chance to make history.

3// *Change the World*

The 1960s

ON THE THRESHOLD OF ADULTHOOD, many of my classmates believed we were going to do something meaningful in a world freshly scarred by the assassination of our President, his brother, and the leader of the country's racial equality movement who advocated non-violent protest as the means to drive social change. Our view of the world was complicated by an increasingly murky war in the jungles of Southeast Asia, the bloody and surreal images of which came through the same TV sets in the same rooms where we had watched *Captain Kangaroo*, *The Three Stooges*, *Bonanza*, and *The Beatles* performing live on *The Ed Sullivan Show*.

Growing up in America in the 1960s, with television cameras providing us raw images long before our young minds had the chance to gain the wisdom of experience, and unfiltered by a historian's perspective, for better or for worse, we teenagers had been overdosing on the dramatic reality of life and death. Before we reached the age of 10, we had practiced for enemy air raids and nuclear holocaust, often wondering what would happen if we didn't race to our bomb shelters in time, or what we would do once we got there. In the fall of 1963, we tried to understand why the inspirational President John F. Kennedy could have his skull blown off in public, then we watched on live TV two days later when his alleged assassin was shot to death while being escorted down a hall by officers of the law in Dallas, Texas.

In 1968, when we were freshmen and sophomores in high school,

we learned of the assassinations of Dr. Martin Luther King Jr. and
U.S. Senator Bobby Kennedy, then of the riots at the Democratic Party
national convention in Chicago, then watched the election night returns in November as Richard M. Nixon narrowly defeated Hubert H.
Humphrey to become the 37th President of the United States. Earlier,
our St. Louis U. High student body had conducted a mock election,
which Humphrey won. That delighted Del Bannister and his politically
inclined family of loyal Democrats. Nixon generated substantial support,
and some even cast ballots for George Wallace, the American Independent Party candidate whose policies advocating racial segregation had
been rejected by the Democratic Party. In the real national election,
Wallace carried five Southern states. In our mock election, many of
us had written in the name of Gene McCarthy, the peace-advocating
candidate whose candidacy flame first flared then ultimately flickered
in the Democratic primaries.

President Lyndon B. Johnson had decided not to run for re-election in
1968, battered as he was by diminishing popularity associated with his
administration's conduct of the Vietnam War. By 1965, tens of thousands
of American combat troops had been deployed to Vietnam, and President Johnson had authorized a bombing campaign over North Vietnam
he thought would break the spirit and resolve of the North Vietnamese
people and their allies in South Vietnam, the Viet Cong. By January of
1967, there were 389,000 American troops deployed in Vietnam, about
one in three of whom had been drafted. At the height of the war in 1968,
there were almost 550,000 American troops in the small Asian country.

In the introduction to her book, *Witness to the Revolution*[4], published
in 2016, author Clara Bingham claims that in 1969-70, *"the sixties went
wide and the nation arguably came close to civil war."* In the book, she tells
the stories of 100 *"leaders and foot soldiers of the sixties peace movement,"*
based on interviews she conducted over three years, four decades after

"*the twelve months that changed the nation forever.*" She writes in the introduction, about the year from September 1969 to September 1970:

> *It is almost impossible to imagine the apocalyptic atmosphere of America in
> those months. From the start of the academic year in 1969 until the beginning
> of classes in September 1970, a youth rebellion shook the nation in ways we
> may never see again. It was the crescendo of the sixties, when years of civil
> disobedience and mass resistance erupted into anarchic violence. Hundreds
> of thousands of young Americans took to the streets in 1969 and 1970. They
> were fueled by marijuana, LSD, and rock and roll; inspired by third-world
> freedom revolutions of Che Guevera in Cuba and Ho Chi Minh in Vietnam;
> disillusioned by the assassinations of Martin Luther King, Jr., and Robert
> F. Kennedy; battered by the police at Berkeley, Chicago, and Columbia;
> and appalled by mounting U.S. casualties and images of napalm-disfigured
> Vietnamese civilians.*

It was this troubled world that many of us in the Class of 1971 wanted to change, stoked as we were, among other things, by what the Jesuit
faculty members were teaching us at St. Louis U. High.

4// *The "Black Robes"*

The 1500s / 1818

SLUH WAS FOUNDED IN 1818 as the *St. Louis Academy* by Louis William Valentine DuBourg, a Roman Catholic expatriate priest from France
who was the bishop of St. Louis. This Latin school for boys held classes
in a one-story house on Church Street, near the corner of Market Street
and Third Street, on what was then the westernmost border of St. Louis,

less than a mile west of the Mississippi River. Bishop DuBourg recruited priests from the Society of Jesus in Belgium to take on the management and teaching at the school.

In 1832, the institution was chartered as a university, and became St. Louis University. In 1888, the academy and university moved to a site on Grand Avenue. Finally, in 1924, the high school separated from the university and moved to Oakland Avenue just west of Kingshighway Boulevard, a few hundred yards south of Forest Park, in the City's central west end. It was built with funding from Anna F. Backer as a memorial to her late husband, George H. Backer, and became known as St. Louis University High School.

The Society of Jesus is a religious order of the Catholic Church established in the 1500s by Ignatius of Loyola in Spain. Saint Ignatius was an accomplished man of the world, an intellect, a warrior, and a lover of challenge whose pursuit of adventure was grounded on a battlefield in Pamplona in 1521 by a French military cannonball that shattered his leg. His companions carried him on a stretcher to his family's castle in Loyola, where they assumed he would die from his wounds.

By his own admission a man "given to the vanities of the world," Ignatius was determined to recover. It was said that he submitted to a series of operations, dubious in nature, in an attempt to conceal the grotesque distortion of his leg, so he would again look handsome in his leg tights. His leg never properly healed, and he walked with a limp the rest of his life.

As he began a nearly year-long convalescence, he hoped to pass the time by reading of the chivalrous adventures of noble knights, but the only literature available to him was spiritual fare, including a story about the life of Jesus Christ, and an account of the lives of the early saints of the Christian faith. During this time, Ignatius was transformed, and inspired to promulgate a process for transforming others.

Ignatius left the castle in 1522 to pursue his spiritual journey, first with a pilgrimage to a monastery in Montserrat, in Spain, then to Manresa, a town near Barcelona. While there, living in a cave with virtually no amenities, he begged for his food and he grew closer to God. After several months, he moved on to Jerusalem, then eventually to Paris, where he studied to become a priest. It was in Paris that he finished developing the Spiritual Exercises, a month-long process of reflection, prayer and discernment the Jesuits have used for centuries to help retreatants and others develop a deeper connection with God. "Finding God in all things" is a primary tenet of this reflection, from personal relationships to viewing a sunset. Another is the call to be contemplative "in action"; that is, being active in the world, trying to make an impact. With six close friends, including St. Francis Xavier, Ignatius formed the "Company of Jesus," or *Societas Jesu* in Latin, and eventually won the approval of the Catholic Church in Rome as a recognized religious order.

The Jesuits' message of conscience-driven activism has not always been well received by society's established institutions and those who run them, as some Jesuits throughout history have wielded that challenge to disrupt convention. Long before Pope Francis began challenging the status quo upon becoming the Catholic Church's first Jesuit pontiff in 2013, men of the Society of Jesus had been advocates for social change. Indeed, one of the most newsworthy Jesuits of the 1960s was Daniel Berrigan, a priest who took the concept of social activism to an extreme, and whose radical, anarchical, illegal acts in protesting the Vietnam War landed him in prison. Rev. Pedro Arrupe, the top-ranking "Superior General" of the Jesuits from 1965-83, though revered within the order, was viewed as a threat by many. Rev. James Martin, S.J., writes, in *My Life with the Saints*[5]:

> *It is difficult to communicate how admired Fr. Arrupe was by so many Jesuits, particularly in the United States and especially among younger Jesuits, for*

whom his commitment to social justice was so important and inspiring.

But Pedro Arrupe was not popular everywhere. Because his efforts on behalf of social justice seemed to carry the whiff of socialism or, worse, communism, Arrupe earned the displeasure of some in the Vatican.

For me, and for many SLUH students on the cusp of an anti-establishment commitment, the Jesuits' teaching and challenge were compelling and inspiring. They taught us to think for ourselves.

The Jesuits long have been a teaching order, and at St. Louis U. High in the 1960s and 1970s the Jesuit priests and "scholastics" who were studying to become Jesuit priests thrived in pursuit of molding young students as "men for others." They traversed the 12-acre SLUH campus grandly, the older ones often adorned in their long black cassocks, buttoned from the Roman collar at their necks to the base of the garments flowing to a couple inches above their black shoes. Some referred to them as "the Black Robes."

Their mission at SLUH was to work the "high end," the intellectually gifted young men who had to survive a rigorous selection process to gain entry. Exceptional academic credentials and male genitalia were the school's primary acts of discrimination. Economic background did not matter, and in fact, the Jesuits endeavored to attract a varied mix from along the family wealth spectrum, as well as from all the St. Louis metropolitan area neighborhoods and ethnic backgrounds. Generous benefactors provided financial relief for families unable to afford the tuition. As "men for others," the young students at SLUH were to come to understand what St. Luke had written: *"To whom much is given, much is expected."*

Change the world, indeed. As young, inexperienced, relatively unaccomplished students, many of us were both naïve and arrogant enough to think we could.

5// *A Season Ruined*

<u>*Autumn 1966*</u>

OF COURSE, most of us spent little time actually *planning* for those meaningful contributions to change the world. After all, our days were pretty crowded already with the pursuit of acceptance—by our teachers who graded us, by colleges we hoped would admit us, by girls who mostly terrified us, and by each other.

As hopeful yet confident eighth graders, Del Bannister and I took the entrance exam administered at the school, and I sat directly behind a fellow candidate named Bill Caputo. Del and I recognized him as the younger brother of Lou Caputo, a star on the 1966 St. Louis U. High football team. I never discovered what it was that Mrs. Caputo was feeding her boys, but it must have been potent nourishment. Built like his older brother, Bill was one of the most naturally strong human beings I ever encountered. He, Bannister and I were among the 229 who received news in the spring of 1967 that we had been granted admittance to SLUH and would enroll there a few months later. I looked forward to competing with him on the football field and in the classroom. What did the next four years have in store for us?

Certainly, my classmates and I were concerned about the troubles that befell our country and world. It's just that after each intermittent dose of those hard realities, most of us retreated into the comfort of knowing that our personal lives had not been encroached. Horrible things happen, we understood, but they happened to somebody else. It was as if we were strolling through a zoo, looking through impenetrable laminated glass at the wildlife on the other side, close enough to see it but at the same time protected from it. So when the evening news broadcasts were over, we went back to the pressing business of the day, a little more anesthetized but no less concerned. Many of those just a few years older were miles from the periphery that protected us, in the middle of increasingly chaotic college campuses or in the middle of Vietnam.

We had classes to take, sports or band instruments to play, girls to pursue, pimples to deal with. Gaining admission into SLUH was hard enough, and enough to celebrate, for the freshmen boys in the SLUH Class of 1971, who just a few months before, on a historic night in November of 1966, had come to know the glory of Junior Billiken football. We were the "Junior Billikens" because the teams at the four-year college that shared our heritage were known as the St. Louis University Billikens. Our mythical mascot, a chubby, squinty-eyed, simian-like creature with a perpetual smile, was said to be *"the god of things as they ought to be."*

In the autumn of 1966, while we restlessly were tolerating the eighth grade and sweating out the high school application and acceptance process, Bill Caputo's older brother Lou, along with quarterback John Houska, Art "Buzz" Demling, Dan Classen, Mike O'Brien, Kevin Shaner and the rest of the St. Louis U. High football team, had won their first eight games, and were on their way to perhaps the greatest football season in school history. That is, until a disappointing defeat in the biggest game of the year.

On that cool, early November evening, from his vantage among 31,526 people in attendance at Busch Memorial Stadium, one hopeful soul among the largest crowd ever to watch a high school football game in the state of Missouri, Mike Wiese sensed the pain his older brother Bob felt while thumping along the sideline on crutches.

Bob Wiese wasn't where he was supposed to be. After all, the three-sport star from North St. Louis County had started as SLUH's defensive end the year before, one of the rare times Coach Paul Martel called on an "underclassman" for a starting role, and he had helped the Junior Billikens to a 9-1 record and the No 4 ranking in the St. Louis area. Now, as a senior, his rightful place was on the field, starting at defensive back and offensive right end. But in the second game of the season, Bob Wiese tore ligaments in his ankle, and he could not play. How different Bob Wiese's life would have been, had it not been for the few seconds of history it took for his ankle to crumble.

Christian Brothers College High School was St. Louis U. High's most reliable and bitter rival, and the annual game had generated so much interest that for several years the two schools successfully staged it inside Busch Memorial Stadium, the concrete coliseum in downtown St. Louis which had debuted in May of 1966 as the new home of the professional St. Louis Baseball Cardinals, and then in the late summer as home for the National Football League's Cardinals, who spent 27 years in St. Louis before moving to Arizona in 1988. In August of 1966, an audience of some 23,000 watched the Beatles perform live in the stadium, in a makeshift shelter over the stage to protect them from a punishing rain. The Beatles would play only four more shows before they stopped touring.

SLUH entered the 1966 game ranked No. 1 among high school teams in the greater St. Louis area, and CBC was ranked No. 2. In 1966, still two years before Missouri would inaugurate its playoff tournament, the state's high school football teams competed for rankings, and the "mythical" elite status that came with them.

At the time, CBC was located less than five miles from St. Louis U. High, west as Oakland Avenue ran to the City of St. Louis' western limit then yielded to Clayton Road and St. Louis County. Proximity and similarity fed the rivalry between these two private, boys-only college preparatory schools, as proximity and similarity have fueled rivalries among feuding parties throughout history. Brothers and cousins played against brothers and cousins. The annual football game was a big deal, bigger than any other game on either team's schedule. Win that rivalry game, it was said, and your season was made, regardless of what happened with the rest of the schedule. It was convincingly argued that the stakes in *this* CBC-SLUH confrontation were higher than for any game in a continuous football rivalry that had begun in 1925. Entering the game, SLUH's offense was ranked No. 1 in the St. Louis area; its defense No. 2. CBC's defense was ranked No. 1; its offense No. 2.

In the first half, the game delivered on its hype, as SLUH finished off an 84-yard drive with quarterback John Houska completing a five-yard touchdown pass to halfback Dave Walsh in the second quarter for the half's only score and a 6-0 lead.

To those who did not know him, Houska seemed the quintessential high school heartthrob, a handsome, blond-haired senior who wore No. 14 and played the most important position on the No. 1 ranked team in the area. He looked splendid in his varsity letter jacket, with the giant blue-trimmed white "STL" letters covering much of the blue fabric on the left breast of the coat, and the number "67" sewn into the creamed-colored right sleeve, indicating his graduation class year. A matinee movie idol to people like Del Bannister and me, impressionable kids and fans of Junior Billiken football. Houska himself didn't see it that way. He knew he was just 5 feet, 8 inches tall, and 148 pounds. And he was mindful of the slight overbite that made it difficult to call out signals while wearing a protective mouthpiece.

"When I was a little kid playing baseball," he recalled, "when I was pitching, and the other team wanted to get to me, they'd call me 'Bucky Beaver.'"

Houska was not one to be deceived by an illusion of invincibility. Humble and realistic, he understood SLUH was fortunate to hold a half-time lead over this CBC team, especially given the absence of Bob Wiese ("probably our best player," he said) and the limited use of star running back Buzz Demling, who had a fractured finger.

The Cadets of CBC would soon prove their worthiness, opening the second half with a devastating assault.

Moments earlier, in a somber and serious locker room, the CBC players had listened as coach Bill Gerdemann explained what they would have to do in the second half if they hoped to prevail. Then, he yielded the floor to someone unaccustomed to speaking. Tom Shine, the Cadets' inspirational but quiet captain, had been knocked out of the game in the first half, having suffered a debilitating hip injury. "Listen up, you guys," Shine called out. According to Phil Pacini, a junior and starting lineman on the CBC squad, the players were surprised to hear from Shine.

"He used up half his normal quota of words just calling the players to attention," said Pacini.

Disappointed at being disabled by what he regarded as a questionable hit, an emotional Shine called on his teammates to crank up their level of intensity in the second half. Amply inspired, the Cadets roared out of the locker room and back onto the Busch Stadium turf.

On its first scrimmage play in the second half, CBC quarterback Tom Hauser detected both SLUH linebackers blitzing, and countered with a quick, short pass to halfback Jack McDonald, who ran 50 yards to the SLUH 23. Four plays later, CBC took the lead with a touchdown and extra point, then recovered a SLUH fumble on the ensuing kickoff on the 31. On the first play of the series, halfback Roger Cerny swept around left end and scored, and CBC led, 14-6. On his next possession, Houska was hit from behind and fumbled on the SLUH 16. Four plays later, the Cadets scored again and took a 20-6 lead.

"In two minutes and 10 seconds, we basically lost the game," Houska said. "It was one of those games."

With that lead, and three interceptions by Pat Deisner, the CBC defense smothered the Junior Billikens in the final two quarters. Young Mike Wiese could only watch in the stands as his brother Bob could only watch from the sideline, and CBC finished off a 33-6 victory. Mike remembers Bob kicking one of his crutches a few yards along the sideline after one particularly disappointing play. It would be SLUH's only loss in another 9-1 season. CBC finished as "mythical" No. 1 in Missouri, voted so in a post-season coaches' poll published in the area newspapers. As my consolation, disappointed as I was at the SLUH defeat, I was happy for Phil Pacini, the CBC junior lineman and my first cousin.

Bob Wiese's ankle recovered enough that he was able to advance to the semifinals of the Missouri state wrestling tournament that winter, then to star as the center fielder on the Junior Billiken baseball team, for which he was voted All-Metro recognition as the best at his position in the metropolitan St. Louis area. This area included schools from the City of St. Louis; the north, west and south sections of St. Louis County; the counties just east of the Mississippi River in Illinois; and the perimeter counties abutting St. Louis County.

Perhaps mindful of the lost promise of his senior season, Bob felt he had more football in him, so when he was later accepted by Notre Dame University without a scholarship, he tried out for the freshman team in the fall of 1967. A national collegiate football powerhouse in the mid-1960s, as it has been for so many eras in its storied history, Notre Dame had won the national championship in 1966 and started the 1967 season ranked No. 1 in the country. That seemed like a worthy environment for Mike Wiese's over-achieving older brother. Bob Wiese "walked on," made the Irish freshman team, and ascended to the second string.

6// *Union of North and South*

1967

LATER IN 1967, less than a year after CBC spoiled SLUH's perfect 1966 season, and three years before we reached the brink of the 1970 state championship game, Del Bannister and I decided we would try out for the sophomore football team, known as the "B" team, even though neither of us ever had played organized football. Why not? What did we have to lose? If we got cut, we were pretty sure we would make the freshman "C" team. After two weeks of workouts, we approached the posted "cut list" anxiously. To my surprise, I saw "Joe Castellano" among the names of six freshmen who had made the roster of the 50-player team. Bannister got cut. Time to escape my comfort zone and make some new friends, I knew. Mike Wiese would be one of them.

I was the son of a man who co-owned a small neighborhood tavern with his brother-in-law and tended it seven days a week, and a woman who tended to our home in the south part of the City of St. Louis. Jim and Leona Castellano raised five children on what he earned at that tavern, and they sacrificed to make it possible for my brothers, sister and me to take advantage of the opportunity they never had but were willing to pay for—to attend a private, college preparatory high school. My Dad had completed just two years of high school during America's Great Depression, when he dropped out to earn money to help support his immigrant, widowed mother and younger siblings—one brother and two sisters—in St. Louis's Italian Hill neighborhood. He didn't spend much time in school, but he knew successful people did, and he was determined that his children would do so, too.

Mike Wiese was one of Claude and Dorothy Wiese's six children, and they lived on the north side, in St. Ann just across the city boundary in St. Louis County. Claude was a machinist who put himself through night school to get a college degree, then ascended to become a project planner at McDonnell-Douglas, the major American aerospace manufacturing corporation and defense contractor which eventually merged with Boeing. It was classic American Dream stuff.

To those of us who grew up south of what was then Highway 40, the area *north* of that boundary might just as well have been in the Bering

Strait. Same was true about the south side, to those who grew up *north* of the highway. It didn't matter, though, because there is something about competing side by side in crusty, sweat-drenched, smelly football pads that renders that stuff insignificant. Mike Wiese and I became close friends, bonded in part because we were among a small handful of freshmen on a team of sophomores. There was something very practical, yet poetic at the same time, about the fact that the St. Louis U. High campus was almost exactly on the border of Highway 40, now known as Interstate 64. The central location long has been a key advantage for the school, as it has successfully attracted students from the north and south, from West County, and from across the Mississippi River to the east, in southwestern Illinois.

Mike Wiese also had not played organized football before we stepped onto that SLUH practice field as 14-year-olds in August of 1967. It was a very big deal to us that we made the "B" team, along with four other freshmen—Errol Patterson, Bill Ziegler, Doug McDonald and Bob Thibaut. We played a little bit that year, on a team that won six games, tied one, and lost two, and entered the fall of 1968 with grand hopes of moving up to the varsity, where sophomores rarely earned their way onto the roster. Turns out, Mike Wiese and I failed to "graduate," while the other four did, along with two others, Tom Milford and Jim Twombly, who had played on the "C" freshman team the season before.

Wiese and I decided to make the most of our repeat opportunity, and we were looked to as leaders among our sophomore classmates. I looked forward to spending the season with Del Bannister, a fellow lineman who would be my teammate on the "B" team, and with whom I would be able to hitchhike home after practices.

Wiese was skinny and bony, but rock hard. None of us had heard much about "body fat" in the 1960s, but it's likely Mike's body fat percentage would have been in the single digits. He was so mild-mannered, though, it was difficult to see how he could be much of a menace on the football field. One of his most significant talents, he was to discover later, was his ability to drink beer while standing on his head. It was remarkable to see. He poured beer into a plastic cup, clenched the cup with his teeth, the mouth of the cup cradling his chin. Then he bent over, and steadily and surely, touched his head and two hands to the ground in a three-point stance, then thrust his legs up into the air. He seldom spilled a drop during this circus act, and was able in that position to slurp up (down?) the beverage, leaving an empty cup and an astounded audience.

"I was always able to stand on my head," he said. "My Mom, she could always stand on her head."

Such genetics served him well in other areas, too, it turned out. Most notably, on the football field, where it was clear he had his older brother Bob Wiese's pedigree.

My pedigree was less certain. It was whispered that my father was a bona fide professional baseball prospect, based on the way he hit and handled pitchers as a catcher on the streets of the Italian Hill Neighborhood in St. Louis, which a few years later produced Major League Baseball Hall of Famers Yogi Berra and Joe Garagiola. No one can say for certain, of course, because Dad gave up his catcher's mitt for the sure thing of the few dollars a week he was able to earn cleaning out the spittoons in a tavern owned and operated by an entrepreneurial Italian immigrant named Armando Pacini.

Dad liked a sure thing, and wasn't much given to pity or regret. He never moaned about the lost opportunity, and besides, he always felt like he ended up ahead of the game, as he went on to marry two daughters of Mr. Pacini, who also staked him and his brother-in-law to their own saloon a few years later. The first daughter, Marie, died childless and suddenly in 1948; the second, Marie's younger and closest sister Leona, my Dad married two years later. Leona was my Mom, and I was the second of their five children. Leona was fierce as a mother, demanding and protective, an inspiration for my siblings and me, as she made it clear to us that nothing should deter us from going where our ambitions led us, nor from doing things the proper way.

The baby of our family, my brother Steve survived a difficult birth but eventually was diagnosed as learning disabled. He struggled to keep pace in school, and had to repeat the first grade, and battled his way through the progression of grades at Epiphany School. Increasingly aware of his limitations, Steve confronted my Mom one day with a brutal question: "Why did God make me different from my brothers and sister?"

I have been haunted and humbled by that question, as I have spent a lifetime trying to reconcile how and why I got such a sweet playing hand while Steve got a crummy one. My Mom was not fazed.

"God makes every one of us different," she responded to Steve without hesitation. "What's important is what we do with the gifts God gave us."

Like Mike Wiese, I had an older brother I looked up to and tried to emulate. Eighteen months older than I, Jim Castellano was below average in size. For most of our childhood we were the same height, and usually I outweighed him by 20 pounds. It was said that I had inherited the "Pacini legs," which I always accepted as a loving mother's euphemism for my hefty bottom half. Jim was fit; I was "husky," a term I came to deplore, particularly when it came time for our annual trek to Famous-Barr to buy two pair of new dress trousers for school. After Jim selected from an array of fashions, we moved on to the "fat boy" section, where a husky lad could try on black or white Levis.

Two classes ahead of me at St. Louis U. High, Jim played on the freshman and sophomore football teams, though he stood only 5 foot, 6 inches tall and weighed about 150 pounds. Remarkably, he played offensive guard. His best sport was soccer, which he played for three varsity seasons at SLUH, then in Kansas City at Rockhurst College, a Jesuit school later upgraded to Rockhurst University. Jim was very tough, as he had to be to survive and prosper, and he never took any crap from anybody. Not on those football fields, nor later in life in business board rooms, where as a Certified Public Accountant and eventually chairman of the RubinBrown firm in St. Louis, he would go on to wield his integrity, his piercing insights, and his mental toughness to influence men and women to do the right thing. He was never better than when, as the newly appointed chairman of the American Institute of Certified Public Accountants in 2002, he found himself defending his profession before Congress and the national news media in the wake of the scandal that destroyed the Enron Corporation and the Arthur Anderson accounting firm. In 2012, the AICPA named Jim one of 125 people who have made a significant impact on the profession since 1887.

My Mom and Dad had died by the time Jim received that honor, but they would have been so proud. At the same time, to ensure Jim was not tempted to feel disproportionately special about the accolade, Leona likely would have tried to bring attention to her other children: me, our younger sister JoMarie, who gallantly taught grade school children for four decades, and younger brothers Mike and Steve. It was her way of keeping us grounded. When Mike was named chief executive officer of Esse Health, a physicians group in St. Louis, the news ran in the *St. Louis Post-Dispatch*, under a headline featuring Mike's name. Probably sensing the need to balance the scales, Mom declared to Jim and me: "Your names never appeared in a headline."

7// *Crazy Joe*

_1967-68_

COACH JOE VITALE KNEW how tough my brother Jim was, and maybe that's why he kept me as a freshman on his sophomore team in the fall of 1967. By that time, I was bigger than my brother, about 5-11, 170 pounds as a freshman, and I, too, aspired to play in the interior line, where my "Pacini legs" would serve me well. Mike Wiese and I had the particular pleasure of witnessing the "Crazy Joe" Vitale circus two years in a row.

Joe Vitale was a man of integrity and passion, a teacher of economics and typing, and a coach whose emotion occasionally carried him to places I believe he later regretted going. Some say it was because he was so conflicted by his father's profession and reputation, which some say was on the wrong side of the law. John Vitale made a living in the company of St. Louis gangsters, most notably Anthony Giordano, who was reputed to be "boss" of the St. Louis Mafia in the 1960s and 1970s. Nothing much was ever pinned on "Johnny V" Vitale, who reportedly became "acting boss" upon the death of Giordano in 1980. As a young man, he had served two years in prison for a narcotics violation. In 1967, the first of two consecutive years Mike Wiese and I were playing football for his son, the U.S. Justice Department identified John Vitale as "representing the national cartel in St. Louis."

That his students and players referred to Joe Vitale so disrespectfully as "Crazy Joe" is a testament to the impertinence of youth. That we did it behind his back but not to his face is a testament to our cowardice. What I remember about Joe Vitale is that he was smart, principled, devoted, and, yes, passionate. Once troubled by an officiating call during a game at Forest Park, he removed his wristwatch and hurled it in the direction of Highway 40, which ran adjacent to the football pitch on Aviation Field. The following Monday in Coach Vitale's classroom, one mischievous soul set up a classmate, a meek and naïve sort, who was led to believe he would get a funny response if he asked Crazy Joe for the time of day. We all took pity on the poor, gullible bastard.

Coach Vitale once punched a student in the nose, when that student spun around from a drinking fountain to spray water on someone he thought was a fellow student. He had not counted on the Coach waiting his turn in line behind him, and the Coach didn't waste a moment pondering the consequences of slugging a student. Fortunately, that student's father understood. "He had it coming," the father was reported to have told a relieved Joe Vitale.

Despite his rogue temper, Joe Vitale was a good man who was devoted to the players he taught and coached. Few came to know him as well as did Steve Walsh, whose searing fastballs I caught for the SLUH baseball team, when we were battery mates playing for the varsity team Vitale coached in 1970 and 1971.

"He was very defensive about his Dad," said Walsh, a left-handed pitcher who earned All-State recognition. "He was being loyal to his father. He used to tell me his Dad wouldn't let him and his brother have anything to do with the family business. To me, he was the most loyal and honest guy I knew, outside of my family. He was one person I could trust to tell me the truth."

After graduating from Michigan State University, where he played on a soccer scholarship, former SLUH quarterback John Houska became a teacher and coach, and spent 10 years on the football staff at St. Louis U. High. He and Vitale became good friends.

"He was a deep thinker," Houska said. "He was very different from what people could imagine. Yeah, maybe he was crazy, but he talked about it. He always wanted to write a book, which he wanted to title *North Side of Nowhere.*"

Joe Vitale also was a very good football coach. For many years, he teamed with assistant coach Jim Murphy to direct the SLUH sophomore team to extraordinary achievement on the field. Damned entertaining, too.

One day at the outset of practice during my freshman year, with the entire squad huddled around the coaches, Vitale announced that we would be working exclusively on running plays that morning—first team offense against second team defense. No passing today. We broke into the two squads, with Crazy Joe leading the offense and Coach Murphy the defense. In the defensive huddle, Coach Murphy deduced that since the head coach had declared there would be no passing that day, the first play certainly would be a long pass play, designed to catch the defense off guard. "Be ready for the long bomb," Coach Murphy said.

Sure enough, starting quarterback Tracy Powell took the snap from the center, and bounced back three or four steps to set up for the long pass, which he barely released before getting crushed by a surprising pass rush. We on defense intercepted the pass gleefully, showing up the starters and infuriating Coach Vitale. Jim Murphy smiled.

"We had a friendly competition, so I wasn't going to let him pull that on me," Jim Murphy recalled many years later. "I was on to that. I knew him well enough to know what he was going to do. He went nuts, and I loved it. That's the kind of thing I loved to do."

Murphy was something of an institution at St. Louis U. High, a 1954 graduate of the school who landed a job there six years later as a young teacher and coach, then spent 41 years as a teacher of history and technical drawing, as an administrator, and as a football and wrestling coach. His father was a quarterback on the first SLUH football team in 1916. For four decades, Murphy was the man in the press box on the public address system, announcing the plays for those in attendance. He knew Joe Vitale better than most.

"He was a little wacko," Jim Murphy said of Vitale. "But I could work with him. He'd do some outrageous things, but it seemed like I could handle it. I know he meant well. He was very good to me. He trusted me. He turned the defense over to me. It was a good partnership, football-wise. And it was actually a good partnership, personality-wise. He was very intense, and very serious. He was great that way. He always wanted to do the right thing. Always wanted to do it the right way. And he was passionate about that."

The following autumn of 1968, I was captain of the sophomore squad, and found myself on one occasion trying to reason with Coach Vitale, pleading for the mercy I suspected was within him. During August in St. Louis, the temperature rarely falls below 90 degrees, and the humidity often soars above 90 percent. Outfitted in our football pads and helmets, and rationed on water as was the custom then, it seemed we were always about one wind sprint away from collapsing in exhaustion or dehydration as we went through our preseason drills. On a particularly hot and muggy day, one of the team's most gung-ho leaders was pushing everyone to go harder. Later generations called this sprint running drill "Killers." Lined up shoulder to shoulder, about 50 guys wide on one sideline of the field, we bent over in a "three-point stance," with the finger tips of one hand touching the ground. At the captain's call, we would blast off the starting line in unison and race at top speed some 50 yards to the other side. Worn down physically from a 90-minute practice, these sprints were a test of our physical and mental endurance. Just when we thought we were finished on this particular day, Tom Schoeck, another legacy player whose older brother Jim was a quarterback on the varsity, shouted out, "Let's do another sprint!"

Apparently, that was the final irritant for reserve lineman John "J.B." Benoist, who had grown weary of hoisting his ample backside up and across that arid, grassless practice field. In a voice likely heard some 300 yards away in the Jesuit residence on campus, J.B. shouted, "Oh, fuck you, Schoeck!"

Certainly, Coach Vitale had no trouble hearing it, and he promptly told Benoist to march off the field and turn in his equipment, he was off the team.

After practice, I nervously entered the coaches' room, and asked Coach

Vitale if I could speak with him. "What is it?" he said.

"Coach, I'd like to ask you to reconsider your decision to kick Benoist off the team," I said. "He has been working really hard out there, and I think he just kind of shouted out what the rest of us were feeling. He regrets doing it, and he's a good teammate we'd like to have back."

A little bit to my surprise, I guess, Coach Vitale agreed to reinstate Benoist. It was good to discover that an appeal to reason and a person's good nature can actually work. That was hardly the most insightful revelation of 1968, but it was meaningful to me nonetheless. And useful perspective for a 15-year-old whose generation at times seemed intent on breaking apart just about anything put forth by the ones preceding us.

Midway through our sophomore team season, we saw another example of the complexity within Coach Vitale. Entering the Bi-State Conference game against the historically weak Marquette High Explorers in Alton, Illinois, Vitale advised us to be mindful of the vulnerability of our opponent, which had barely enough players to field a team. We had won our first five games by an aggregate score of 104-6. Perhaps proving that a football team cannot function properly when adjusting gears downward, we found ourselves trailing in the game. Coach was unambiguous during a spirited halftime address. We began the second half recharged, and went on to salvage an 18-7 victory, and finished our season 8-1. The blemish, a 13-0 loss to CBC.

8// *"Part of a Greater Organism"*

1968-69

THE YEARS 1968 TO 1970 were among the most tumultuous of the 20th century, a century Elie Wiesel, a Jew, had survived the Nazi concentration camps at Auschwitz and Buchenwald during World War II in the 1940s. His mother, his father, and his younger sister did not survive. In 1979, U.S. President Jimmy Carter appointed him Chairman of the President's Commission on the Holocaust. Elie Wiesel's perspective was heavily influenced by what he called two fanaticisms: "Political fanaticism: capital, Moscow. Racial fanaticism: capital, Berlin. And therefore, that century has caused more deaths than any time before."

Awarded the 1986 Nobel Peace Prize, Elie Wiesel devoted his life to the message that we as citizens of the world must get involved when we see injustice.

"The greatest commandment, to me, in the Bible is not the Ten Commandments," he once said in a university commencement address[6]. "My commandment is, 'Thou shall not stand idly by.' Which means when you witness an injustice, don't stand idly by. When you hear of a person or a group being persecuted, do not stand idly by. When there is something wrong in the community around you—or far away—do not stand idly by. You must intervene. You must interfere."

There is something very Jesuit in that message. Del Bannister, Mike Wiese and I, and our classmates from the SLUH Class of 1971, had been hearing it for a couple of years by the time we were 15 and 16 years old in 1968. Yes, there was a lot of stuff going on out there, and it kind of bothered us, and we kind of figured we should do something about it. Then again, we were just kids, and it was time for football practice.

In an epic protest anthem he published in 1965, the songwriter P. F. Sloan had painted a dark, pessimistic picture from his view of life in a troubled world. We had been hearing the Barry McGuire cover of *Eve of Destruction*[7] regularly on our AM radios for a couple of years, and it came to mind often as we digested the troubling news in a decade turning decidedly somber.

The eastern world, it is explodin'.
Violence flarin', bullets loadin'.
You're old enough to kill, but not for votin'.
You don't believe in war, but what's that gun you're totin'?
And even the Jordan River has bodies floatin'.
But you tell me, over and over and over again, my friend, you don't
believe, we're on the eve of destruction?

Don't you understand, what I'm tryin' to say?
Can't you feel the fears, I'm feelin' today?
If the button is pushed, there's no runnin' away.
There'll be no one to save with the world in a grave.
Take a look around you, boy, it's bound to scare you, boy.
And you tell me, over and over and over again, my friend, you don't
believe we're on the eve of destruction?

Well, P. F. Sloan might not have convinced my pals and me that the world was on the brink of extinction, but I must admit I was a little daunted by the world's events. Barry McGuire went on to sing about "hatred in Red China" and troubles in Selma, Alabama, among other things, and then delivered this, with killer cynicism:

You may leave here for four days in space, but when you return it's the
same old place.

Fair enough. In July of 1969, the United States National Aeronautics and Space Administration fulfilled the challenge President Kennedy had issued less than a decade before, when Neil Armstrong and Buzz Aldrin walked on the moon, then with fellow Apollo 11 astronaut Michael Collins returned safely to earth after their eight-day mission. It was an almost unfathomable feat of the ingenuity and competence of humankind, an event that inspired so many Americans to feel we could do just about anything. Of course, when the astronauts returned, earth was "the same old place," with war and discrimination and suffering resuming their share of the nightly news.

A month later, at the onset of our junior year, we started the football season on the dreaded date of August 15, 1969, the first day high school teams were allowed to begin organized practices. Dreaded because it was the official end to our summer vacation. Dreaded because it was so hot and humid on that godless, arid lower field on the SLUH campus, the site just east of the erstwhile Walsh Stadium, which is where midget auto races and football games and various daredevil shows had been staged for more than two decades, until it was decommissioned and demolished in 1957. In 1969, our "lower field" was an empty dirt wasteland, where grass refused to grow. And dreaded because it was the day Coach Paul Martel would have us run a mile on the dusty, cindered track that circled the field—four and a half laps, in full football gear. Linemen had to complete the mile in less than six minutes, 30 seconds. Backs had to make it in less than six minutes.

On that very same day, some 1,100 hundred miles to the Northeast, on a 600-acre dairy farm owned by Max Yasgur in Bethel, N.Y., some 500,000 people came to hear four days of music in an event that became a defining moment of our generation. The Woodstock Music & Art Fair featured more than 30 acts, including inspiring artists who influenced our souls with their melodies and lyrics. While those just several months or a few years our elder were stretched out or tripped out among the sweet, chaotic humanity at Woodstock, taking in the musical poetry of legends such as Jimi Hendrix, The Who, Janis Joplin, the Grateful Dead, Richie Havens, Joe Cocker, Joni Mitchell, and Crosby, Stills, Nash & Young, we were mixing dust and our own sweat into a cake that hardened into a crust in the creases of our football gear on a miserable field in the center of St. Louis.

Joni Mitchell called Woodstock "a spark of beauty," where 500,000 kids "saw that they were part of a greater organism."

Many of us in the SLUH Class of 1971 desperately longed to be part of that greater organism, too. We just weren't sure how to do it. So we went to football practice, and then to class.

I played sparingly, mostly on special teams, that autumn of 1969, as the SLUH varsity won eight of our 10 games. For Del Bannister, Mike Wiese and me, and the rest of our classmates, our time would come the following August, in the summer and fall of 1970. For the time being, we were pretty content to ride out the relatively carefree winter and spring of our junior year.

9// *"He Was My Hero"*

February 1970

AS WE IN THE JUNIOR CLASS REACHED our second semester, U.S. troops had been deployed in the War in Vietnam for longer than they had been in World War I or World War II. Certainly, it was on our minds, especially as we contemplated the idea of being called to serve in it before long, if—as had been debated and eventually would be enacted—the "college exemption" were to be eliminated. Many of our older brothers were temporarily excused from involuntary induction because they were in college, through a provision that allowed draft-eligible young men to defer their military service while enjoying the privilege of attending college.

Mike Wiese was one of the few guys in our class who had a brother in the Armed Services. Despite his magnificent debut at Notre Dame in the fall of 1966, Bob Wiese had decided college was not for him, and he had dropped out to enlist in the U. S. Marine Corps in January of 1968. As always a leader, Robert James Wiese came out of boot camp as a corporal.

"He was home in mid-December of 1969," Mike Wiese remembers. "He left just before Christmas. We weren't too worried, though, and thought he was far away from the fighting. We thought he was safe and sound."

What Corporal Bob Wiese had told Claude Wiese, and had asked his father not to tell the rest of the family, was that he had volunteered to be a machine gunner on a combat helicopter. Four years before, Bob Wiese had sat in the same classrooms we occupied now. Classrooms far away from the fighting in Vietnam.

On a chilly February morning in the winter of 1970, St. Louis U. High assistant principal Charlie Conway opened the door to the class Mike Wiese was in, interrupted the teacher, and asked Mike to step outside. "Mike," said Charlie Conway somberly, "Do you have a brother Bob who is in Vietnam?"

Charlie Conway did not have to say anything else. Mike Wiese's heart accelerated, his legs weakened, his stomach cramped, and he started to weep.

En route to the USS *Repose* on the night of February 16, on an emergency mission to retrieve a supply of transfusion blood that would preserve life for wounded soldiers, Corporal Bob Wiese and four mates from Marine Medium Helicopter Squadron 161 navigated through a dark, foggy sky in their Boeing-Vertol CH-46 twin engine, tandem-rotor helicopter. In this ill-fated "20 seconds of history," the helicopter clipped a hilltop and crashed hard into the earth, in the Thua Thien Province in South Vietnam. No one survived.

Thoughtfully, Charlie Conway asked Mike if he wanted to take a friend home with him. Accompanied by classmate and good friend Steve Walsh, and driven by assistant varsity football coach Ebbie Dunn, Mike Wiese headed home.

"I'll never forget going into that house, and seeing my Mom on the couch bawling," said Mike Wiese, many years later. "She was there with Dad. I was devastated."

Many years later, Mike had often wondered what his life would have been like, had his brother Bob not died in Vietnam. It would never be the same.

"He was my hero," Mike said.

10// *Thoughts of the War*

1968-70

THE DEATH OF BOB WIESE in Vietnam made the war more personal for us, as the deaths of more than 58,000 Americans lost in that war affected the lives of millions of family and friends. For one thing, it affected us because we saw our friend Mike Wiese carry the heavy burden of his most personal loss with him every day. For another, we knew this war was being fought by young Americans just a year or two older than we were. The average age of the American soldier in Vietnam was 19, well below the average age of 26 for the GIs in World War II. In World War II, American combat troops faced combat, on average, an estimated 40 days per year. In Vietnam, on patrols in search of a hidden enemy or in sustaining frequent ambushes, and facilitated by the mobility of the helicopter, the troops saw combat an average of 240 days per year.

This war, this world, had suddenly become a bit more real.

In the summer of 1968, people of our generation created chaos in the streets of Chicago as the Democratic Party convened to nominate Hubert Humphrey as its candidate to succeed Lyndon Johnson as President of the United States. The Chicago police tried to keep order, but people of our generation were beaten and arrested.

Inspired by the very public protests against the Vietnam War, John Lennon wrote and recorded *Revolution*[8] that year with the Beatles.

You say you want a revolution
Well, you know
We all want to change the world
You tell me that it's evolution
Well, you know
We all want to change the world

Rock 'n Roll and Top 40 music stations commanded large audiences in the 1960s, and both reflected and fed the protest culture that was rising in America. Even songs like *For What It's Worth*[9] (*"There's a Man with a Gun over There …"*) by Stephen Stills of Buffalo Springfield, and the Rolling Stones' *Street Fighting Man*[10], written for other purposes, were appropriated for the anti-Vietnam sound track of the Baby Boomer generation.

In November of 1969, a crowd estimated at 500,000 people, the great majority of whom were from our generation, paraded on Pennsylvania Avenue to the Washington Monument in Washington, D.C., to protest the War in Vietnam. It was called the "Moratorium of War" March on Washington. Gene McCarthy, the U.S. Senator from Minnesota who had lost in his bid to become the Democratic Party candidate for President in 1968, was at that demonstration, where he challenged those gathered to continue to assert their criticism of the war.

"The record of history, I think, is clear," Senator McCarthy said, "the cases in which political leaders out of misjudgment or ambition in ancient time and in modern times basing their action on the loyalty of their people, have done great harm to their own countries and to the world. The great loyalty of the Roman citizens moved the Caesers to war. The great loyalty of the French moved Napoleon to actions which should never have been taken. Let us in the United States take warning from that experience."

A U.S. Senator, in clear and unambiguous terms, was imploring the citizens of our country to speak out in defiance of our government leadership on the subject of the War in Vietnam. It was a message that resonated with many of us, particularly since so many of us failed to understand the reasons our country continued to fight that war, and why American families had to continue to lose their loved ones in a place so far from home. It had become difficult for many of us to accept the commonly provided rationale of a "domino effect," that if South Vietnam fell to Communist governance, then, like descending dominoes, other countries in Southeast Asia and around the world also would fall to Communism.

Senator McCarthy's call to action, and a growing culture of public protest, ignited first by a crusade for racial equality and civil rights in America, then amplified by the outrage of casualties in Vietnam, stirred something deep inside many of us teenagers. In spring of 1970, people of our generation were gathering and marching and protesting on their college campuses across the United States.

11// Getting Involved

Spring 1970

DULY INSPIRED, many of us in the SLUH Class of 1971 were willing to carve out time from drinking beer, goofing off, clumsily trying to impress girls, playing sports, and arguing with our parents to do something serious. Something besides trying to learn something useful and to compete for the grades that would help us get into a good college. Student government, for example.

At St. Louis U. High, the Student Council served as a representative voice for students with the faculty and administration, sponsored and supervised student events, and served as a liaison between SLUH and other area schools. There were four elected offices of the Student Council, but following school tradition, there was to be no campaigning for those offices: President, Vice President, Secretary, Treasurer. Each student in the incoming senior class was to vote for four classmates, with four points assigned to his first choice, three to his second, two to the third, one to the fourth. Points would be tallied, and the four officers would be elected based on total number of points.

In the spring of 1970, Whayne Herriford viewed the Student Council as a platform to make a significant difference for the school and our classmates. He made it clear to his close friends that he was interested in becoming an officer for the coming year, and he allowed himself to think he could be the first African-American President of the Student Council in school history. One of six African-Americans among the 209 students in our graduating class, Whayne had immersed himself in the national political news of the day. He felt the calling to get involved, and for him that meant getting elected to the Student Council.

When the results of the April 24 Student Council election were announced three days later, Whayne was quite pleased to have been voted in as the Secretary, with the third highest total number of points. Whayne, who years later added the "H" to the spelling of his first name, lived in the city, on the north side, with his father Merle, a physician, his mother Barbara, a registered nurse, and his younger siblings Carla and David.

I was elected President. Elected Vice President was Ed Hawk, the son of Mary and James Hawk, an attorney, who lived in the affluent suburb of Des Peres, in West St. Louis County. Our fourth officer, our Treasurer, was Phil Schaefer, one of three brothers being raised by widowed mother Elizabeth Robeff Schaefer in Shrewsbury, a small St. Louis County community just across of the city's southwest boundary. Until that day, none of us knew the others well. However, we knew we would be spending a lot of time together over the next 12 months, and we were quite excited at the prospect of doing great things together.

Two days before our Student Council election, activities for the first Earth Day were staged in communities across the United States. Having been organized by activists concerned about the environment of our planet, Earth Day inspired millions of Americans to celebrate an official acknowledgement of concern for the quality and sustainability of the world's land, water and air.

On April 10, news had emerged that Paul McCartney was leaving the Beatles, thus making official the rumors that had circulated for months that this iconic voice of a generation was breaking up for good after a 10-year collaboration.

On April 30, less than a week *after* we were introduced as the leaders of the SLUH Class of 1971, President Richard Nixon announced he had authorized U.S. combat troops to cross Vietnam's border into Cambodia to attack Viet Cong supply positions there. "We take these actions not for the purpose of expanding the war into Cambodia," he explained, "but for the purpose of ending the war in Vietnam, and winning the just peace we all desire."

Many were not mollified by that explanation. On college campuses across the country, students accelerated their protests, in response to the Cambodia incursion. On May 1, on the campus of Kent State University, 560 miles to the east of the campus of St. Louis U. High, about 500 students gathered around the Victory Bell on the Commons, a natural site for staging student rallies. Students came and went over the course of that weekend, voicing their dismay over the war in Vietnam. The Ohio National Guard was called to the campus, and established a visible, menacing presence.

On Saturday night, May 2, there was a disturbance in the town of Kent, when protestors clashed with police, and demonstrators set on fire the school's Army Reserve Officer Training Corps building. On Sunday, May 3, Ohio Governor James Rhodes arrived in Kent and held a news conference. The protestors, he declared, were "the worst type of people we harbor in America, worse than the brown shirts and communist element ... We will use whatever force necessary to drive them out of Kent." He was running for the U.S. Senate, and the primary was to be held two days later. In his view, the protests were organized by a small band of "revolutionaries." His comments did not serve to calm down the campus.

The next morning, Monday, May 4, students returned to the Commons, and by noon an estimated 1,500 protestors had gathered. The 116 members of Troop G of the Ohio National Guard attempted to disperse the crowd, and after they achieved some success in doing so, there remained a small group of students exchanging angry words and throwing stones. A group of Guardsmen had moved into a three-walled practice football field, and felt trapped there. Another group was entrenched a few hundred yards away. Tensions escalated. Could any of the young men in National Guard uniform that day, armed with an M-1 rifle, have anticipated being in this situation, facing off with contemporaries of his generation?

Suddenly, the tension yielded to panic, and in just 13 seconds, 28 of the Guardsmen fired a total of 67 rifle shots, hitting 13 people. Four were mortally wounded, including two students who were not among the demonstrators. They were walking to class, caught in the wrong place at the wrong time. Four dead in Ohio. Ages 19 and 20. Less than 20 seconds that changed history.

The next day, four million students went on strike, forcing 450 schools to shut down, many for the remainder of the second semester. At St. Louis U. High, we finished the school year peacefully, and looked forward to the summer break.

12// *Black in America*

<u>1953-70</u>

THE FOUR NEWLY ELECTED OFFICERS of the St. Louis U. High Student Council began our final high school summer vacation with grand ambition, excited by the challenge we accepted to inspire the best year of our lives for the members of the Class of 1971. The four of us were a microcosm of the diversity of the SLUH student body: south city, north city, near county, west county; a couple affluent, a couple not so much; three white, one black. It was our goal to inspire the most inclusive, service-oriented, fulfilling experience possible for our classmates. There were committee leadership positions to fill, agendas to set, events to plan. Though we had summer jobs that would command our time and attention, and I had a full summer schedule of American Legion baseball games to play, I welcomed the thought of getting to know these three guys better.

The one I knew least was Whayne Herriford.

From 1953 to 1968, which coincided with the first 15 years of my life, there was, in my estimation, an almost unfathomable crucible for African-Americans in the United States. In this era of the Civil Rights Movement, a high-wattage light shined on issues of oppression, disenfranchisement, discrimination, violence and suffering. An unwitting, and certainly unsophisticated, passenger along for that ride, I marvel at what transpired during that period of time. In 1954, the U.S. Supreme Court ruled to integrate public schools in "Brown vs. Board of Education," and less than two years later Rosa Parks inspired the Montgomery, Alabama bus boycott when she was arrested for refusing to yield her seat on a bus to a white patron. In the fall of 1957, President Eisenhower sent U.S. Army troops to Little Rock, Arkansas, to secure the peaceful integration of Central High School, after Arkansas Governor Orval Faubus attempted to block it with the Arkansas National Guard.

As a toddler and for many years beyond, I was oblivious to these matters of history. These are my earliest memories of my experiences with Blacks in America, from the late 1950s:

- The *"Amos 'n Andy"* show was popular on television, as it had been for years on radio with white actors playing African-American characters. The TV show featured a pair of African-American actors playing the roles of pals who operated a taxi company, and an assortment of numbskull friends, including the scheming George "Kingfish" Stevens and the dim-witted Lightning. Not exactly Sidney Poitier and Denzel Washington. I recall watching the reruns of this show, and thinking it was pretty funny, largely unaware as I was of the societal implications. It aired in 1951-53, with syndicated reruns broadcast through 1966, when complaints about ethnic stereotyping convinced series owner CBS to cancel it.

- My mother hired a black maid to clean our house. I have no idea how we afforded that, but Mary Jane Clark was a sweet, caring person upon whom Mom often relied to supervise my siblings and me as she attended to her numerous volunteer activities.

- Steve Greenfield was the "porter" at Jimmy & Andy's Bar, which meant he mopped the floor and scrubbed the rest of the tavern at dawn before my Dad or Uncle Andy opened the place to the public at 6 a.m. every day.

- At the Epiphany of Our Lord elementary school I attended, there was a single African-American student. In a "Special Education" group segregated from the regular class grades, there were kids with physical palsy, Down's Syndrome, and various forms of learning disability, one of whom was African-American. I was such an ignorant and uninformed

10-year-old that I had assumed the boy's skin color was the reason he would be schooled in a special class.

Within a few years, Freedom Riders entered the South in 1961 to bring attention to the fact that interstate transportation laws banning segregation were being ignored; James Meredith enrolled as a student at the University of Mississippi despite threats on his life; Commissioner of Public Safety Eugene "Bull" Conner ordered the violent fire hosing of civil rights protestors and even children as young as six years old in 1963 in Birmingham, Alabama; and civil rights leader Medgar Evers was murdered in Mississippi. Dr. Martin Luther King Jr. emerged as a messianic leader and advocate of nonviolent protest, and gave us a lasting legacy with his actions and the words calling for the end of racism in America in his famous "I have a dream" speech, which he delivered in August 1963 during the March on Washington for Jobs and Freedom.

In 1965, the city of Los Angeles erupted in violence in the streets of Watts, and 34 people were killed in the rioting.

In Oakland, California, in 1966, Huey Newton and Bobby Seale formed the Black Panther Party, established for the purpose of protecting the black community from oppressive police brutality. With sharp rhetoric, militant posturing, and loaded weaponry, the Black Panthers certainly raised racial awareness in counterpoint to the non-violent approach to civil disobedience advocated by Dr. King, and stirred sentiments among both blacks and whites in America. At a political gathering in 1968, Bobby Seale declared the following:

Everyone falls into two categories. You are either part of the problem—or part of the solution. Being part of the solution means you're willing to grab a shotgun and take to the barricades, killing if necessary. Being part of the problem means you're on the other side of the shotgun. There is no in-between.

Black Panther chapters were founded in major cities across the country. FBI Director J. Edgar Hoover labeled the Black Panthers "the greatest threat to the internal security of the country."

In July of 1967, President Johnson appointed an 11-member group called the Kerner Commission to find out what could be done about the country's racial tensions. Seven months later, the Kerner Commission released *The Report of the National Advisory Commission on Civil Disorders*. The 426-page report cited failed housing, education and social services policies, and claimed the rioting resulted from black frustration at lack of economic opportunity.

One of its most notable passages warned, *"Our nation is moving toward two societies, one black, one white—separate and unequal."* Martin Luther King Jr. pronounced the report a *"physician's warning of approaching death, with a prescription for life."* Among its recommendations were investment in housing that would better integrate neighborhoods, creation of new jobs, and hiring more diverse and sensitive police forces.

Two months after the report was published, Dr. King was assassinated on a motel balcony in Memphis, Tennessee. Washington, New York, Boston and Chicago were among 100 American cities that raged with rioting, which led to an estimated 20,000 arrests. St. Louis was *not* one of those cities confronted by a riot, but our community certainly was troubled.

On that April afternoon in 1968, St. Louis U. High freshman Tim Rodgers was hitchhiking home from school, which he often did. Tim's father was an executive with Ozark Airlines, and the family lived in the near North County area, not far from Lambert Airport. Soon after exiting the car of a driver who dropped him off on Easton Avenue, still far from home, the 14-year-old Rodgers wondered why he was being verbally assaulted by one African-American after another.

Suddenly, a police patrol car whipped around the street corner and pulled up next to him.

"What the fuck are you doing?! said the animated officer, an African-American, addressing the startled Rodgers. "Don't you know Dr. Martin Luther King was assassinated today?!"

It would have been easy to understand if the officer had moved on after warning Rodgers. But he did not. He directed Rodgers to get into the squad car, and drove him to his house, surely well out of his police jurisdiction.

The assassination sparked rioting in more than 100 U.S. cities, though St. Louis was spared. In Washington, D.C., President Johnson directed more than 13,000 federal troops to restore order in the nation's capital, and Marines mounted machine guns on the steps of the U.S. Capitol. Thousands of rioters were arrested around the country.

A few years later, Easton Avenue in St. Louis was renamed "Dr. Martin Luther King Jr. Boulevard."

The world of sports always seemed to have been a few steps ahead of the rest of the American culture on confronting racial issues. Olympic sprint champion Jesse Owens had deflated Adolf Hitler's theory of Arian supremacy in the Berlin Olympic Games of 1936, heavyweight boxing champion Joe Louis had given hope to the country's oppressed of all races in the 1930s and '40s, and Jackie Robinson had integrated professional sports with Major League Baseball's Brooklyn Dodgers in 1947. But the decade of the 1960s was particularly impactful.

Cassius Clay cracked our consciousness with his boastful self-promotion, backed by his shocking upset of the menacing and sullen St. Louisan Sonny Liston in the heavyweight boxing championship fight in 1964, then his title defense a few months later. By converting to the Islam religion, by changing his name to Muhammad Ali, by enduring a banishment from boxing for his refusal to be inducted into the Army in 1967, this one man forced Americans to confront their racial biases in ways they had never before had to. There were sides to be taken, and most people chose one or the other. Love him or hate him.

Other athletes, such as the tough and serious Jimmy Brown of the NFL Cleveland Browns, Bill Russell and Kareem Abdul-Jabbar of the NBA, and Curt Flood of the St. Louis Cardinals, were among the influential and charismatic national figures who were changing and shaping racial attitudes across the United States, all the way down to ignorant high school teenagers such as I, who had grown up with a perverse, uninformed perspective on race.

On the sports fields and courts, I had played with and against African-American athletes. Fluent in the language of sport, I found the associations easy and comfortable. Whayne Herriford was decidedly *not* an athlete, and his was a language of politics and policy and human relations that required a depth and commitment to which I had not been accustomed. Over the next 12 months, he was to become one of my dearest and closest friends.

13// *"Whites Live Yet Blacks Die!"*

1967-70

WHAYNE HERRIFORD SPENT MOST of the summer of 1970 in Belmont, California, with a cousin who owned a printing company. It was near Haight-Ashbury, which had gained a reputation as the world epicenter of the "hippie" culture. And near the Black Panthers headquarters. In early July, Whayne sent me a letter addressed to "J. 'Boss' Castellano," a fanciful reference to our relative SLUH Student Council offices, and concluded it with the following:

> *Well, far be it from me to take up the precious time of His highness the President.*

Just remember—ALL POWER TO THE PEOPLE!!!!!!!!
and KEEP THE FAITH BABY.
Your cousin, Sec

Later in the month, two weeks from the start of our senior year, Whayne sent me a post card, with this message he wanted me to convey to our fellow Student Council leaders and Father David Wayne, who was to be the special advisor for our senior class and the Student Council:

> *Would appreciate it if you would prepare a meeting of Internal, External, Academic, Ed, Phil, you and Fr. Wayne for Monday or Tuesday because I will be prepared to distribute the report I have made of racial attitudes and I have copies for these people. I want to talk about it and I think that the sooner the better. It is important to me that we do something before we go back. It is about 30 pages long, and it's kind of bitter in spots, but it truly "tells it like it is."*
>
> *Thanks, Wayne*
>
> *I will call you! Don't call me!*

Well, by that time it was becoming clear that the coming Student Council session was to be something other than a social club. Being Whayne Herriford's classmate, being Whayne Herriford's fellow Student Council officer, being Whayne Herriford's friend, was not something that was to be done passively. When he returned to St. Louis from California, Whayne gave me a copy of his report. It was 34 pages long, and it featured this title page:

WHITES LIVE
YET …
BLACKS DIE!

Racism at SLUH
Wayne Herriford
1971

14// *"How Does It Feel To Be A Nigger Lover?"*

BEING WHAYNE HERRIFORD, it turns out, was not so easy, either. One of just six African Americans to enroll among the 229 freshmen in the Class of 1971, Herriford had been told by one of the nuns at the Holy Rosary Catholic School he attended, "You are Slum Scum. You won't make it there (at St. Louis U. High)." Despite that stark admonition, Herriford still thought the private Catholic high school was a better alternative than Beaumont or Sumner High, the public schools representing his neighborhood. Somehow, he had the impression those public school kids would antagonize, harass or even physically harm the Catholic kids, especially those as slightly constructed as he.

During his first two years of high school, Whayne rode the Taylor Avenue bus south on Kingshighway Boulevard, then back home north on the same line. "I just wanted to go there, finish class, then get the hell out," Herriford recalled. The first two years, he lived with stress and a knot in his stomach. Whayne saw the other SLUH students as many nervous freshmen saw other students: connected, in cliques, well adjusted, comfortable and sure of themselves. Certainly, very few actually were those things. But as a stranger in a new environment, as easily identified as "different" by the color of his skin, it was understandable that he might start with the assumption that he didn't belong. He recalls most classmates regarding him passively, with neither animosity nor warmth, but he clearly remembers certain classmates who made him feel welcome, such as Bill Grieser, Mark Graham and Tom Weber. He also recalls hearing another classmate crudely utter this challenge, not meant for his ears, to one of those kind classmates who had befriended him, "So how does it feel to be a nigger lover?"

After two years, Herriford felt he was at a crossroads, and recognized he had to make a decision: continue to struggle as an outsider, or get involved. Encouraged, in particular, by Dennis Duggan, a young Jesuit scholastic who taught a social studies course called *American Problems*, Herriford decided to assert himself. It was time, he concluded, to confront race, to challenge his classmates, to ensure people *thought* about things, to break down stereotypes. To trust people, and to make friends. He got a taste of this as a sophomore when he volunteered and was selected to announce the Democratic candidate for President of the United States at an all-school assembly, a "mock election" to generate awareness for the 1968 race between Richard Nixon and Hubert Humphrey. He wrote the speech himself, and delivered it with enthusiasm, building to the payoff line like a seasoned politician:

If these accomplishments and qualities I've mentioned describe the kind of person you believe should be President of the United States, then I urge you all to cast your vote for Hubert H. Humphrey, the next President of the United States!

Herriford liked the sound of the applause he received. Junior year, and the rest of his life, would be different.

By the spring of our junior year, his heart was set on being elected to the Student Council. Whayne had made his case to enough classmates, through what he described as an underground campaign, that it was time to elect to our Student Council someone who represented the "little people" or "outsiders" who seldom got the chance to work on the inside.

"Whayne was becoming the school social activist and social conscience," said Phil Schaefer. "I liked him. He was operating on a different wavelength, and I found that intriguing. He could get you off-balance, but I didn't mind that at all. I thought even in those days how challenging it might have been to be a black kid in an upper-crust white school."

Herriford vividly recalls that Friday in April, when the results of the Student Council election of officers were read over the school's public address system, starting with Treasurer, then Secretary, then Vice President, then President.

"When they announced Phil (Schaefer) as Treasurer, I thought that I had probably not made it," he said. "Then they said I was elected Secretary with 302 vote points and I was shocked and ecstatic at the same time." St. Louis U. High had its first African American Student Council officer.

15// *The Roy Rogers Hotel in Springfield*

1962

COACH PAUL MARTEL HAD BROKEN the "color barrier" for the SLUH varsity football program in 1962, when he kept Bennie Davis on the team.

"Are you going to let that Negro play for SLUH?" Coach Martel was asked by a number of parents of the white kids on the team.

"Well, yes," he said in reply. "If he beats out a white kid, you bet he's going to play."

A game that season in Springfield, Missouri, presented a couple of challenges for Martel and the Junior Billikens. First, the Coach had to find a place for Bennie Davis to sleep, since so many establishments at that time were racially segregated: *Whites Only or Colored.* Martel was determined to find a hotel that would accept the entire team; not one hotel for the whites and a second for Bennie Davis.

"After being turned down by a few hotels," Martel said, "we finally got the whole team in at the Roy Rogers Hotel in Springfield."

Next, he had to find a roommate for Davis. Some of the players' parents had expressed concern about the possibility of their sons sleeping in a room with a Negro.

"Put him in with me," said Al Chettle, one of the team captains. Considering the time and context, it was an act of courage and leadership. Of course, it hardly deserves mention on the same page as the courage it took Davis to persevere in the face of the indignity he suffered. But it was the kind of simple, quiet gesture that builds community and advances the civilization. That changes the world. And made it easier for young men like Errol Patterson to play the game with so much less social drama just a few years later.

Patterson was one of the six African Americans who entered St. Louis U. High in the autumn of 1967 as part of our Class of 1971. From my first encounter with him, it was easy to see Errol was a special talent, and a special person. Extremely gifted as an athlete, Patterson was fast and fearless on the football field, a talent impossible to overlook. Off the field, unlike Whayne Herriford, he seemed self-assured, easy going, and incapable of an uncomfortable or awkward encounter. It turns out, though, it was something of a miraculous coincidence that he was even a student at St. Louis U. High.

16// "They Always Tried To Reach High"

1950s / 1960s

THE SECOND OF Dr. Relford and Gloria Patterson's three children, Errol grew up in Tuskegee, Alabama. Professor Patterson, a native of Lenoir, North Carolina, had met the lovely Gloria Cooley when they were undergraduates at Howard University in Washington, D.C. Gloria was from St. Louis, but she moved with her new husband when his career took him to Shaw (Raleigh, N.C.) and Wilburforce (Ohio), two of the Historically Black Colleges & Universities, to pursue his career in music education. In 1956, Dr. Patterson was recruited by Tuskegee Institute, the university founded by the freed slave Booker T. Washington in 1881, to become director of its renowned Tuskegee Institute Choir. Relford and Gloria moved to Tuskegee with their three children: Relford, age 4, Errol, 3, and Myrnae, 1.

It was an idyllic setting for the young Pattersons. Under their father's direction in 1958, the Tuskegee Choir performed as part of the 25th anniversary celebration gala at Radio City Music Hall in New York City, with the Atlanta Symphony Orchestra, and at Expo 58, the World's Fair in Brussels, Belgium. In 1962, the Choir performed at the White House Christmas Tree Lighting Ceremony as guests of President John F. Kennedy. The family once spent more than six months in Madagascar, where Gloria home schooled her three small children.

"My folks made a point of showing us the world," Errol said.

Back in Alabama, the kids attended St. Joseph Catholic School in Tuskegee, which is about 40 miles east of Montgomery, the state capital. Montgomery is about 50 miles east of Selma. In the mid-1960s, a young African-American family in the middle of Alabama was quite aware of the social turmoil brewing. A decade earlier, Dr. Martin Luther King Jr. had begun his ministry in Montgomery. It was there in 1955 that he organized a 13-month boycott of the city's buses in protest when Rosa Parks was disciplined for refusing to yield her seat on a bus. In 1963 in Birmingham, 90 miles north of Montgomery, a bomb was detonated before Sunday morning services at the 16th Street Baptist Church, and four young girls were killed by the blast that generated national attention and triggered protests that became the epicenter of the national movement for desegregation and the civil rights movement.

"My Mom did a good job of insulating us," Errol remembered. "We saw things on the news, and it was dinner-time conversation. We lived in this little carve-out community, and we never went into town. But that could only last so long."

In March of 1965, Dr. King Jr. organized a series of marches from Selma to Montgomery to bring pressure to pass the Voting Rights Act, designed to prevent racial discrimination and remove the obstacles African-Americans had encountered in a systematized effort to keep them from registering to vote. The first of the three marches disintegrated into what became known as "Bloody Sunday," when Alabama state troopers and local law enforcement used tear gas and clubs on protestors at the Edmund Pettus Bridge. Much of the American public was stunned by what they saw of the event on their television sets, which helped provide an impetus for President Lyndon Johnson to push legislation through Congress. By the fall, the Voting Rights Act was passed and signed into law.

By this time, the Patterson children were entering their teenage years, and Relford and Gloria wondered if there might be a better, less-volatile environment for their kids as they prepared to enter high school. In the spring of 1967, they looked hard at moving the children to St. Louis, where Gloria's parents lived. Almost any place would be better than central Alabama, they reasoned, though by then, St. Louis' reputation for its racial climate was mixed. While deep, institutional divisions were being manifest in housing and zoning practices, the community had been spared the rioting that had shaken many urban centers around the country. And it was Gloria Patterson's childhood home. When Gloria's father, Dalton Cooley, died, she and Relford decided to send young Relford and Errol to live with their newly widowed grandmother Mattie Cooley in her home on the near north side of the city, near Page Boulevard and

Vandeventer Avenue.

Gloria Patterson was aware of St. Louis University High School, and believed its Jesuit pedagogy and stellar reputation for academic excellence would provide the proper environment for her sons. Those in the school's admissions department had other ideas, perhaps concerned that the non-traditional path these young men had traveled would diminish their ability to prosper in the highly competitive academic environment. The Pattersons were advised that McBride High School, a private school run by the Catholic Archdiocese of St. Louis and not far from Mattie Cooley's home, might be more suitable. "It was a little rough at first," Mrs. Patterson recalled many years later, of her quest to have her sons accepted at SLUH. But she was determined, she and Dr. Patterson persevered, and the boys were admitted in September of 1967—Relford in the sophomore class; Errol as a freshman.

"Knowing my parents, they always tried to reach high," Errol said. And so he became one of the six African-American freshmen in the SLUH Class of 1971. Without him, I would say, we would have had trouble winning more than half our games in the autumn of 1970.

Despite his pedigree, Errol Patterson was not much of a musician. "I wanted to play football for as long as I could remember," he said.

17// *"Will You Be a Championship Team?"*

Summer 1970

WITH THE SUMMER VACATION of 1970 came the realization that our final high school football season was to begin in less than 100 days. In June, July and August, there were American Legion baseball games to play, summer job duties to endure, streets to drive up and down in search of some type of alluring but unattainable action, weekend dates with girlfriends to navigate. And, inescapably and always, the looming and somewhat haunting sense that we had to get into shape for the opening of football practice. Coach Martel had published his eight-page *"Summer Conditioning Program for Football"* guide, which he had typed himself and copied on the school's mimeograph machine. It was not something a serious SLUH football player cavalierly ignored. It began:

> *Conditioning may be defined as the progressive preparation of athletes for the severe physical exertions necessary in competitive athletics. Through the use of graduated amounts of activity, the endurance and the capacity of the individual will increase to a point of peak efficiency.*

In the deliberative, meticulous, and prescriptive style with which this serious man approached most things in life, the guide laid out the summer conditioning program we were to follow from June 1 right up to August 15, when we were to report for the first official practice. This is the July 15 through August 1 prescription, to be done five days a week:

1. Jog 1/4 mile—walk 1/4 mile............*Repeat four times. This will total one mile of jogging and will not cause muscle cramping.*
2. Do 30 Push-Ups...............*10 at a time.*
3. Do 40 Sit-Ups....................*10 at a time.*
4. Wind-Mills............................*20 - 4 counts.*
5. Jumping Jacks...................*20 to begin with – add one each day to Aug. 1.*
6. Neck-Bridge......................*One minute – Increase to two min. by July 22.*
7. Leg-Lifts..............................*10 on a 4 count.*
8. Trunk Rotation...................*20 – Clock and counter-clock.*
9. Stretch Exercise................*Feet extended – touch the ground behind the heels on a 4 count. Repeat 8 times.*

10. Speed, Stamina and Skill Drills ....*Perform 4 times weekly*

   (Stance and Start – 10 fast starts and sprint 15 yards)

   (Pull out of line – Right 8 times and turn left – Left 8 times and turn right)

   (Reaction Drills – Football position from all fours, rise to two point,

   backward, lateral and forward reaction against an imaginary object)

   *WATCH YOUR WEIGHT ** YOU MUST BE ABLE TO MOVE IF YOU*

   WANT TO PLAY FOOTBALL.

The "Aug. 1 – 15" schedule was similar, though with guidance for more intensity. And this admonition: *50% of games are won or lost on physical conditioning.* YOU MUST BE IN BETTER SHAPE THAN YOUR OPPONENT. The guide also included a weight-training regimen with very descriptive instructions on how to lift weights.

Two-hand curl: Stand close to the bar and grasp barbell with both hands, palms out. Stand erect with the weight hanging at arms length. Slowly, without moving the elbow from the sides, move the weight in a circular path to the shoulders, then lower to the starting position. Begin with a minimum of 6 repetitions and work to a maximum of 12 repetitions before increasing weight. Breathing: Inhale when lifting—Exhale when letting the bar down.

Coach did infuse his own brand of "selling" into this literary masterpiece.

In the past years, coaches have been very much concerned with the physical condition of football players in the off-season, especially freshmen, sophomores and juniors. There is definitely a lessening of desire on the part of athletes to continue to keep physically fit in the off-season.

Since World War II it has become apparent that the physical fitness of our nation's youth leaves a lot to be desired. To participate in a football program it is extremely important that the athlete is in top physical condition.

Statistics show that most games are won or lost in the last quarter. If a player is not in good shape physically, he cannot be expected to perform up to his capabilities. This affects his mental attitude; his determination to do the job with maximum effort is decreased; and his contribution to the team morale is decreased. There is no easy road to success. Every player must work hard if we are going to meet the measure of success that is desired.

Top physical condition cannot be emphasized enough in preparing for the coming football season. Anything worth doing, is worth doing well—do not overlook any points when it comes to training. Champions train conscientiously, practice long hours, and follow closely the rules of good living.

A foundation has been laid—it's up to you to build upon it. Do you have the courage? Are you going to work hard this summer? Will you be a championship team? Only you hold the answers!

Will we be a championship team? Well, that certainly was motivating. Equally motivating was the commitment we felt to each other, an unspoken sense that each of us would prepare ourselves so we would not let down our teammates.

The Missouri State High School Activities Association, which governed high school sports in the state, prohibited practices supervised by coaches or school officials before August 15. So if we were going to show up in shape, it was up to us. In the summer of 1970, jogging was nowhere near the widely practiced enterprise it had become in America by the end of the 20th century, and weight training, for most of us, was nonexistent or, at best, unsophisticated. A common weight set consisted of two large coffee cans full of cement, adhered to opposite ends of a metal bar—courtesy of our entrepreneurial fathers. My dad had mixed up one of those for our family, though I must admit it did not wear out from overuse. Once in a while, I recall, Del Bannister walked down the alley the 100 yards from his house to mine, and we hoisted it a few times.

As for running that summer, a few of us started the informal practice of running a one-mile lap around Aviation Field just across Highway 40 from St. Louis U. High in Forest Park three times a week, followed by calisthenics. And sprints. Yeah, like the sprints Tom Schoeck had challenged us to run at the conclusion of an exhausting practice one hot afternoon when we were on the sophomore team. Without prompting by our coaches, we players would adopt this custom for the season—at the conclusion of every practice, we would run 10 full-speed sprints across the width of the field.

The last paragraph of Coach Martel's conditioning instructions contained this ominous message:

At the first practice every man on the squad will be timed for one mile. All linemen must be able to run under six and one-half minutes while the backs should be able to run it under six minutes. Anyone falling short will run a 440 each day until he can meet this standard.

For some of us, running a mile in full football gear, in the time allocated, was the equivalent of President Kennedy's challenge to the nation in 1961 that we would put a man on the moon by the end of the decade and return him safely. So we wouldn't embarrass ourselves, or, worse, vomit right there on the soft cinder-covered track surrounding the practice field in front of everyone at the conclusion of our timed mile run, most of us took that running regimen pretty seriously that summer.

18// *"Keep Refilling the Glasses"*

TIM KELLETT GOT IN a little running one memorable day that summer, as we pursued frivolous things as a diversion to our job of delivering rented party supplies for Weinhardt Catering. Kellett landed that job, because his older brother Tom had done it two summers before. Invited to recruit two friends, Kellett asked Bob Thibaut and me to join him, and we quickly accepted. It was a dream job. Physical, pretty mindless labor. Pretty good pay, at $3.30 an hour. Not cooped up inside, except when we had to wash glasses and dishes at company headquarters. Most appealing of all was the chance to work in a virtually unsupervised way with our pals. Unsupervised, I say, because the "grownup" who drove the delivery truck, a happy fellow named Dale, a few years our senior, was as interested as Tim, Bob and I were in goofy things.

Goofy as in the great challenge race around the sports track at Parkway West High School in west St. Louis County. We had just dropped off a few hundred folding chairs that would hold the keisters of the school's graduating seniors and their families the next day, and we thought it was time to have some fun in the absence of any discernible security from the high school. Dale in the truck would have to traverse the entire quarter-mile track, while Kellett would start a half-lap ahead on his 220-yard sprint. I lowered my arm to signal the start of this classic event. Kellett took off, pumping his arms and striding steadily heading into the first curve. Dale floored the truck's accelerator and, after slightly fishtailing as the rear wheels spit out loose cinders at its hind end, bore down fast on his human foe. He was closing in on his two-legged adversary, a few hundred horsepower churning that old box truck's axles, charging into the final curve. Again, the back wheels shot out loose cinders before Dale straightened out for a sprint to the finish. Kellett, ever the competitor but perhaps realizing the potential calamity as a lunatic in an eight-ton truck was getting nearer by the yard, kicked into a higher gear and glided across the finish line the winner. Thankfully, Tim was not run over.

I loved that job, as much as anything for the chance to become closer friends with Kellett and Thibaut.

The son of John, a physician, and Kay, a homemaker, who raised six children, Kellett was from Webster Groves, the quaint St. Louis suburb that was featured in a CBS Television documentary entitled *16 in Webster Groves*[11] in 1966. Narrated by the noted Charles Kuralt, the program depicted Webster Groves teenagers as overly status-conscious, conformist, materialistic, and clique-ridden. The community's citizens, many of whom happily cooperated in the filming, mostly felt betrayed by what they deemed were unfair characterizations in the program that aired.

Tim Kellett was none of those things. The younger brother of Tom Kellett, a fullback and linebacker two years older who starred as captain of the 1968 St. Louis U. High team and went on to play for the University of Missouri, Tim was thoughtful, fun-loving, and inclusive. And generous. He didn't hesitate to offer his football cleats to an absent-minded fellow freshman, who was on the sophomore team, and had forgotten to bring his to a game. Tim had just finished practice for the freshman team. "Uh, I better not wear those because they are muddy," said the oblivious I, mindful of Coach Crazy Joe Vitale's regulations for clean uniforms. Stupidly, I wore my clean sneakers to that game instead. Another Kellett trait is a wicked sense of humor, and I suppose that if somehow we transcend space and time and survive into the 22nd century, he still will rib me about that. "Remember when you thought my football shoes weren't good enough for you?" I will hear him say.

Bob Thibaut was the only child of Gayle and Robert Thibaut, who progressed from a beer truck driver to a successful sales executive for the Falstaff Brewing Company. He was transferred from New Orleans to St. Louis when young Bob was in the third grade, and enrolled his son in the Seven Holy Founders Catholic grade school in southwest St. Louis County. Strong, thick and quick, Thibaut knew pretty early in life that he was meant to play football. His father played the game on a city championship team in New Orleans, though he was not the family's best. That honor belonged to Bob's uncle, Jimmy Thibaut, an All-American at Tulane University who went on to play for the New York Giants in the National Football League.

When a volunteer at Seven Holy Founders organized the boys to practice football, he had to dismiss young Bob Thibaut from the group.

"He wouldn't let me hit people," Thibaut said. "I was big, and he said, 'Bob, you can't come out here and do this.'"

Thibaut found another outlet, joining with boys in the neighborhood, wearing makeshift gear, calling themselves the Grantwood Gophers, and challenging boys from nearby neighborhoods to games of tackle football. "It was like Norman Rockwell," Thibaut said of the unsupervised, Americana setting. "One guy had a war helmet, another had an old football helmet. Whatever we had, we put on. We played a lot. And we played a lot of 'kill the man with the ball.' I mean, we just beat each other to death. Somebody had to go to the hospital almost every other week, it seemed. I was always the meatball. Ran the ball. I loved running the ball."

When it came time for high school, the Thibaut family was strongly influenced by the family of Seven Holy Founders classmate John Sondag, whose older brother Dave attended St. Louis U. High. Thibaut attended the 1966 SLUH vs. CBC football game at Busch Stadium, and spent the first half on the CBC side with grade school classmate Mike Geary, who had declared his intention to attend CBC. In the second half, Thibaut watched from the SLUH side with the Sondags. "If I could get into SLUH," Thibaut thought to himself, "I'd rather do that than march around in uniforms (at CBC, which at the time required military protocols as part of its ROTC tradition)."

In August of 1967, having been accepted into the SLUH Class of 1971, Thibaut decided he would try to make the sophomore football team. Since the Falstaff headquarters at the time was just to the west of St. Louis U. High on Oakland Avenue, on the land once occupied by Walsh Stadium, Bob's father drove him to the first day of tryouts on his way to work. He pulled the car over, and waited for Bob to exit.

"I'm not going," Bob declared. "I'm not getting out of the car."

"What?" Mr. Thibaut responded.

"I think I'll just go out for the 'C' team," Bob said.

"I'm here, I drove you here, and you're going," Mr. Thibaut answered firmly. "You get your ass out of this car right now."

And so it was that Bob Thibaut made his debut on the practice field for Joe Vitale's "B" team. He made an immediate impression on Vitale.

"He took a liking to me, he really did," Thibaut said. Vitale liked him so much that he made him his starting tackle on both offense and defense, very rare for a freshman on the sophomore team. The first week of school, Vitale gave Thibaut a special assignment in his freshman typing class. "Type up this list and post it," the coach told him. It was the "cut list," the list of players who made the team. "That's how I found out I made the team," Thibaut said.

The following year, when we sophomores attempted to make Paul Martel's varsity, Thibaut had a bold idea.

"I hated tackle," he said. "I said to myself, I'd rather not play if I can't touch the ball. So I asked Vitale what he thought, and he encouraged me to try out for fullback. Martel went for the idea, and Thibaut was one of the six sophomores he kept on the varsity for the 1968 season.

Ed Weinhardt was the successful, under-educated, parsimonious, literally toothless entrepreneur who founded and owned the catering company that bore his name. I am grateful he hired Kellett, Thibaut and me to deliver and pick up his party rentals during the summer of 1970.

And pour champagne. Certain that we could handle the bartending duties at wedding receptions and other private gatherings for which he supplied the bubbly, glasses, plates, silverware, 60-inch round wood tables, and folding chairs—and apparently averse to paying seasoned bartenders— Mr. Weinhardt relied on us 17-year-old minors to take care of business. One had to love that about him. Looking dapper in our white shirts and ties, we gladly embraced the assignment. It was the first time I had ever been in homes like that, in some of the wealthiest neighborhoods in the most affluent areas of St. Louis City and County.

One evening, Thibaut and I served drinks during the funeral wake for Mark Eagleton at the Eagleton home. The deceased, whose body lay in state in the parlor, was the father of Missouri Senator Thomas Eagleton. Two years later, in the summer of 1972, Senator Eagleton would be invited by Democratic Presidential Nominee George McGovern to be his Vice President running mate as they would challenge incumbent President Richard Nixon. Eighteen days later, after news broke that Eagleton suffered from depression and had undergone electroconvulsive therapy, McGovern dumped him from the ticket.

Despite the turmoil that had encircled us for much of the previous decade, those months in May, June and July of 1970 were about the most blissful and carefree in our lives.

"Keep refilling the glasses," Mr. Weinhardt instructed us. "They have to pay for every bottle we open up."

There was a lot there for a distrustful, college-bound teenager to reject and rebel against. Personally, I guess the three of us didn't think much about it at the time. We were having fun.

I also spent that summer falling in love with the beautiful and buoyant Katie Rhoades, whom I met after one of my baseball games that spring. She was a radiant spirit untroubled by the way I morphed into a shy, awkward klutz in the presence of girls. We called her Cougar Kate, because she drove a cool Lincoln Cougar. She was the youngest of four children of Lois and Roy Rhoades, who was the plant manager of the Ford Motor Company factory in St. Louis. As such, he was entitled to lease late-model automobiles produced by Ford and Lincoln, and since Lois did not drive, Kate commandeered that vehicle. In September, Kate would enter her senior year at Nerinx Hall, the private, all-girls college preparatory school in Webster Groves, and I would enter mine at SLUH. Until then, we had a summer to savor.

19// *"We Were Invincible"*

ED HAWK, TOO, WAS ENJOYING a carefree summer. The second oldest of James and Mary Hawk's seven children, our incoming Student Council Vice President saved most of the money he earned busing tables at Westwood Country Club to buy the car his father did not want him to have. It was a 1966 red MGB convertible. Price tag: $1,000.

"I was the one who talked my Dad into letting him buy that car," recalled John Hawk, 19 months younger than Ed and one class behind us at St. Louis U. High. "The two of them bucked heads a lot. I was always the one who could keep things calm."

The two brothers were very close. "As close as two brothers could be," John said. Still, they had a spirited rivalry. "Growing up, he was always bigger than me," John said. "He used to sit on top of me. He found out if he hit me in the nose, it could make me sneeze. He thought that was funny."

With the family expanding in the early 1960s, Jim and Mary Hawk converted the basement of their West St. Louis County home into two bedrooms, each with a bathroom. Ed and John shared one bedroom; their older sister Maggie shared the other with younger sister Bridget. The younger children, Joe, Anne and Beth, were upstairs with their Mom and Dad. In many ways, it was an idyllic childhood for the Hawk kids. A successful attorney, Jim Hawk took his boys hunting and fishing, and with Mary they supported the children's activities at St. Clement of Rome Catholic School. The boys enjoyed playing sports, and at one time Ed was captain of the 8th grade soccer team while John captained the 7th graders. "Ed always won the 100-yard dash at the school picnic," John said. "He was faster than me, but I'd say I had more skills."

Certainly, John admired his brother, and frequently sought to follow his footsteps. But he was satisfied with his position in the family's birth order. "I was the third kid," he said. "That was a good place to be, because you could hide. Ed was always getting in trouble, either because of discipline or grades."

Even so, in his first three years at St. Louis U. High, Ed had put together a formidable high school resume, including landing the role of Vinnie Barella in SLUH's theater production of *The Odd Couple* as a sophomore, and getting elected Vice President of the Student Council for our upcoming senior year. He had spoken with John and others about his plans for the future. Perhaps college at Notre Dame University. He was developing an interest in medicine, and mentioned an interest in learning more about the St. Louis College of Pharmacy. He had things to do.

And he had life to live, which he did, at times, as if he were in a hurry. Bob Thibaut and Tim Kellett were among his close friends. "Beer and booze," Thibaut said. "We had that in common." An only child, with no relatives in St. Louis other than his parents, and with his Dad often away at work, Thibaut relished those evenings he could spend at the Hawks' home, with the activity and life abundant in a large family.

One evening during our junior year, Thibaut, Hawk and Kellett were idling on a parking lot when Ed issued a challenge.

"I bet that if I got on the hood of your car, you couldn't buck me off," Hawk said. It is difficult to believe, from the perspective today of a grown adult, that this sounded like a reasonable idea. To Kellett and Thibaut at the time, however, their only act of discernment was deciding who would go first.

"I went first," Kellett recalled. "I just kind of drove in circles, and Ed stayed on. It was impressive."

Then it was Thibaut's turn. Steady behind the wheel, looking into Hawk's eyes as he gripped the hood of the car, Thibaut went left, then accelerated quickly as he sharply reversed the steering wheel to the right.

"Ed just went sailing," Kellett said. "Just sailing." He got up, nicked and scraped from the gravel into which he landed. "We all just laughed like crazy."

Like many adolescents in search of their limits, Ed was pursuing the natural separation from his family. In late July of 1970, he had talked his parents into letting him leave early from their annual summer vacation retreat in the rented cabins of Macatawa, near Holland, Michigan. The one concession he accepted was that his grandmother, Dee Maruska, would stay at the Hawk home with him while the family was away.

Saturday nights in the summer were to be savored for Don Martini, the son of a bricklayer and one of Ed Hawk's closest friends. He wasn't due back to work at the Scullin Steel plant until Monday night at 11 p.m. for the midnight shift. At the plant, just a couple miles from St. Louis U. High, Don would shovel sand, shake iron scraps from the steel molds, do "all kinds of crap," while laboring for oxygen in the hot plant. "I hated it, but it was good money," said Martini, a fellow member of the SLUH Class of 1971. It was certainly no Weinhardt Catering gig, nor table busing at a country club. The highlight for Martini was "lunch" at 3 a.m., when he and a dozen or so fellow workers headed across the street to eat.

During the week, he coped with the grueling shiftwork in the Scullin plant, because he was making great money for a 17-year-old, he was getting in good shape, and—as was *not* the case for most of his co-workers, most of them African-Americans for whom there was no finish line—he knew the experience would sunset once school resumed in late August.

On August 1, one of the final Saturday nights of the summer, Martini looked forward to a night with friends, and he would be traveling with Ed Hawk. Ed would be driving that night, after working his shift at the Westwood Country Club until 4:30 p.m. Later in the evening, he left his family's home in the upscale suburb of Des Peres in west St. Louis County and drove to Webster Groves to pick up Don, who crawled into the narrow passenger seat of Hawk's red MGB convertible, and they headed toward the city. Ed worked three summers to earn the $1,000 he spent in May to buy that used car.

The two of them and Bob Thibaut were among a small group of our classmates who earlier in the summer had solved the problem of finding a place to party: renting a dumpy apartment on Pershing Avenue, in a neighborhood of the city that offered a rate suitable to the budget of 17-year-olds who preferred to spend the little money they had on beer, not housing. For young men of that particular age, buying beer and drinking beer were illegal activities, a prohibition to be scorned by those on the threshold of their last year of high school, at the conclusion of a decade when all of America, it seemed, had lost its innocence. What was the big deal? Weary of being hassled by adults who didn't understand or accept our delusion that we already were adults, we regarded the apartment as a logical thing to do. Of course, the parents were not to be told of it. "We had tried everything else," Martini said. "Parks. People's houses when their parents were out of town. We were just looking for some place to be able to go every night. Somewhere where you could go and just relax."

This particular dive was on the city's near northwest side, just east of the border separating St. Louis from University City, and just a block north of Forest Park. Phil Schaefer and the SLUH cross-country team ran through that neighborhood during conditioning runs, but not after dark. "Living in St. Louis, we knew there were places you didn't want to go," Schaefer said. "It was too dangerous."

This neighborhood was one of the city's most celebrated and majestic during the time of the 1904 World's Fair, when St. Louis was one of the country's most populous cities. But it had deteriorated during the previous decades, as the gentry class moved to the suburbs to avoid racial integration.

Many years later, Don Martini would reflect on the decision to get that apartment. "It was a pretty stupid thing to do," he said. "But we were in high school and invincible. The worst thing was, the craziest thing, stupidest thing was, none of the girls ever wanted to go down there. They were smart. They were deathly afraid of the neighborhood. They would think up excuses not to go down there."

Katie Rhoades never went there. "It was something for the guys," she recalled. "On the periphery. A random place, in not a very good part of town."

"The girls were smart," Martini said. "We were invincible."

20// *"You Got the Time?"*

August 1970

ED HAWK FELT particularly invincible in his MGB, and he picked up Don Martini for a night of kicking back at the apartment. They parked, went in to greet Bob Thibaut, Tim Kellett, John McElroy and others already there, and quickly headed back outside. "We had just gotten there," Don said. "Not enough beer. Had some, not enough. Not enough alcohol. We collected some money, and went out on a beer run, as somebody had to do every night." It was very civilized, when you think about it. All for one, one for all.

Driving down DeGiverville Avenue toward DeBaliviere Avenue, just a few blocks from the apartment, toward one of the joints they knew would sell alcohol beverages to minors, Hawk and Martini weren't thinking about much. Slowing as they neared a stop sign, the two barely noticed as two young African-American men approached the car.

"You got the time?" one of them asked. An old ploy, Don Martini was to recognize much later. He wasn't wearing a watch, but Ed Hawk was. "Ed always had a watch on," Don said. "We were nice guys. We stopped."

"Eleven o'clock," Ed called out, as he turned to his left to greet this stranger. He noticed a shiny object in the clutch of the young man's hand.

"Next thing, I look down and there was a gun pointed at us," Don said.

"Give me your money," one of the assailants said.

"My first reaction was one of shock, then to give them what they wanted," Martini said. "Not Ed. Ed hit the gas. He gunned it, and I think we both kind of ducked. Shots were fired."

The young stranger with the revolver fired once, then again, then again.

"Why would the guy have fired?" Don Martini asked himself a thousand times after that night. "We were gone. The episode was over. He should have just faded into the night. I don't know why he didn't. Maybe he was shocked that Ed sped off. Maybe he panicked."

Martini reached over to help Hawk steer away from a parked car, and the two landed in the parking lot of a Burger King restaurant.

"You all right?" Don asked.

"Yeah, I'm all right," Ed said.

But he wasn't all right. One of the .38 caliber bullets had hit the luggage rack on the back hood of the MGB and deflected downward into Hawk's back. It went through a lung, his spleen, his pancreas, then lodged in his right hip. A moment after declaring he was all right, he started hacking. "I've been hit," he said, contorting his face. Then he passed out.

In the span of a minute, maybe "20 seconds or less," in the flash of a gunshot, in a random moment when two young men from the pastoral safety of west St. Louis County found themselves in a dangerous place at the wrong time, many lives would be changed forever.

21// "When Are We Going To Have Our Meeting?"

A PATRON OF the restaurant called the police, who arrived quickly. While Martini stayed with the car and described what happened, Ed Hawk was rushed to nearby St. Luke's Hospital.

Dee Maruska got the call from the police, and desperately tried to reach Ed's parents—her daughter Mary and son-in-law Jim Hawk in Michigan. She was unsuccessful, but was able to contact Jim's sister, Margaret Warner.

"Aunt Margaret called Mom and Dad," said John Hawk, Ed's brother. "They came in and woke up Maggie and me, but let the other kids sleep."

The news was dire.

"Everyone thought he was going to die that night," John said. "That's the way it came down, based on what the doctors told my aunt in St. Louis."

While Jim and Mary rushed to St. Louis on the next flight, they arranged to have Mary's brothers drive to Michigan to pick up the six children and drive them home in two cars. Jim and Mary reached the hospital Sunday. With Uncles Bill and Paul Maruska driving, the kids got back late Monday night.

The Sunday morning after the shooting, Tim Kellett answered the phone at his house. Pat "Del" Bannister was on the line with the somber news. "It seemed like it was always Del who called, who always had the news first," said Kellett. Hawk and Martini never returned from their beer run Saturday night, he suddenly remembered. The night before, he and others just figured they found something else to do.

Word of the incident spread quickly among our SLUH classmates and other friends. I phoned Katie Rhoades to tell her Ed had been shot. "At first, I was in denial," she recalled. "I couldn't wrap my head around the news." We all were stunned by the news, and I had difficulty processing it. We all wanted to go see Ed, despite the admonition we received that he was not to have visitors.

"They didn't let me into his room that night," said Don Martini, who persisted. "The Hawks got me up there one time, but the hospital really fought that. I think a lot of guys tried to sneak in."

Remarkably, despite the extent of the damage inside his torso, Hawk's condition stabilized. For the first days, he was conscious, and it appeared he would recover. Those looking for anger or a bitter reaction or self-pity, were not going to find that from Ed Hawk.

"I just can't imagine being shot in my own city," he said more than once.

When you think about it, that's a rational response from a 17-year-old who was full of optimism, dismissive of the concept that bad guys doing bad things was inevitable and unavoidable, flush with the potential of a harmonious society. It surprised him.

"That first week he was getting better and better," John Hawk recalled. "He was watching TV and talking."

While visiting, John and Ed watched a John Wayne movie in the hospital room. Big John Wayne got shot in it. Ed told his brother, "They act like it doesn't hurt. It hurts."

We were buoyed by the news that Ed was awake and conscious. A number of us gathered, embraced each other, and we prayed for our friend's full and fast recovery. With every day, we awaited news of Ed's progress.

"I didn't believe he would die," Katie said. "We were praying. We were taught that our prayers got answered. We thought he would pull through, and refused to believe he wouldn't."

"There was this huge sigh of relief, because Ed was doing well," Kellett recalled. "A horrible thing happened, but thank goodness, he was going to be fine. There was this unbelievable feeling of relief. The fact that he was up and talking, was an indication that it was almost 100 percent that he was going to be fine."

Kellett remembers his reflections during that first week, while Ed lay in his hospital bed recovering.

"You just don't believe it," he said. "And then I just felt crushed. I thought about his parents, his family. And at that point, it crystallized how stupid, how dangerous having that apartment was. There are so many things you are told are dangerous, so you shouldn't be doing that, and you went ahead and did them anyway. And you never really suffered the consequences. This time, it happened. This time, we were wrong, really wrong."

Bob Thibaut and I decided we would not be deterred by the hospital's visitation embargo, and we headed to St. Luke's Hospital, determined to see our friend for ourselves. We walked boldly through the lobby, careful to avoid eye contact with anyone smelling of authority, rode up the elevator to Ed's floor, and walked confidently past the nurses' desk toward Ed's room. We walked to the threshold of the room, and stood in the doorway.

It was disturbing to see Ed lying there, colorless and connected to so many tubes. But he was lucid, and recognized us immediately. He smiled.

"Hey, Bob," said Ed when he noticed Thibaut.

"Joe, when are we going to have our meeting?" he said to me. We had Student Council business to get under way, and it was clear Ed was planning to be there.

"As soon as you get out of this place," I said. "You'd better make it soon."

"At that point," Thibaut recalled, "I didn't think it was serious. I wasn't thinking this is a real serious thing."

Bob and I bounced out of the hospital, encouraged by Ed's buoyancy and optimism, and anxious to tell the others of our visit. It was, however, the last time we would see Ed alive.

22// *A Price Way Too Steep*

BACTERIA HAD ATTACKED Ed's badly damaged pancreas, and the doctors could not stem the infection. It spread, and started attacking his other organs. On August 12, Ed was transferred to Barnes Hospital, which had the equipment that could take over for his failing kidneys, with the hope that he could stabilize and recover.

It did not work. With his parents and brother John at his hospital bedside, Ed died during the afternoon of August 14.

We didn't believe the news at first. How could that happen? We had just seen him. He was awake, he was joking around. He was just 17 years old. Gone forever? We would never see him again, never work with him, never play with him, never grow old with him? Impossible.

"This can't happen," Bob Thibaut thought. "It was so unreal."

"It was horrible," Tim Kellett said. "It was almost cruel that there was an expectation, or belief, that he was going to make it, based on the news that he was getting better. And then he died."

"I was shocked," Katie Rhoades said. "It was horrible, traumatic. For me, it was the end of innocence. I had experienced people dying, but they were old, and that was the natural order of things. This was the first time something penetrated this bubble we lived in, where we were safe and special. It was scary and so sad, and it ripped your heart out. And I felt so sad for his parents."

Most of Ed's classmates were unprepared to comprehend the news, to accept the reality and permanence of what had happened. It was another body blow to be absorbed by teenagers whose world had been beset with national tragedies, who struggled to find a perspective from which we could continue to hope for a better world. Ed was someone so full of promise, so full of life. His was a life to be devoted to goodness. Were he to lose that life, certainly it would be in the path of goodness, sacrificed nobly for a cause, inspiring to others. Instead, it was lost to a whimsical act of irrationality and randomness, a price way too steep to be paid because young men, feeling invincible, had ignored the risks of being in a tough neighborhood.

At the beginning of Act II in *The Fantasticks*[12], just after the rescue of Elisa, El Gallo sings:

So we would like to truly finish
What was foolishly begun.
For the story is not ended
And the play is never done
Until we've all of us been burned a bit
And burnished by—the sun.

Getting "burned a bit … by the sun" makes me think of the price we sometimes pay for not paying close enough attention to risk, something for which adventurous youth are noted. This passage in the musical presaged things to come, rather than rued things past, and so it a fair criticism to say this is an odd, and possibly inappropriate, reminder of a friend's tragic death. So be it. I ask forgiveness, both from the play's ardent fans and from those who have mourned my friend.

23// *One Lap Short*

THE BEGINNING OF FOOTBALL practice in any year was difficult, the sporting equivalent of a military boot camp, and it was to be dreaded even by those who loved the sport. Especially dreadful was the one-mile run test on the first day of practice, when the coaches would find out what kind of shape we were in. The prior year's run, our junior season, was notable for a couple of reasons.

First, it turns out at least a couple of daring, creative scofflaws had rested behind the equipment shed on the far side of the practice field, just inside the track's backstretch, hidden from the view of the coaches and skipping a full lap as their running mates rounded the track to start lap 4, then resumed running when the pack came by to complete the last half lap to the finish line. Not exactly a monument to Jesuit influence and strong moral character. The culprits had plenty of energy left, as one might imagine, and they sprinted toward the finish line, where a timekeeper was stationed to call out the time, second by second. "Five thirty. Five thirty-one. Five thirty-two." We runners were to note the time called out as we crossed the line, and we would be asked to report the time later, when Coach Martel called out our names in front of the entire squad.

Second, Fred Daues provided a moment of comic relief, with his spasm of honesty. His thick build served him well in battles at the line of scrimmage, but was not well suited for distance running. Daues was particularly challenged by the thought of completing a 4.5-lap mile in less than six and half minutes, in full football pads. Certainly, 25 percent of his weight was in the beating organ that kept alive this man-child, one of the friendliest and most generous spirits any of us knew. At the same time, dressed in football pads and lurching out of his four-point stance from the defensive tackle position, he was one of the fiercest football players on the team.

"I thought I could make it," Daues recounted many years later. "I had no intention of stopping behind the shed. On my second lap, I saw seniors stopping behind the shed. I was falling farther and farther behind. On lap three, I stopped."

Hidden from the view of the authorities across the track at the finish line, Daues took a breather until the pace-setting "rabbits" leading the pack approached behind the shed on the way to their last half lap. When that group of rabbits came upon their finish, Fred was right there with them; they finishing the four-and-a-half-lap mile; Fred stopping at three and a half. When Coach Martel, clipboard and pencil in hand, went player by player asking us to report our times, Fred dutifully responded on his turn by calling out, "Coach, they said the time was five minutes, twenty seconds, but I think I must have stopped one lap short."

A year later, now seniors, we were at it again.

For some, the lure of the shed was as compelling as the Sirens were to Ulysses. Bob Thibaut has acknowledged he was one of those guys. "Yeah, I hid behind the shed," he said. "Senior year. I did jump behind the shed. Which I have hated to this day. To this day, I regret doing it. I shouldn't have done it. I'm thinking to myself, 'Here you're supposed to be one of the leaders of the team, and you're jumping behind the shed.' But it happened. That wasn't one of my shining moments."

One could rely on the St. Louis temperature to be in the 90-degree range and the humidity to approach 100% during the middle of August. We were to cram our bodies into tight pants stuffed with hard-foamed pad inserts, clumsy shoulder pads, and helmets seemingly designed to ignore the fact that we had ears. As an added attraction for the 1970 season, someone in the SLUH administration ordered the dirt excavated to make room for the new school library to be spread on the surface of the notoriously barren "lower field," where we practiced. The thought was, maybe grass finally would grow through the newly deposited soil. What nobody realized, until it was too late, was that the excavated dirt was full of rock and concrete chips. For three months, that stone debris tore our hands, forearms and knees to shreds.

As difficult as the physical conditions could be, that field also served as a therapeutic arena, where we could go to escape the real world of academic demands, social challenges, a troubled society, and, now, the death of a classmate and close friend.

On August 15, one day after Ed Hawk died at Barnes Hospital, we football players endeavored to run the distance of a mile around the cinder track in full gear. It was the long anticipated moment of truth. We linemen hoped to beat six minutes, 30 seconds; backs and receivers tried to make it in under 6:00.

In waves, we were sent off the starting line. After four and a half laps around the track, as we neared the finish line, we listened for the timekeeper calling out the times. "Five forty-five. Five forty-six. Five forty-seven." Lucky showoffs. As I neared the end, I heard, "Six twenty. Six twenty-one. Six twenty-two." Sprinting with legs bounding and lungs burning, as if being chased by an axe-wielding lunatic, I lurched across the line as "Six twenty-five" was called out. I was euphoric. And I did not vomit. A sense of epic accomplishment swept over me. Five seconds to spare.

24// *"Has Anybody Here Seen My Old Friend Ed?"*

SO, THE FOOTBALL SEASON officially was under way. There was no postponement to allow for mourning the death of Ed Hawk. There was no grief counseling. I do not recall craving a sensitive touch from our coaches, faculty or school leadership, and that is good, because none was forthcoming.

Dick Keefe, the young French teacher early in his 43-year SLUH career, was in Europe on an educational tour with Father George Pieper and SLUH students when he heard the news of Ed's death. That era, he said, was different from today. "The atmosphere at the school was more formal then," he said. "We didn't talk about issues, as openly as we do now."

Paul Martel contemplated his options. "You knew you lost a student, even though he wasn't a member of the football team," Martel reflected, many years later. "But he was a person out of the SLUH family. The ballplayers lost a classmate and a friend."

He made the decision that we would carry on without postponing practices, though he later wondered if that was the right call. "It got down to the point, you don't think about a lot of things the way you should have thought about them," he said. Such is the fate of leadership, when the man in charge must choose, and choose now, sometimes between two lousy options. Del Bannister and I took turns driving to practice, and for the first few days, neither of us felt compelled to interrupt the silence in the car. I dwelled on thoughts of Ed Hawk, trying to picture him, to keep him alive, at least in my mind. For me, it was good to have the regimen of practice to occupy my mind and help exhaust my energy.

Still, we knew we still had to bury our friend, and we wanted to pay him the respect he deserved. Collectively, we reacted in the way we knew, together and without much supervision. "The parents just did not seem to be that involved," recalled Tim Kellett. "None came to our football practices, only a few came to the games. I always had the feeling when I was in high school that I was in charge and responsible for all aspects of my life, including taking care of any problems, including with teachers, and also getting back and forth to school. We hitchhiked, took the bus, or carpooled to and from school and practices, regardless of the time of day."

That is not an indictment of negligent parents; it is just a fact of the way things were at that time. For my part, I knew my parents were busy working and tending to my younger siblings, and I appreciated the independence and trust they showed in me.

After Ed Hawk's death, we gathered in the chapel at St. Louis U. High, we embraced each other, we reflected three years of Christian Jesuit indoctrination and avoided any temptation to fixate on bitterness or blame. There were 309 homicides in the City of St. Louis in 1970, more than in any other year before or since. The St. Louis Police Department never discovered the identity of the young man who ended Ed Hawk's life. It is quite possible that young man never knew he ended a life.

Individually, we reacted in a variety of ways. Some wanted to talk about it, some didn't. Some were driven to question their Christian faith, most were comforted by it. Most wept, often and openly.

"Being together with everyone was cathartic for me," said Katie Rhoades. "We could be with everyone going through it. I didn't have to be alone. Guys were crying, girls were crying. It wasn't awkward. We had a community to hold each other up."

Mike Wiese, more than ever, thought of his late brother Bob and tried to comprehend this tragic loss of life.

Back from his summer job in San Francisco, Whayne Herriford was in the Ozarks with his family in mid-Missouri when he heard of Ed's death. He booked the first Greyhound Bus available, and arrived that evening at the downtown St. Louis station. Driving his father's car, Tim Kellett picked up Herriford, and together they headed to Herriford's home in North St. Louis. Just under two miles from their destination, the car broke down, near Penrose Park, south of Highway 70 at Kingshighway Boulevard. The two young men abandoned the car and walked to Herriford's house. Whayne took the keys to his mother's car, and drove Kellett to his home in Webster Groves, almost 20 miles away.

Kellett's grief was compounded by the loss of his revered maternal grandfather, who died eight days after Ed Hawk. "Eddie Burke and my grandma always called me 'Little Timmy Burke,' because I was always over at their house, and always wanted to be over at their house," Kellett said. A crusty old Irishman with a big heart, Eddie Burke was a member of the St. Louis Soccer Hall of Fame. "He was really special to me."

Fred Daues was working on a van in his father's warehouse when he learned of Ed's death. "My Dad broke the news to me," he said. "He came up to tell me that Ed was gone. I wept in the truck for 10 minutes. Dad said, 'You can't go home like that. You don't want your Mother to see you like that.'"

Phil Schaefer was devastated when he learned the news.

"How do you deal with that?" said Phil, our Student Council Treasurer. "It was the beginning of our senior year in high school. It shoved death into our padded world. It changes you. We lived in a bubble in high school. We were under the care of our parents. We were safe with the Jesuit community watching over us. How does this work? It was frightening. It does something to your head. It did something to our whole class. We tried to be positive, but it took the wind out of us. It cast a shadow over everything. How could it happen?"

Me? I did not cry. I could not cry. I could not feel it. Desperately, I wanted to feel it, but it was as if I was hovering a few feet off the ground, detached and watching the physical me on the ground and watching others interact with me. Is that what it means to be numb? Bob Thibaut reacted similarly. "I don't remember shedding a tear," he said. "At least not until I saw Mrs. Hawk."

I felt an obligation to act, to do something constructive. So I joined a group of class leaders to plan a tribute Mass to honor our friend's life and memory. Since I was class president, I accepted the responsibility to speak on behalf of our classmates at the Mass.

How in the world would I say something meaningful? How in the world would I say anything without breaking down in sobs?

Soon after Bobby Kennedy's assassination in June of 1968, the song-writer Dick Holler wrote the soulful song, *Abraham, Martin and John*[13], a tribute to charismatic Presidents Abraham Lincoln and John Kennedy, who were murdered while in office, and to civil rights leader Dr. Martin Luther King Jr. and Presidential candidate Bobby Kennedy, whose lives were ended by gunshot in 1968. Recorded by Dion and released late in 1968, *Abraham, Martin and John* was a wistful, longing ballad that bemoaned the lost potential of people who had tried to make a better world.

Has anybody here seen my old friend Abraham?
Can you tell me where he's gone?
He freed a lot of people,
But it seems the good they die young.
You know, I just looked around and he's gone.

It seemed fitting to include this song in our tribute to Ed. The good die young.

Hundreds of friends, classmates and family crowded into the SLUH Chapel. The Reverend David Wayne, the Jesuit priest who served as Student Council Moderator for our Class of 1971, was the principal celebrant. Father Wayne was a humble, unpretentious man who over the course of the next nine months was to become more of a psychotherapist than a simple moderator to Whayne Herriford, Phil Schaefer and me, the three Student Council officers who survived Ed Hawk, our class vice president.

I sat in the first row during the service, and, when the time came, I dutifully rose to take my place behind the simple pulpit to eulogize Ed. Certainly, the words were trite and forgettable. Something about cherishing our class rings as a physical reminder of Ed's presence, and grabbing the ring at those points in the coming year when the going got tough. Somehow, perhaps still numb and still unable to cry or feel, I got through it without breaking down.

To encourage all in the congregation to join in singing the concluding song of the service, we distributed the song lyrics, with one alteration to Dick Holler's lyrics—we inserted Ed's name in place of Bobby.

Anybody here seen my old friend Ed?
Can you tell me where he's gone?
I thought I saw him walk up over the hill,
With Abraham, Martin and John.

The service over, we trudged back to reality. The beginning of academic classes for our senior year still was several days away, but it was time to resume football practice.

25// *"Think About Your Ring"*

OUR INNOCENCE SEVERED, our idealism depleted, we retreated limply back into that part of the world to which we had access. The thoughtful Tim Fleming had a pointed perspective on it. The teammate we had nicknamed "the Old Man" because of a stern countenance and the gray specks that had infiltrated his black hair, reflected on the battle we fought against the generation in charge.

"Great things were expected of us," recalled Fleming, a senior tackle who was an able substitute on defense, and who started two games when starter Al Fahrenhorst was disabled by injury. "Our own expectations and those others had for us. To live within the rules others made for us. Yet somehow to rise above the decay of the old order and make the world right again. The problem was, making the world right again required doing things in a new way—leaving the '50s and early '60s behind, and the old guard did not want to hear that. We knew there was no returning to the good old days, but the generation in charge of us did not. The old ways had gotten blacks lynched, students shot, Kennedys and King assassinated, and an ugly war started.

"We were expected to change this old order with our bright new ideas. But when we spoke those ideas, the old guard did not want to hear them. We were stuck: we were smart, spirited, and idealistic … but too young and powerless to do anything. So we transferred this brilliance, this creative energy, this capacity for dreaming big to the only outlets they let us have—academics and extra-curriculars. Excelling in football became the one way we could fulfill the great expectations heaped upon us."

To Fleming and to many of us, our focus on football gave us a tangible purpose.

"We could show them how much talent we had," Fleming said, "how driven we were, how great we were—as a generation and as sons of those who wanted better things for their children—on a football field."

In an act of mild anarchy, I used a felt-tip pen to mark the football helmet I was assigned for the 1970 season. The helmet was several years old, having been commissioned to, worn by, and returned to the stable by previous St. Louis U. High varsity football players. It was school property. Above the ear hole on the right side of the helmet, in permanent marker ink, I wrote: *Ed Hawk '71*. This was a direct violation of Rule Number 3 of Paul Martel's "Responsibilities of a Football Player" manifesto, under the section "PLAYER CONDUCT":

> *Players will not intentionally mutilate or place any identifying marks on their personal equipment.*

While this was not exactly Black Panthers stuff, and clearly I did not *mutilate* the headgear, it was in my view an act of willful civil disobedience. I didn't ask permission, and I didn't talk about it. I just did it. My teammates and I devoted our senior football season to our fallen classmate, and his name just outside my right ear would provide comfort and inspiration during every practice, every play, every game. After all, I couldn't wear my class ring on the football field.

Heading somberly with my teammates to our first full-contact practice on the lower field, the grassless and hard ignominious pit of hell, I was soothed by the "clack, clack, clack" sound of our metal-tipped cleats as we descended the 34 concrete steps. At the lower elevation, the practice-field playing surface was not visible from the school's main campus, giving us a sense that we were in our own world, isolated and maybe even in-sulated from the pressures of the outside world. That was okay with me. Football is a violent sport, barbaric almost, with its future in question due to the condition known as Chronic Traumatic Encephalopathy, first diagnosed by Dr. Bennet Omalu in 2002. Dr. Omalu was featured in the motion picture *Concussion*[14], released in late 2015, that dramatized the damage done to professional football players from years of undiagnosed or ignored brain injuries resulting from crashing contact in the sport. I don't recall anyone even thinking about that in the fall of 1970. For me, football was an escape.

On this day, I was anxious to release some tension, and football practice was a sanctioned way to do so. I felt the blood pumping through my veins with a great fury. Two weeks of emotion had begun to move, apparently in search of an outlet. With an unusually intense adrenaline rush, I bounced through calisthenics, drills, and contact as if possessed by a demon. I had experienced this pronounced physical state on football fields before, though never this acutely, and in a way it alarmed me. This savagery was useful for a football player seeking an advantage, and the game provided a sanctioned outlet for it. But I was concerned about being capable of such violence. More than once on this day, at this practice, I slammed into my opponent in a one-on-one drill, and jumped up to take on the next man, ignoring the protocol of going to the back of the line.

After 90 minutes of this, Coaches Paul Martel and Ebbie Dunn called the team to the center of the field. The 1970 season was off to a fierce start. We retreated to the locker room.

I took off my helmet, jersey and shoulder pads, and sat down on a bench, away from the main flow of the locker room and away, I thought, from the view of my teammates. The emotion in me that had been building for a fortnight, had just energized my bones and muscles to a 90-minute sprint through practice, but now it was doing something very different. I was thinking about Ed Hawk, and trying to picture him, and trying once again to understand. I lowered my head, covered my face with my hands, and started sobbing. Lost in the moment, I didn't notice Tim Fleming approach me. Tim put his hand on my shoulder.

"Think about your ring," Tim said.

PART II

REFUGE

26// *"Around Here We Shower AFTER Practice"*

August 1970

WE CONTINUED OUR GRUELING PRESEASON PRACTICES, one in the morning, one in the evening, on the desolate, dusty, rock-filled lower field, in the hot, humid hell of the St. Louis August. It was a survival contest, in which we exhausted ourselves in executing Paul Martel's colorfully named "agility drills": *seat roll, crab circle crab, butt roll ("same as the seat roll, except it starts from the two point position"), wave drill, crabbing seat roll, face drill, and running backwards.* And we bloodied and bruised ourselves, knocking into each other in full contact drills.

One of the most diabolical drills was the "Bull in the Ring." Standing in the center of a small-circumference circle carved into the thick dust, a single player stood surrounded by five adversaries, each assigned a number. Mr. Robert Voss, a Jesuit scholastic who helped the coaches run drills at practice, seemed to take particular delight in his duty, which was to call out a number, randomly from one to five, that prompted the assigned attacker to launch aggressively toward the Bull in the Ring in an attempt to knock him on his ass. The Bull's challenge was to brush off the attacker fast, then ready himself for the next onslaught, then the next, then again the next. Very few players made it through the entire series of thrusts without hitting the deck in this drill, which I came to appreciate many years later as a fitting metaphor for life itself.

The pressure of competition to distinguish ourselves and gain the attention of Coach Martel could be intense. We senior class veterans knew we would make the team, but only a few were certain we would be starters, and fewer still knew we would be featured players. And then there was the sheer exhaustion of the drills, in our thick padded practice uniforms, and the outdoor sauna created by the searing August sun and humidity. We found relief in the sanctuary of the locker room.

To us, Fred Daues was both larger than all and larger than life. He was the biggest player on our team. And with a penchant for broad humor, he often was either instigator or target of comical pranks. Fred practically saw himself as a fictional character.

"When I was a kid I read every book Clair Bee ever wrote," he said. "Chip Hilton. I was living a dream. For me, playing football at St. Louis U. High was like going to Valley Falls High School, with all the various characters in those stories."

Clair Bee was a college basketball coach at Rider and Long Island universities, whose teams won more than 400 games from 1928-51, a record that earned him election into the Basketball Hall of Fame in 1968. While still coaching, Bee authored the 24-book *Chip Hilton Sports Series* of novels about the exploits of the mythical Chip Hilton, a three-sport athlete who starred for Valley Falls High and State University. Published between 1948 and 1964, the series featured an idealized version of sports and its heroes. Fred Daues consumed those stories like so many cookies and glasses of white milk.

Often, in the midst of the area of our locker room reserved for the seniors, Daues willingly accepted the stage we eagerly yielded to him, a clearing among the sweaty bodies in various phases of dress. Swaggering like legendary tough-guy actor John Wayne, Fred would boom out his scripted challenge, imitating Wayne playing G.W. McLintock in the 1963 classic movie, *McLintock!*[15]:

"Pilgrim, you've caused a lot of trouble this morning. Might've got somebody killed. And somebody oughta belt you in the mouth. But I won't. (Pause.) I won't. (Another pause.) The *hell* I won't." (Feign a booming left hook to the jaw of the imaginary offender.)

We would erupt in applause and laughter, and plead for more. Occasionally, Fred would claim to be legendary outlaw Black Bart, the real-life robber who menaced stagecoaches in California and Oregon in the 1870s and 1880s. His Black Bart voice was indistinguishable from his John Wayne voice, but we let that ride. We nicknamed him Duke, in honor of the actor.

With his bias toward humor and remarkably even temperament, it was damned near impossible to rile Fred Daues to anger. Of course, we had a reputation as smart asses to uphold, so a reasonable person would understand our undying efforts to do so. On one random day, between our morning and late afternoon preseason practice sessions, a couple of the fellows broke out the itching powder.

Itching powder can be made from parts of ground plants such as rose hips or velvet beans, and seems to exist exclusively as an agent for practical jokes. That was the intention of mastermind Al Fahrenhorst on that hot afternoon in August of 1970. We nicknamed Fahrenhorst "Bubba," who at 199 pounds was the second-largest player on our team. A tackle who would go on to start on both offense and defense, Bubba Fahrenhorst feared no one. With Fred Daues's attention diverted away from his locker, Bubba sprinkled an ample dose of the itching powder directly into the business section of Fred's jockstrap. He calmly retreated to his own locker, and waited for the drama to unfold.

Del Bannister and I were among a group of teammates encircling

Daues, trying to be inconspicuous but keen on maintaining our "front-row" access. Bannister took particular delight in anything that would rile Daues. This would be a classic, he thought. We anxiously watched as Daues slowly, deliberately put on his gear. Nothing. Damn, was it a dud, like a firecracker that failed to ignite? Tim Kellett looked at Fahrenhorst with his arms extended, as if to signal, "What's up?" Bubba shrugged his shoulders. We finished dressing, and headed outside to practice. Daues had not noticed us watching him. But indeed he did begin to feel uncomfortable.

"By the time I got down there, my balls were already itching," Daues recalled. "It got worse and worse and worse. When you start sweating down there, it gets really acute."

The discomfort became unbearable, and Daues was compelled to approach Coach Ebbie Dunn for a reprieve.

"Coach," said Fred, "I need to take a shower."

Coach Dunn replied calmly, "Around here, Fred, we shower *after* practice."

"Not today, Coach. I gotta go."

And go he did, without regard for anything else Coach Dunn might have to say. Ebbie did not say anything. He just shook his head.

27// 50½ *Players on the Roster*

AFTER CLOSE TO THREE WEEKS of this business, we weren't sure how good we were going to be, but we sure were tired of scrimmaging each other and wanted to start banging into people from some other team. In the final week of preseason practice, Coach Martel finalized the roster, which meant those not selected were disappointed, relieved, or both. A total of 51 players made the final squad: 26 seniors, 23 juniors, and sophomores Tim Gibbons and Don Behan. Perhaps more accurately, a total of 50½ players made the roster, as Tim Gibbons was to split his season between leading his fellow sophomore-laden "B" team as its quarterback, and placekicking for the varsity. The Missouri State High School Activities Association allowed for such timesharing, but had a regulation governing it, presumably to protect players from what it must have regarded as over-competition. Gibbons was to be limited to 40 quarters of competition during the season, and it was up to "B" Coach Joe Vitale and the varsity's Paul Martel to parcel that playing time strategically, to ensure an optimal use of this 15-year-old's considerable talents.

Having just spent two weeks of intense two-times-a-day practices in the midst of a hot and humid St. Louis summer, and destined to be together nearly every day for the next 75 days, this was the group of classmates who would author the history of the 1970 St. Louis University High School football team, whatever that was to be. We couldn't help but wonder how good we could be if we had one or both of our school's best athletes on the team.

Handy Lindsey was one of the six African-American students in our class, but that was not the reason I stared the first time I saw him. It was at our freshmen orientation night, and he appeared in the gymnasium. He was a physical marvel. When he grabbed the thick exercise rope suspended from the ceiling of the gymnasium, I stood and watched in awe. In dress shirt and slacks and street shoes, Handy ascended that rope one grab at a time, with his muscular legs extended straight out at a 90-degree angle. Up the 40 or so feet to the ceiling he climbed, before slapping the steel girder holding the rope, then descending briskly, with no visible sign of exertion. Lindsey went on to star for the SLUH track and field team, and regularly won his 100-yard dash events with 10-second speed. Man, imagine that strength and speed transporting a football down the field. "I never liked football," Handy would say.

Steve Walsh was six feet, six inches tall and he could have been the best quarterback in the St. Louis area. We imagined him hovering over center, barking signals, flinging bullets downfield, running the option like an extra fullback. Trouble was, football ranked behind baseball and basketball on his playlist, and he decided to refrain from risking his formidable potential earning power on a football field full of angry defenders. No one ever blamed him for that. After all, he started for the varsity baseball team as a *freshman*, and a 13-year-old freshman at that, since he had moved from the third grade straight to the fifth grade at St. James the Greater Catholic School in the city's Dogtown area. As humble as he was talented, Steve was a loyal and devoted friend to many, and he would have been a natural leader on the football team, just as his older brother Joe Walsh had been in 1967, when he was voted co-captain of the team before the season and All-Metro First Team at center at its conclusion. Steve was the close friend Mike Wiese chose to accompany him home after receiving the devastating news that Bob Wiese had been killed in Vietnam.

A left-handed pitcher with a wicked fastball, Steve Walsh went on to become a first-team all-Missouri player, and a 31st-round draft pick of the St. Louis Cardinals in 1971. Some Major League club likely would have picked him in an earlier round, had he not already declared his intention to accept a full scholarship to St. Louis University after earning all-state distinction as the center of the Junior Billikens basketball team. He had a distinguished career on the basketball court at St. Louis U., and seemed a sure bet for a Major League Baseball career, especially when the Chicago White Sox selected him in the 24th round of the 1975 draft. However, while playing basketball during his junior season, he had jammed the elbow of his shooting and pitching arm and dislodged the ulnar nerve out of place. He never recovered, and finally relinquished his dream of a big league career when he failed to make the Montreal Expos in 1976 spring training, then got cut from an independence league team in Victoria, Texas.

"I knew I was done," Walsh said. "I was done with it. I knew I had to get a job. But at least I had a girl to come home to."

The girl was Gina Spesia, whom he married and with whom he raised two sons. The job turned out to be with Bill Bidwill, who owned the St. Louis Football Cardinals and needed someone to run his tickets operation. Walsh did that in St. Louis, and then in Phoenix when Bidwill uprooted the Cardinals and moved them to Arizona after the 1987 season.

28// *Captain Jim Castellano*

THOSE OF US WHO MADE the 1970 Junior Billiken football team were handed ballots, on which we would list the three teammates we wanted as our captains. In the playbook and football manifesto Paul Martel distributed at the start of the season, he included this passage about team captains:

> *The captains are elected by you to lead the team. They have been selected because of their experience and your confidence in their leadership. They are our assistants and are the coaches on the field while the game is in progress. Be ready to assist them in any way throughout the entire season.*

Being elected captain certainly was a worthy honor.

"That was one of my goals," said Bob Thibaut. "I really wanted to be captain, more than anything. I really thought I was a fairly good leader, and I took it seriously."

My cousin, Phil Pacini, was a junior on the CBC team that ruined SLUH's season in 1966, and he was elected captain of the Cadets the next year. I would be this team's starting center, and I would share duties at inside linebacker on defense. I allowed myself to think that maybe I, too, could be a captain.

In the team huddle at the conclusion of our final preseason practice,

Coach Martel announced the results of the balloting. "Let's give our congratulations and support to the three captains you elected," Martel said. "Bill Ziegler, Bob Thibaut, and Jim Castellano."

Wait, what? *Jim* Castellano? Did Coach Martel forget my name? Who IS this guy? How can this man have such a thorough grasp of every minute detail of his football program, down to the breakfast menu of our state championship game road trip, and mess up something like the first name of one of his captains, one of his "coaches on the field"? Well, nobody is perfect. I thought of my older brother and smiled.

29// *"Talk about Embarrassing Moments"*

1910s – 1959

PAUL MARTEL'S FATHER John emigrated to the United States from Russia as a 19-year-old, just before the overthrow of Czar Nicholas II during the Bolshevik Revolution. A generation earlier, lured by an offer of free land, John's parents had moved to Russia from the Alsace-Lorraine region, and settled near the Volga River. Though his formal schooling ended in the fourth grade, John spoke five languages and was resourceful and ambitious. He joined the U.S. Army, and was deployed as a soldier in World War I in Europe. Upon his return to the USA, he moved around chasing work in the wheat fields of Texas, Oklahoma and Kansas, then he moved to St. Mary's, Kansas, where his brother had settled. He became a U.S. citizen, and landed a job as a maintenance worker at St. Mary's College, which at the time was run by the Jesuits.

It was in St. Mary's that John Martel met and married Eva Brungardt, and with the birth of Leona, they started a family. The family moved around as John sought laborers' work in Kansas City and Chicago and pursued an ill-fated dream of owning a farm in Minnesota. Paul was born in Kansas City, while his father was working for a structural steel company. Eventually, the family returned to St. Mary's, where the last three of the seven Martel children were born. Though Eva was born in the U.S., her family held hard to its German traditions, including speaking German as its primary language. Though that was fine with John Martel, whose German was better than his English, it made life a little difficult for their children.

"My older sister flunked first grade because she couldn't speak English," recalled Paul Martel.

Paul was determined to avoid a similar fate. With their house right across the street from the school he would attend, young Paul watched when the older boys broke for recess, then raced across to the schoolyard to play with them and learn English.

In St. Mary's, he did indeed master the language, and he blossomed into a formidable athlete. St. Mary's High School had no football team, but Martel prospered on the basketball court, where he encountered "the best coach I ever had." A Jesuit scholastic, still a couple years from his ordination as a priest, Maurice Van Ackeren was a teacher of the game who emphasized its fundamentals.

"Having him was the greatest thing that happened to me," Martel said. "He was so particular about the way you maneuvered around the court. He was the one who focused us on the basics on how to play offense, how to play defense. He was so particular about what you needed to do, and if you didn't do certain things, he was very critical. He would get after you, wanting to know why you did certain things under certain conditions. He was the best teacher I had. He was the greatest coach I ever had, and that included college and even semi-pro. He taught me so many things."

Martel starred on the basketball court, and was a good candidate for a college basketball scholarship. However, it was 1942, just a few months after the Japanese had attacked Pearl Harbor and drew the U.S. into World War II. He enlisted in the U.S. Navy, and headed to midshipmen school in New York. Given three choices for what assignment he preferred, Martel responded: serving on a PT boat, or on a submarine, or as a translator in Europe (fluent as he was in German). None of his choices was granted. Instead, he was deployed on a landing craft ship that delivered soldiers, equipment and supplies to invasion battlefront beaches in the Pacific theater. He saw action in the Philippines and Okinawa, and spent time in Japan after the war ended. Upon his discharge, he enrolled at Rockhurst College in Kansas City, where he would star in basketball and play organized football for the first time.

Four years in the service enhanced the buff athletic frame he had honed through hard, physical labor during the summers of his youth, when he baled hay in the farm fields of eastern Kansas. He was good enough to start as a freshman on the Rockhurst College basketball team, and found himself awestruck upon entering the 10,000-seat Municipal Auditorium in Kansas City for a game against the Kansas University Jayhawks. "Man," he thought, "this place would really hold a lot of hay."

He would never forget the first shot he attempted. Having spent so much practice time on an outdoor court, often confronted by a stiff wind that required an extra *oomph*, and jacked up by the excitement of that opponent and that grand auditorium, he launched his first shot over the top of the backboard.

"Talk about embarrassing moments," Martel said.

30// *"Did You Sell Your House Yet?"*

UPON GRADUATION in 1948 from Rockhurst, where he had played three seasons of football in addition to basketball, Martel became football coach at Immaculata High School in Leavenworth, Kansas. Two years later, he became coach at St. Agnes High School in Kansas City, Kansas. With a new building to accommodate a growing student population, St. Agnes became Bishop Miege High in 1958. That autumn, Paul Martel's football team achieved a 9-0 record and a No. 5 ranking among Class AA schools in Kansas, while outscoring its opponents, 300-39. He also coached the basketball team to a 19-5 record. Then he learned of a job opening across the state of Missouri in St. Louis.

Gene Hart was the coach at St. Louis U. High, and under contract for the 1959 season, when he got an attractive offer to become assistant athletic director at St. Louis University. Father Gerard Sheahan, the Jesuit priest who was principal at SLUH, told Hart he would release him from the contract on the condition he found a qualified replacement. Hart thought of the perfect candidate, and headed to Kansas City to speak with his old Rockhurst College teammate. Paul Martel was managing a swimming pool at a country club that summer, but agreed to drive to St. Louis on a Monday, when the pool was closed. Father Sheahan met with Martel that Monday, then after deliberating with colleagues, he decided to offer him the job. "I got a call from Father Sheahan that Thursday," Martel said. Father Sheahan told him, "The job is yours if you want it."

Proud of what he had accomplished in nine years at St. Agnes / Bishop Miege, mindful that his undefeated football team would return eight starters on offense and his basketball team would return four starters, steeped in his Kansas City roots and largely unaware of or unmoved by St. Louis U. High's deep tradition, Martel acknowledged it was not an easy decision. At the same time, he and his wife Therese had four children under 10 years old and another soon on the way. "In the final analysis," he said, "it was money." With an almost 30 percent increase in pay, he took the job, doubling as athletic director and the 14th head varsity coach in a SLUH football history that began in 1916. None of the previous 13 had lasted more than six years. It was of some comfort that his old coach, Father Maurice Van Ackeren, had gone on from Rockhurst to serve as the St. Louis U. High principal from 1946-51.

"I had to tell my kids why we were going to St. Louis," he said. "Because you're getting a little bigger, you're eating a little more, and you're costing me more."

One of the first SLUH parents he encountered upon arriving in St. Louis had a startling question for him.

"Have you sold your house in Kansas City yet?" she inquired.

"No, why?" Martel answered.

"Well, don't sell it until after the CBC game."

Featuring a roster whose defense inspired the colorful nickname the "Hungry Huns," his first SLUH team won seven games, tied one, and lost none. They outscored their eight opponents, 142 to 21, shut out six of them, allowed opponents just 100 yards offense per game on average, and easily defeated archrival CBC. It was just the fifth undefeated team in the 43 seasons of SLUH football that had been played to that point. After the CBC game, the mother who earlier had cautioned him about his Kansas City home hosted a party, and invited the coaches. "OK," she told Martel, "you can sell your house now."

31// *"Blocking Is Generally Weak"*

1959-70

DR. MIKE SHANER, A LONG-TIME professor at St. Louis University, played on Paul Martel's first two SLUH teams. During his second summer, in 1960, Hollywood came to the Oakland Avenue campus for filming of the movie, *The Hoodlum Priest*. The critically acclaimed film was based on the true story of Father Charles Dismas Clark, a Jesuit priest who was a teacher and assistant principal at SLUH in the 1930s and went on to counsel desperate young St. Louisans in trouble with the law. The producers shot much of the film in St. Louis, and spent a day at the high school to record the 30 seconds that made it into the final product. One with a sharp eye and sophisticated video equipment can spot both Martel and Shaner in the scene. Actor Don Murray played the role of Father Clark, who founded Dismas House in 1959, a "halfway house" where ex-convicts could live before integrating into society.

The previous summer, Shaner was a junior anxious to welcome Paul Martel as St. Louis U. High's new coach. After his sophomore season on the varsity, when he experienced the tough and demanding hand of Coach Gene Hart, Shaner was at a football team party when he heard the news of the coaching change. "Somebody said Gene Hart wasn't going to be coach, and I said 'Yes!'" Shaner recalled. "Gregg Hilker, our quarterback, came at me and said, 'He's the best coach you have ever had, and you shouldn't be like that.' But I was. I was just as happy as I could be, because Hart was such a hard-ass, such a hard-nosed person."

The new coach, *any* coach, Shaner reasoned, would be a welcome change.

"Junior year," Shaner said, "we show up for practice August 15, and out comes this young stud in his shorts and T shirt, looking like Clark Gable." The 35-year-old Paul Martel had arrived.

Shaner and his teammates welcomed Martel, and tried to size him up. "He said he was from Bishop Miege," Shaner said. "We didn't know Bishop Miege. Where in the heck was that? We didn't know anything about him." Shaner was surprised that someone that young and fit was a World War II veteran. "It was 1959, so it made sense, but to me World War II vets were all ancient." Before long, Shaner and his teammates realized Martel was a tough but fair leader who definitely knew the game of football. "He was good, but he was distant. It's not like we hung out or did anything. He was the coach, like a teacher. You had him for this period of time, and that was it. He was a good coach, and you worked your ass off for him. He was tough, but he wasn't vindictive. He certainly knew the game. Without a doubt, he knew the game." They admired and embraced their new coach, and the affection was mutual.

The *Hungry Huns* nickname came from one of the team's seniors, who thought the barbaric, conquering tribe of that name, which menaced Europe in the first half of the first millennium A.D., was a fitting role model and inspiration. The players prided themselves on their suffocating defense. And all but one of the starters applied adhesive tape forming the letters H-U-N-S on their helmets. "My dad wouldn't let me do it," said Shaner, whose father, Dr. John Shaner, was the SLUH football team physician for many years. "He said the Huns were not good people." Well, the original Huns *did* plunder under the command of Attila, who was known *"The Scourge of God."*

Martel established residence in St. Louis, and went on to 29 seasons as head coach of Junior Billiken football. By the time my class came around in 1970, we had heard often of that great Hungry Huns team of 1959. "The 'Hungry Huns' this, and the 'Hungry Huns' that." Blah, blah, blah. Yeah, that team was formidable. Indeed, three of those players received scholarships from Notre Dame—two-way end and punt returner John Simon, and two-way tackles Jack Anton and Scott Videmschek. Simon and Anton took their scholarships and played for the Irish; Videmschek played for the University of Missouri. Desperate for praise from our stoic coach, we aspired to eclipse his fondness for that 1959 team. What would we have to do to earn a lofty accolade from him?

In the playbook Paul Martel created and distributed to his players at the start of our season, he unabashedly offered his philosophy of sports, which to him clearly reached beyond the playing of a game.

Why play football? Football is fun. I hope you will play football because you enjoy playing. If you do, you should be very successful.

However, besides football being just plain fun, there are other advantages to be derived from this sport. It is true that being a football player will add to your stature with your fellow students. Success on the football field automatically means a certain amount of respect by the student body; and I will expect that you will be worthy of that respect. It is also true that for some of you football may mean an athletic scholarship and a college education.

The most important values derived from athletics are not quite so tangible. Nevertheless, they are very real and available for all who love the game and are willing to try their best, whether you be a "star" like Johnny Unitas or a "benchwarmer" as was President (Dwight) Eisenhower.

What are these values? Football teaches us to win. Not just winning a game but more important, winning the great battle over ourselves. It is not to win at all cost, but winning because we played the game by the rules, because we met our opponent fairly and defeated him at his best.

Charles Martel, an 8th century Frankish military and political leader, led his fighting troops to defeat an invading Muslim army at Tours in north central France in 732 AD. Some historians credit that victory for preserving Western Europe for Christianity, and it earned Charles Martel the nickname *"The Hammer."* There is no evidence today that Paul Martel descended from this decorated military victor whose surname he shared, and whose nickname he certainly *could* have shared, but a few dozen boys who aimed to play football at St. Louis U. High would have feared and respected the two men equally. It is almost inconceivable that in 1970 a group of teenagers, whose generation spent much of its energy in battle with its parents over everything from military intervention in Southeast Asia to the length of their sideburns, could have succumbed so feebly to the authority of a single adult.

Paul Martel was 45 years old in 1970, at the start of the 54th season of St. Louis University High football. It would be his 12th season in charge of the Junior Billiken program, and his legend was fairly well established by then. Jim Bruno, who played for Martel in the mid-1960s, recalls that the coach once figured out when an opponent was going to run or pass, based on the position of its linemen's knuckles before each play began. "Knuckles tucked in, run; knuckles pointed out, pass," Bruno said. On another occasion, while scouting the CBC team coached by his brother-in-law Jack Kersting, he noticed the quarterback tipping the direction of the offense's running plays. Right foot pointed out, play goes to the right. Left foot out, play goes to the left. That SLUH team went on to lose just 7-0 to a superior CBC squad that season. On its lone touchdown, the Cadets ran up the middle.

Martel was tall, with a serious countenance, his head always cocked slightly back, and a jaw seemingly constructed by U.S. Steel. He moved and spoke slowly and deliberately, with the confidence of someone who knows he won't have to say anything more than once. My teammates and I were willing to do what this man demanded. Some out of fear, some out of respect, all because we wanted to play football. We called him "Tall Paul." Most of us worked very hard to earn this man's endorsement and his praise.

Some unabashedly adored the man; others regarded him more warily. For some, he was like a father they wished they had, and they were eager to earn his approval. For others, he was rigid and insensitive, and they were eager to earn his approval. Almost desperately, we yearned for his approval. To all, he was the gatekeeper. The arbiter who decided which boys made the team, which boys made the starting lineup, which boys played, and to some degree which boys were to be rewarded with post-season award recognition.

"I played to please Coach Martel," said Tim Gibbons many years later, expressing a sentiment many of our players felt. As a sophomore, Gibbons was our team's placekicker. Two years later, as a senior quarterback in 1972, Gibbons led SLUH to a perfect 9-0 season, but those Junior Billikens were denied entry into the state championship playoffs because their "strength of schedule" hurt them and they did not qualify. Not enough of their opponents had winning records. "That's why I played the game," Gibbons said. "I wanted his acknowledgement that he knew I did my best." Coach Martel dispensed compliments as if he were rationing a limited water supply to a group lost in the desert.

Before our first game, in an interview with a *St. Louis Post-Dispatch* sportswriter who was writing about the upcoming season's prospects for teams in the Bi-State Conference, in which SLUH played with five other schools, Coach Martel did yield that he might have the best two defensive ends and one of the top backs in the area. Defensive ends Jim Twombly and Mike Wiese were worthy of that accolade, and certainly our star player Bill Ziegler would live up to his Coach's kind words. As for the offensive linemen, well, we convinced ourselves that Coach Martel was sending us a motivational message. Asked to assess the prospects for the Junior Billikens, Martel told a reporter for our school newspaper, the *Prep News*: "Blocking both in the line and the backfield is generally weak and will necessitate extensive bolstering." Not exactly Knute Rockne, inspiring the Notre Dame squad to run out and cream somebody. We also got the message: we were not exactly the "Hungry Huns" of 1959.

32// "I Didn't Know Where It Came From"

September 1970

FINALLY, WE FLIPPED the calendar to September, and inched closer to the threshold of our regular season. Soon, Jack Warner would begin casting for _The Fantasticks_[16], which he would produce and direct that autumn for the stage in the SLUH auditorium. The role of El Gallo would go to classmate Steve Keller. These many years later, I can recall Keller delivering the lyrics to open the musical:

> _Try to remember the kind of September_
> _When life was slow and oh, so mellow._
> _Try to remember the kind of September_
> _When grass was green and grain was yellow._
> _Try to remember the kind of September_
> _When you were a tender and callow fellow._
> _Try to remember, and if you remember,_
> _Then follow._

Later in Act I, El Gallo speaks to the audience:

> _You wonder how these things begin._
> _Well, this begins with a glen._
> _It begins with a season which,_
> _For want of a better word,_
> _We might as well call—September._

> _Recall that secret place._
> _You've been there, you remember:_

That special place where once—
Just once—in your crowded sunlit lifetime,
You hid away in shadows from the tyranny of time.

In the Sunday, September 6, 1970 edition of the *St. Louis Post-Dispatch*, there appeared a photograph accompanying the story about the prospects for the upcoming Bi-State Conference season. Coach Paul Martel had told Jerry Stack, the reporter, "The big thing lies in our quarterbacking. If we can find a kid who can throw the ball …"

That comment inspired the reporter to have the photographer Fred Sweets pose a most unusual shot. The four candidates for quarterback would crouch over, hands poised behind the center's posterior as if ready to take the snap. *Who Gets the Ball?* read the photo caption.

> *St. Louis U. High center Joe Castellano will be giving the ball to one of the four Junior Bills behind him this season, but the quarterbacking job hasn't been settled yet. Candidates (from the left) are: Tony Behr, Dan Calacci, Gregg Hannibal and Doug McDonald.*

The strained expression on my face had less to do with the fact that eight of my teammates' hands were hovering around my rear end than with the extraordinary effort it took to arch my head up high enough, with my hands on the football in the hiking position, so that my mother would recognize me. Quarterbacks become accustomed to the limelight; interior offensive linemen live largely anonymously. I didn't want to miss this opportunity for some face time. Since the photo was snapped on the practice field right after a hot, sweat-inducing practice, I had no opportunity to tame my wildly curly "helmet hair," nor to change out of the disgustingly crusty football pants that had not been threatened by laundry detergent for several days. In preparation for the photograph, the sole deference to vanity was the opportunity to put on the brand new blue game jerseys, for the first time, that we would wear to open the season against Cleveland High School the following Saturday. Our school colors were blue and white, and we wore them unadorned with logo or lettering. No team name on the helmets or jerseys' front; no individual names on the back. Just like Penn State and its legendary Nittany Lions. We called ourselves the "Blue Buddies," and we extended that beyond the players to include the community who supported us. It felt special.

It is difficult for a football player to know how good his team will be until measured against a few opponents, especially in high school football, and especially at St. Louis U. High, a program in which underclassmen seldom broke into the starting lineup under Coach Paul Martel. Every year, a brand new team steps forward to find its place. That certainly was true in the four weeks prior to the season opener on September 12, 1970. Out of fear, respect, or lack of an alternative, we blindly followed the instruction of Coach Martel and Assistant Coach Ebbie Dunn. We learned their offensive alignments and ran their plays; we absorbed their defensive schemes and accepted on faith that what they told us would work. We did not know for sure.

We were about to find out, as we would open against the Cleveland High Dutchmen, the defending champions of the rugged Public High League, which was comprised of the public high schools within the limits of the City of St. Louis. Located on the near south side of the city, Cleveland High turned out tough young men, mostly Caucasian, who were not intimidated by schools like Sumner and Central and Soldan and McKinley, fellow PHL teams from the near north side of the city that turned out some of the finest athletes in the St. Louis area, most of whom were African-American. And, at least from our perspective, they were not very impressed with what we assumed they believed to be the boys of privilege from St. Louis U. High.

We were thankful Cleveland High's legendary coach Ray Cliffe had agreed to schedule us. Upon taking the SLUH job, Paul Martel was told the area's formidable schools would not schedule us, because they were convinced SLUH "recruited" athletes, in violation of state association rules. When Father Philip Kellett, the Jesuit priest who served as the SLUH moderator of athletics, learned Martel indeed had convinced top schools to put the Junior Billikens on their schedules, he was desperate to know how.

"Several beers, for one thing," Martel told him, meaning he spent time getting to know the rival coaches socially, in a non-competitive setting. And he promised any coach willing to play his team, that if the coach could prove SLUH had recruited any players, then those players would not play in their scheduled game. One such coach was Cleveland's Cliffe, a renaissance man who was a brilliant scholar, artist and painter in addition to being a legendary coach and teacher. "You couldn't think of a more ideal school to open against," Cliffe told reporter Myron Holtzman of the The St. Louis Globe-Democrat newspaper. The season before, Cleveland opened its season against SLUH, losing 34-8. From there, it blasted through the rest of its season with nine straight victories, allowing an average of just 5.5 points per game and winning the Public High League championship. From 1967-69, the Dutchmen won 25 of its 29 games, tying one and losing just three. "St. Louis U. High can really get you ready for the season. They hit hard and play good, fundamental football." It helped Coach Cliffe that good, tough players lived within the neighborhoods near the school and wanted to play for the Dutchmen.

On the Friday before our first game, Bob Thibaut was asked to speak at an all-school pep rally during the lunch break. A gifted speaker, a rare three-year member of the varsity, a team captain, Thibaut was a worthy choice to inspire us. He wrote out his remarks, and earnestly began to read them.

"I'm not going to say a whole lot," he began, with the undivided attention of an auditorium full of hyped up students. We on the football team stood a few feet in front of Thibaut, wearing our football game jerseys over our dress shirts. "We have three goals this year as Junior Balls ..."

What?! Did Bob just say "Junior Balls"?

"... er, Junior Bills," he said, trying to recover.

Too late. The student body reacted to the Freudian slip with a rousing round of cheering and applause. Thibaut let the laugh play out, coolly—so coolly, some of us thought, that we were convinced he said it on purpose. He swears otherwise.

"We have three goals this year," he continued. "To win the Bi-State Conference championship. To win the state championship. And to have an undefeated season. But, this week, it's to beat Cleveland."

Once again, the audience erupted in applause and whooping cheers. We were inspired.

The opening game of the 1970 season was a "home game" for SLUH, which did not have a home field. The school had contracted to play all its "home" games on the field at O'Fallon Tech High School, located less than a mile south of SLUH, just off Kingshighway Boulevard. And on that field, we were to find out what kind of team we had.

One thing we had not prepared for that day was nausea. In addition to his construction business, Fred Daues Sr. owned and operated a vending machine company, and one of his products was a relatively new sports drink developed in 1965 by a team of scientists at the University of Florida School of Medicine. They were commissioned by Florida Gators football coach Ray Graves to find a drink that could help players efficiently replace body fluids lost during physical activity, especially in the hot, humid summers and autumns in Florida. "Gatorade" was designed to replace carbohydrates and electrolytes in perfect balance, as it helped rehydrate athletes sweating heavily during competition. The

Gators tested the drink during the 1965 season, and many of them were convinced it helped them outlast favored opponents to forge a 7-4 record. The following season, Florida went 9-2 and won the 1967 Orange Bowl for the first time in school history.

Mr. Daues generously donated Gatorade in powdered concentrate for our football games. "I thought it was going to give us the edge," said Fred Daues Jr. Perhaps it would have, had it been hydrated and diluted properly. "About half the guys who drank it got sick," recalled young Fred. Fortunately, this malady was short-lived.

The quarterback who "got the ball" for the Cleveland game was senior Doug McDonald, a serious young man and a talented athlete who was one of those rare players to have made the SLUH varsity as a sophomore. He doubled as a defensive back. Deliberate in his movements, McDonald had earned the start based on his considerable athletic ability, his disciplined approach to the game, his grasp of the playbook, and his steady attention to Coach Martel's instructions. After the two teams pushed each other around without much forward progress for much of the game's first quarter, and after SLUH gave up the ball once on a blocked punt and again on a fumble, McDonald moved the Junior Billikens to the Cleveland 12-yard line. From there, he dropped back four steps while looking to the right side, then pitched a perfect pass to speedy junior halfback Tim Leahy, who grabbed the pass and eluded a single diving defender on his way to our team's first touchdown of the season. Bob Thibaut booted the extra point. SLUH 7, Cleveland 0.

True to his word, Paul Martel also had senior quarterback Dan Calacci guide the offense, having him alternate series with McDonald. A brilliant young man, not one so bound by convention, who often free-lanced when his free spirit moved him, Calacci worked the edges while McDonald plowed the center stripe. Midway through the second quarter, on a nifty play in which he barely escaped the rush of a Cleveland defender, Calacci arched a perfect pass nearly 40 yards downfield in the direction of Mike Wiese, who was being smothered by the defensive back covering him. Wiese reached and grabbed the ball just as he was being tackled on the Cleveland one-yard line. Thibaut, the fullback, took the next handoff over the line for SLUH's second touchdown, then converted the extra point. For the most part, the offense was working for the Junior Billikens, and we reached halftime with a 14-0 lead.

Certainly, the defense was working that day. Inspired by the spirit of his fallen older brother, Mike Wiese was almost unblockable. On one play, Wiese came roaring in from his right defensive end position, separated from his Cleveland quarterback target by a blocker who went low toward Wiese's legs. Mike sprang right over the blocker without being touched, as if hopping over a puddle of water, then zeroed in to greet the quarterback just as SLUH defensive right tackle Al Fahrenhorst was getting there after shaking a block in the interior line. Quarterback Charles Granda clutched the football close to his chest, then crumbled to the ground under the crunching tackle of Wiese and Fahrenhorst.

On another play, Wiese encountered a double team. He improvised a spin to elude both blockers, then zipped in to sack Granda for a loss. "It was just an instinct," he said. "I don't know where it came from."

Wiese had dedicated his season to his brother Bob. "I put up the cardboard schedule of our season in my bedroom," Mike said. "Before each game, I said a little prayer to him."

Surely, Bob Wiese's presence was on the field that day, as Mike led the Junior Billikens to limit the Dutchmen to 29 total yards. With the benefit of another Doug McDonald touchdown pass, a 30-yarder to fullback Tom Schoeck in the third quarter, and despite 99 yards in penalties, two blocked punts, and three turnovers, SLUH wrapped up a satisfying 21-0 victory to open the season. "We didn't do anything very well, did we?" Ray Cliffe told Dave Dorr of *The St. Louis Post-Dispatch*, which named Mike

Wiese the *Defensive Player of the Week* for the St. Louis area. Paul Martel was uncharacteristically satisfied. "We're already running 75 options on defense," he told the reporter Dorr. "Our kids react well and as long as they can cover their responsibilities we could have a heckuva year with this defense of ours. I'll admit it. I'm really pleased, I mean really."

33// *"Whaddaya Gonna Do?"*

FOOTBALL HAD BECOME a therapeutic sanctuary, an endeavor that required attention to prescribed commands and a significant physical commitment through which young men's energy could be exhausted. There was little time for reflection and little need for thoughtful decision making. I welcomed the free pass from having to process things like the Vietnam War, my future, and, especially, the tragic and sudden death of my friend Ed Hawk. In our classrooms, though, the opposite was true, particularly in the class taught by Father Richard Bailey, who in 1970-71 was tripling as the St. Louis U. High President, Principal and teacher of philosophy and religion. Among the reading Fr. Bailey assigned us was the work of Jean Paul Sartre, the existentialist whose dark view of life was troubling. "Existence precedes essence," Sartre once said. "But the essence of my argument is, he no longer exists." Hmm. Another offering: "I exist, that is all, and I find it nauseating." He won a Nobel Prize.

In *No Exit*[17], Sartre's play that debuted in Paris in 1944, one of the main characters goes through the process of discovering his afterlife.

> GARCIN: This bronze. (*Strokes it thoughtfully.*) Yes, now's the moment; I'm looking at this thing on the mantelpiece, and I understand that I'm in hell. I tell you, everything's been thought out beforehand. They knew I'd stand at the fireplace stroking this thing of bronze, with all those eyes intent on

me. Devouring me. (He swings round abruptly.) What? Only two of you? I thought there were more; many more. (Laughs.) So this is hell. I'd never have believed it. You remember all we were told about the torture-chambers, the fire and brimstone, the "burning marl." Old wives' tales! There's no need for red-hot pokers. Hell is—other people!

For a 17-year-old whose close friend was just murdered, who was trying to find a light of hope and a reason to embrace life, this fare was bleak. On the embers of my despair, this gloomy philosophical angle was a gallon of gasoline. Fortunately, my classmates and I were in the embrace of people like Father Bailey and Father Edward O'Brien, Christian men of God who themselves had waded through nihilism and come out the other side, confident in their faith that Jesus Christ provided the alternative, a pathway to a blissful eternity.

Tim Fleming had a good idea what these Jesuit priests were up to.

"They were walking contradictions—men of faith who taught us that science, philosophy, literature, and history challenged the very foundation of that same faith," he said. "What they were teaching me eluded me then—the idea that faith without empirical evidence is a hard faith … a leap from the cliff without knowing if you'll fall into the abyss. But it is the only faith worth having. How valuable is faith that goes unchallenged? How secure these learned men must have been; men of God who gave nihilist dogma its due. For knowledge makes men more deliberate and thoughtful and open than blind faith does. And the Jesuits knew this. Looking back now, I could not be more grateful for this gift, the ability to think for myself."

Among the Jesuit priests we encountered at St. Louis University High School was Father William Bowdern, who had taught philosophy and religion to our class when we were freshmen. Twenty-one years earlier, when he was 52 years old, Father Bowdern was called on to perform the exorcism of demonic possession of the young Maryland boy "Roland Doe," first at the home of family relatives in Bel-Nor, a village in near northwest St. Louis County, then at Alexian Brothers Hospital in St. Louis. The events associated with this incident inspired novelist William Peter Blatty to write and publish *The Exorcist*[18] in 1971, and the story of the same name became a blockbuster movie released in 1973. On an early afternoon in August of 1970, my spiritual needs were far less extreme, but significant enough for me to seek help. It was Father O'Brien who rescued me that afternoon, when I was struggling with doubt about the meaning of life and the merits of carrying on, and I drifted into his office for an unscheduled counseling session.

"What is the point?" I said. It wasn't really a question.

"Well, you can give up if you want," said Obie, which is what just about everyone called him. It was a fitting nickname for a man so approachable, so genuine. He was a rock, comfortable with the decision he had made a long time ago to sacrifice personal material wealth and a loving connection with a spouse so that he could devote his life to the intellectual and spiritual development of young people. He did not appear alarmed by my inquiry.

"It's sometimes hard to go on," Obie said.

I don't really remember what else he said. I do know he did not lecture me, belittle me, or chastise me. And I do recall walking out of his office reinforced by his serenity and his faith. And determined, perhaps for the first time in my life, to accept and rise above the world's dark side and the tragic turns in store for me.

Two years later, I had a similar encounter with a gentleman of Father O'Brien's generation, with a similar outcome. Struggling to cope with the dissolution of my relationship with Katie Rhoades, after we had tried unsuccessfully to maintain it during our freshman year of college, she at the University of Kansas and I almost 600 miles away at Northwestern

University, I caught the eye of my Dad.

"You seem pretty torn up," Jimmy Castellano observed.

"Yeah," I said.

"I know, it's hard," he said. "When I was younger, not much older than you, I had a serious girlfriend and she wanted to get married. I wasn't ready for that, and wanted to take more time. She said no, and she left me."

I sat silently, somehow strangely captivated by this rare insight offered by my Dad, and by the display of empathy. Then I waited for the inspirational message.

"Whaddaya gonna do?" he said.

While I suppose that will not capture the attention of the editors of *Bartlett's Famous Quotations*, it had a mystical effect on me. Immediately, almost magically, I snapped out of my funk right then and there. Yeah, what was I going to do?

34// *Bring on the State Champions!*

AFTER OUR VICTORY over Cleveland in the opening game, the first in our 10-game schedule, Jesuit scholastic Jerry Snodgrass called out, "Nine more to go!"

The irrepressible Tom Schoeck boldly corrected him: "We've got 11 more to go!" The extra two games would be the Missouri state semifinal and championship contests, which were two and a half months away and a considerable long shot.

Next on our schedule was McCluer High, which had won the first two official Missouri Class 4A playoff championships, in 1968 and 1969. The Comets certainly had the talent to win a third, including a 6-foot-8 giant named Gary Scott and a junior quarterback named Steve Pisarkiewicz. We would play them on a Friday night, on the field of Ferguson Junior

High in north St. Louis County. The Ferguson community would attract the world's attention four decades later, for tragic reasons a world away from a high school football game. Our visit on this particular weekend was decidedly less newsworthy, but so very important to us.

On Fridays during the football season, in what had become a favorite school tradition, all students were invited to gather in the auditorium to participate in a pep rally during the midday lunch break. Bob Thibaut successfully managed the stage in the first pep rally, with his "Junior Balls" message before the Cleveland victory. After that, we gladly granted the stage to Tim Rodgers, whom we had named Chairman of the School Spirit Committee. Irreverent, witty, and widely popular, Rodgers was a natural entertainer, who embraced the assignment of whipping the student body into a cheering frenzy. On the Friday of the McCluer game, Rodgers and classmate Rick Spurr dressed up as "comets" and performed a slapstick routine for which the script is long erased from parchment and memory. What IS remembered, is that (1) Rodgers performed in the voice of host Johnny Carson as the pseudo-psychic Carnac on the *Tonight Show*, (2) the antics generated more student attention than any academic class ever could, and inspired most to feel there was something special about all this, and (3) the pep rally ran longer than the scheduled midday lunch recess break, meaning everyone's first class of the afternoon started several minutes late. For the latter, we regarded Tim Rodgers as heroic, especially so because he alone paid the price.

Every student carried a demerit card, which he had to produce at the demand of a faculty member who observed an infraction, from rowdy behavior to tardiness. Upon accumulating five demerits, a student had to report after school to "Jug," where he was assigned a punishment such as memorizing an arcane chemistry formula, or performing menial labor. In my four years, I was "jugged" just twice, and for one of them had to spend the afternoon carrying the track team's jump hurdles from the lower field up to their summer storage space.

"Every pep rally went long," Rodgers said, "and every week Father Wayne jugged me. But he wasn't mad. He enjoyed them as much as anybody. It was almost as if he thought, 'I've got to do this.' Almost with a wink."

The Class of 1971 was the first for which Father David Wayne served as Jesuit moderator, and he had come to understand and accept us. In just a few months, he evolved from the man aggravated by the academic indifference we exhibited when he revealed the long list of our class's failing grades, to a sympathetic counselor who knew how much the death of Ed Hawk had affected us.

"I think he enjoyed our class," Rodgers said. "Our shenanigans weren't mean-spirited. I think he was able to separate real issues from seeing guys who really enjoyed each other and really cared about each other."

A few hours after the inspirational pep rally, the football team members gathered to dress for the game in our St. Louis U. High locker room. Some players preferred supporting their ankles with white adhesive tape, and took their turns on the metal tables in the training room, where Ebbie Dunn applied the tape to their feet, about five inches up the base of their shins. Somber and silent, we dressed in our game uniforms, including the same new blue jerseys we had worn in the victory over Cleveland the previous Saturday. Ready for battle, we headed to the team bus.

The Junior Billikens honored a few traditions on the bus ride to "away" games. For one thing, we maintained a serious tone, generally refraining from speaking, a silence meant to reinforce the idea that we were thinking about the game and the ominous task before us. Often on those bus rides, in what always seemed an illogical manifestation of pre-game tension, I would doze off asleep.

Another custom was praying the rosary, a Catholic tradition featuring repetitive recitation of the prayers *Our Father, Hail Mary, and Glory Be to the Father*. Beads are strung together on a rosary and divided into five sections (or decades, signifying 10 beads per section). Each decade represents an event from the life of Jesus Christ, and the events are grouped in sets of four "Mysteries": the Joyful Mysteries, the Sorrowful Mysteries, the Glorious Mysteries, and the Luminous Mysteries. For me, there might as well have been a fifth category; that is, the mystery of why I could never remember the other mysteries.

It was the responsibility of the team captains to lead this prayer, including the recitation of the Mysteries, and while my Mother regularly and avidly worked her rosary beads and I had a couple of them in my possession, I never really learned the Mysteries. Fellow captain and co-conspirator Bob Thibaut shared this ignorance with me. "I never knew it," Thibaut said. "I had no idea. Plus, I wasn't concentrating on the rosary. For me, I was trying to remember the plays. Which way to go, you know?" So when it came time for one of the captains to commence the rosary, we looked to Bill Ziegler. Not only was Ziegler our team's best player, he was tops at rosary. "My parents made sure I knew the rosary," he recalled.

The truth is, I was a good candidate for prayer for the McCluer game. In addition to my duties as the starting center, I would be starting at left inside linebacker against the Comets. On the sideline just before the start of each game, Coach Martel would read the names of every player on every squad: first team offense, first team defense, kickoff team, kickoff return team, punt team, punt return team, placekicking team. He read my name on each team except punt team and placekicking team. On the kicking teams, Del Bannister snapped the ball to punter Gregg Hannibal, and Hannibal lined up at the center position to snap the ball on extra-point and field-goal attempts. Except for those infrequent occasions, I would be on the field almost the entire game.

There were a couple other reasons I was a good candidate to benefit from a merciful God's attention. For one thing, I couldn't see very well, a challenge for a linebacker responsible for pass coverage. For another, Mc-Cluer coach Bob Johnson had decided that the 6-foot-8 Gary Scott would line up occasionally at the nose guard position, directly across from me. This would be a considerable test for me, a 5-foot-10 center responsible for keeping him away from our quarterback and running backs.

Significantly nearsighted, I had given up trying to wear athletic glasses under my football helmet, as they tended to get steamy and jammed into my head upon contact with opponents. I managed okay without spectacles in the Cleveland game, which was played on a bright, sunny afternoon. This would be the first time I would attempt this during a night game, and I recall being struck by the hazy, psychedelic visual effect created by the stadium lights and colors. I made up my mind that on pass plays, I would drop into coverage and just tackle anybody near me in a white jersey, whether or not he had the football.

In what one might have interpreted as a troubling omen before the game, our team bus stalled as the driver tried to ascend a steep hill leading to the playing field. We had to exit the bus, so he and the bus could make it up that hill without the cargo. About that same time, I found out later, Katie Rhoades was lost and panicked in her Cougar as she tried to find Ferguson Junior High. Fortunately, she found her way.

The game started, and we understood quickly that the Comets would be difficult. They were big, strong and fast, and our offense had difficulty moving the ball against them. On defense, we faced a nimble quarterback in Pisarkiewicz, who carried out his play action moves with quickness and precision. Somehow, despite spending much of the first half deep in our own territory, either trying to move out of there on offense or to stop McCluer's offense from crossing our goal line, we entered the third quarter in a scoreless tie.

Then we struck first, early in the third quarter.

The play was the "45-4" pass. I snapped the ball to quarterback Doug

McDonald, then bolted to the left to block the charge of the McCluer defensive guard, who was intentionally ignored by Bill Caputo, our left guard who cut behind me and raced to the right to pick up any McCluer player rushing in from that side. Right guard Tom Moore and right tackle Jim Twombly provided additional protection on the right side, where McDonald positioned himself behind his blockers to throw after faking a handoff to fullback Tom Schoeck, rushing up the middle. Errol Patterson, one of our fastest players, sprinted from his left end position on a crossing pattern over the middle and toward the right side, which had been cleared when two McCluer defenders went to cover right end Tom O'Shaugnessy on his deep post pattern down the middle. McDonald located Patterson and threw him a perfect 20-yard pass, which he collected behind the Comets' linebacker and in front of their defensive backs, whom he easily beat in a 20-yard race to the goal line. "I was surprised that no one was there immediately to tackle me," Patterson recalled of the first touchdown he ever scored. "I got a couple strides, got near the sideline, then was running as fast as I could. It was exhilarating." We had taken a 6-0 lead on the defending state champions, and our glee was only slightly diminished when we missed the extra point.

That glee was short-lived, however, as Pisarkiewicz went on to show the skills that would eventually earn him status as the No. 1 choice of the professional St. Louis Cardinals and 19th overall in the first round of the 1977 National Football League draft after an exciting and successful career at the University of Missouri.

On the second play from scrimmage after our kickoff, he dropped back to pass, quickly found receiver Wally Feutz on a deep post pattern, and launched a ball more than 40 yards in the air downfield. Beyond the coverage of the SLUH defensive backfield, which by then was deprived of the injured Patterson, the Comets' receiver glided under the ball, grabbed it and coasted into the end zone to complete the 67-yard touchdown play.

A few series later, Pisarkiewicz stepped back into passing position while looking to the left, dropped his right shoulder to elude a rusher, then flipped the ball 20 yards to receiver Steve Barth, who finished the 35-yard play and the Junior Billikens with his dash to the end zone. With a successful extra-point kick by Pisarkiewicz on each touchdown, McCluer had the 14-6 lead it would take to the finish.

Fred Daues was particularly impressed with Pisarkiewicz, who completed 10 passes in the game for 279 yards.

"I got close to him on one play, but he got off the pass," Daues said. "It whipped by the side of my helmet and I felt a 'whoosh.' Never before or since did I *feel* a pass like that. Maybe he was trying to intimidate me."

Daues made an impression of his own. On defense, he reached Pisarkiewicz for two sacks, and fended off the rotation of blocking guards McCluer Coach Bob Johnson sent in to contain him. On offense, from the tackle position, he battled the 6-foot-8 Gary Scott when Scott lined up across from him. After the game, Coach Johnson greeted Daues. "Son, you're a hell of a football player," said the Comets coach. SLUH Assistant Coach Ebbie Dunn greeted Daues with a hard slap on the rear end, at the sideline after an impressive series. "That was a great sign of approval," Daues acknowledged. On the Monday after the game, Coach Martel called Daues into his office, and handed him a page printed with red ink on both sides. At the top it read:

"Crimson Tide"
"National Champions 1961 – 1964 – 1965"

Martel was using the discretion he had as coach to encourage Daues to complete the form, which he would submit to the University of Alabama's Coach Paul "Bear" Bryant. In his judgment, Daues had merited consideration for recruitment by the legendary Crimson Tide coach.

35// *"Joe, What Do I Need To Know?"*

LIKE THE PLAYERS on any team with high hopes, we had aspired to an undefeated season. A single loss on a 10-game schedule was difficult to swallow, and we knew this loss to McCluer was likely enough to ruin our chances of qualifying for the state playoffs.

The loss made Bob Thibaut sick. "I thought the season was lost," he said. "I wanted the state championship, but I also thought we could do an undefeated season. And to lose the second game, in that way, just made me feel ill. I remember getting sick. That sticks in my head today, that game. I hate this."

In Paul Martel's 29 years as the SLUH football coach, the Junior Billikens lost just 79 games. Long after he stopped coaching, he could remember painful details from those losses. "We lost that game to McCluer, and I still had a feeling we should not have lost that game," he said in 2015, when he was 91 years old. He also understands that to survive, a coach has to let it go. "Had we done something different," he said, "we could have won the ball game. But those things happen."

Exhausted and so disappointed by the loss, I was almost consoled when the Comets Coach Bob Johnson sought me out on the field after the game, as he had done with Daues. "Where is that center?" I heard him ask, as he approached and located me. "Great game, son," he said, offering his sturdy hand, which I grabbed. "Thank you, sir," I said. Football is a consummate team sport, and I had not spent much time pondering the potential for individual accolades. I allowed my mind to think maybe there was college football in my future. That didn't last, however.

Next on the schedule was Assumption High, the Catholic high school in the notoriously rough community of East St. Louis, Illinois. The Pioneers were one of the two Catholic high schools on the Illinois side of the Mississippi River in the six-team Bi-State Conference, along with

Althoff of Belleville. The Missouri schools in the league were Augustinian, Christian Brothers, DeSmet and St. Louis U. High.

Assumption High had some notable athletes in its 60-year existence, including 1970s era professional tennis legend Jimmy Connors, All-Pro defensive back Eric Wright of the NFL's San Francisco 49ers, and running back Jerome Heavens, who starred in college at Notre Dame. In the fall of 1970, however, the Pioneers were not much of a threat, and the SLUH Junior Billikens looked forward to an easy victory.

With the Saturday kickoff scheduled for the unusual time of 5 p.m., few of our players thought twice about breaking Coach Martel's curfew, which was *"be in bed by 10 p.m. on the night before a game."* No one had ever been busted for a curfew violation, as far as we knew, and there was little reason to be worried about it, given the late-afternoon starting time and, more significantly, given the *Fall Frolics*, the annual fund-raising social event scheduled for that Friday evening, the night before the game. While sleeping was of significant interest to the boys of the Junior Billiken football team, especially when it was time to wake up to go to school, it definitely was not something to be desired when there was some life to be lived.

The SLUH *Fall Frolics* was an annual tradition, a themed, co-ed "mixer" dance held in the auditorium in the middle of the main school building, a room that had served as the school's original basketball court before a larger, modern gymnasium was built in the late 1950s. A young "Easy" Ed Macauley had starred on that basketball court before graduating, then heading off to lead St. Louis University to the 1948 National Invitation Tournament championship, then on to a distinguished pro career with the Boston Celtics and St. Louis Hawks. The Student Council orchestrated the *Frolics*, and on this night that old auditorium was transformed into a hippie haven, borrowing heavily from the Woodstock experience a little more than a year before. Del Bannister and Whayne Herriford would wear long-hair wigs, headbands, and T shirts with the "Dove on Guitar Neck" Woodstock logo.

I did not think much about it at the time, but have come to understand the choice of that theme was almost inevitable for our class. Phil Schaefer, my fellow Student Council officer, offered a thoughtful perspective on the tension we felt, whipsawed back and forth between the world's somber reality and the universal temptation of youth to test our boundaries in pursuit of excitement, fun and pleasure. Woodstock, it seemed to us, had captured our generation's defiant response to propriety and social norms, and we wanted to recreate that spirit in the hallowed halls of our high school, at least for one evening.

"That was a moment in time at a crossroads of society," Schaefer said. "Ed (Hawk)'s death brought a reality to everything. You don't think about death at 16 or 17 years old. But there it was, in your face. Sure, there was social unrest, but in many ways we were insulated from that. You could read about it. We felt it. We dabbled in it. We were pressing it. But we were kids just having fun, rather than jumping into it.

"We were drinking the Kool-Aid of the rock 'n roll rebellion. We *did* select Woodstock as the theme of our *Fall Frolics*, which I think was our way of trying to say we *are* going in this direction. Some guys were trying pot, seeing where that took them. Guys were experimenting, something that was rampant in society then. That was going on in our senior year. The societal stuff was coming at us in a powerful wave. We were caught in a rip current."

An important social activity and fund-raiser intended to generate money for other student projects, this was my first major event endeavor as the Student Council president. Of course, I had to be there to ensure it was successful, curfew or no curfew.

What happened next was a blur, one of those moments in which a being senses trouble and realizes, probably reflexively, that something had to be done, and done immediately. A little after 10:30 p.m., about halfway through my informal inspection tour to ensure the event was going as planned, I noticed a commotion through one of the four main entranceways of the auditorium. Walking briskly with a small entourage, Coach Martel entered the room.

"Had he seen me?" I wondered, as I ducked, pivoted, and sped for an exit. If the will alone could render a physical body invisible, then surely I would have been a ghost. I got out of the building as quickly as I could, headed straight for my parents' 1962 Chevy Impala, which they had been allowing me to wheel around in. My girl friend, Katie Rhoades, left the party, met me at the car, and we sped away, with the grand hope that I had escaped the notice of a coaching mastermind who could watch one scrimmage play and yell at any of the 22 players (11 on offense, 11 on defense) who had missed his assignment. "Do you think he saw you?" Katie asked. "I don't think so," I said. I was an optimist.

The next afternoon, dressed for the first time in our white game jersey, I warmed up with my teammates on the field at Assumption High, anxious to build on the solid performance I had in the loss to McCluer the week before. I felt good, and was ready to serve as center on offense, inside left linebacker on defense, ball hawk and tackler on the kickoff team, and blocker on the kickoff return team. As kickoff approached, I relished the luxury I had allowed myself to block out everything but the next hour of football. I was entering the zone. Or at least I was until my singular focus was cracked by teammate Bill Caputo, the fellow behind whom I had been positioned when we took our SLUH entrance exam as eighth graders. Bill started next to me as a guard on the offensive line and was my backup at inside linebacker on defense.

"Joe, I'm starting on defense," Bill said. "What do I need to know?"

My first thought was that my tenure as a two-way starter was being aborted, for reasons I could not calculate. Yes, it was something of a rare privilege on a Paul Martel team of that era for a player to start on both offense and defense. But I had not received any indication that Coach Martel had been disappointed in my performance.

Briefing a teammate on our defensive schemes, just several minutes before a game's kickoff, was a preposterous assignment, but Bill Caputo knew he could count on me to do it discreetly, since he did not really want anyone else to know he had not paid much attention to that side of the ball. The strongest and perhaps the most natural athlete on our team, Bill was the personification of Li'l Abner, the cartoon character created by Al Capp that ran in newspapers from 1934 to 1977. The younger brother of Lou Caputo, who starred for SLUH in the mid-1960s and played in that ill-fated 1966 loss to CBC at Busch Stadium, Bill seemed to play football not because he loved it, but because he was so damn good at it. "Coaching" him on the defense at the 11th hour, I reasoned, was best done by suggesting he line up across from and somewhere just to the left of the Assumption center, wait for the ball to be snapped, then brush aside any nuisance blocker bold enough to take him on, and then obliterate the guy with the football. "OK, got it," Bill responded.

A few moments later, when pre-game warm-ups were concluded and Coach Martel proceeded with his ritual of reading the starting lineups for offense, defense, and special teams, it finally hit me. I had *not* escaped the coach's eagle eye the night before, and I would be paying a penance for breaking curfew. I made the mistake of thinking that after a few series, he would call my name and send me in. Late in the second quarter, he finally called my name, and I sprinted to a spot next to him, inches from the sideline, ready to charge onto the field.

"I suppose you know why you're not playing," he said.

"Yes, sir," I said, crushed by the realization that I would not be entering the game.

"We will talk about it after the game."

Ouch. So just like that, I would miss the entire game, 10% of our season; 20% of our conference competition. I retreated back to my place on the sideline, kept on my helmet, and endeavored to refrain from weeping. I sensed this was a crossroads for me. Already, by the third of 10 scheduled games, our dream of an undefeated season had been deflated, and with it, the realistic chance to qualify for the state playoffs. For me individually, missing a conference game would diminish a realistic chance to earn the post-season all-star recognition usually required to get the attention of college football recruiters. For me as captain, I had just suffered a humiliating indignity that I feared would compromise my ability to lead. After quickly abandoning the thought of punching Coach Martel in the nose, I was tempted to cope by yielding to those who argued that football was a trivial endeavor, generating way too much attention and reverence in a troubled world. I was tempted to cope by rationalizing, by trying to convince myself that this was not very important after all.

36// *"Babe, If It Was Up To Me, You Would Have Played"*

ON THAT MUDDY FIELD, on that windy day in East St. Louis, the Junior Billikens played like champions without me, shutting out the host Pioneers, 29-0. Bill Ziegler rushed 12 times for 98 yards and two touchdowns to lead our offense, and Bob Thibaut sprinted around right end for a 52-yard run that surprised us. "That can't be you, Thibaut," teased Tim Fleming when we watched film of the game the next Monday. "You can't run that fast." Bill Caputo did just fine on defense. Certainly, Assumption could not have scored *fewer* points had I been in there on defense.

There was one great consolation for me in the Assumption game: Del Bannister got to start in my place at center, an honor he had deserved, and had worked just as hard for as I had. A selfless friend, he would make proud his Dad and nicknamesake, and his three older brothers, Junior Billiken alumni Tom, Bob and Joe Bannister.

We on the football team laughed often about the Althoff game from the prior year, when we juniors mostly watched as SLUH defeated the Crusaders on their muddy field in Belleville, Illinois. A senior named Keith Miller played an inspired game, most of it in a jersey on which mud had obscured the bottom horizontal stroke of the numeral 2, which fooled the game's radio broadcaster into believing player No. 67 was having that inspired game, not Keith Miller, who was player No. 62. Player No. 67 was Pat Bannister, whose Dad and other fans listening to the broadcast in St. Louis thought something must have gone haywire for young Del not only to be playing in the game, but to be starring in it.

Not exactly gifted with the athletic body of a Greek god, Bannister nonetheless was a good athlete and an effective blocker, as he used his long, skinny legs to launch his soft, rounded shoulders into the shins of the defenders he was charged with stopping or moving out of the way. And he was flawless as the "long snapper" on our punt team, taking the football in my place as the center, with responsibility for shooting it more than 10 yards to Gregg Hannibal, our punter. Two things made this task particularly difficult: (1) the long snapper has to make this accurate pass while bent over, his head pointing down, and looking back through his legs, and (2) he knew that as soon as he launched the ball, a rushing defender would try to knock him over or elude him in an effort to block the punt. Not once all season did Bannister make a bad snap.

Also, he did have one physical talent above the rest of us, which he displayed memorably on one random day in a corridor in the center of the main St. Louis U. High classroom area.

I believe it is fair to say that most who have traversed adolescence in the last five decades, have at one time or another come across the barbaric, humiliating rituals of the "titty twister" and the "wedgie." At SLUH, we had coined our own brand names for these juvenile rights of passage. The wedgie was known in our circles as "the Creeper," most likely because of the way the victim's underpants would creep up the crack of his ass when the perpetrator grabbed them by the rear of the waistband and yanked violently upward.

Del Bannister was particularly gifted at delivering the titty twister, upon which someone from our class had bestowed the name, "Jerry (Tit) Monger." It is possible but difficult to verify that the name was drawn from Mungo Jerry, the British pop group whose hit song *In The Summertime* had animated our carefree summer of 1970. On that random, memorable day, Whayne Herriford posed an innocent question.

"Who is Jerry Monger?" he asked.

Bannister's eyes lit up, in the way I imagine a California metals prospector's eyes lit up upon discovering a vein of gold in the summer of 1849. Tim Kellett and I looked at each other. Simultaneously, our faces contorted into a weird combination of smile and grimace, and we knew what was coming next. Each of us considered issuing a warning. Each of us refrained.

"Come with me," Bannister said. "I'll introduce you to him."

Del put his arm around Herriford's shoulder, and walked him around the corner, just out of our sight. "Three ... two ... one," Kellett and I counted silently to ourselves. We could just picture Bannister drawing his victim close, then striking like a cobra with the quick, sure lunge of his long, lithe digits ... clutching Whayne's vulnerable nipple and turning 90 degrees to the right.

"Eee-YOWWWWWWW!!" screamed Herriford, in a way that certainly cracked the paint on the walls. The two of them walked back into our sight, a grimacing Herriford clutching his wounded breast and Bannister smiling, smugly and satisfied. "Whayne just met Jerry Monger," Del said. St. Ignatius of Loyola would have been proud, I'm sure.

After enduring the Assumption game alone on the bench, then the bus ride back to the SLUH campus, where we showered and dressed, I was summoned to Coach Martel's office.

"We have rules for a purpose," he lectured. "You broke our curfew, and it doesn't matter that you are a starter, and it doesn't matter that you are Student Council President."

Coach Martel told me the story of an important game from his tenure at St. Agnes High in Kansas City. The school's nuns needed help carrying crates, and they recruited five of Coach Martel's senior football players for the job. The young men fulfilled those duties, then decided they would exempt themselves from football practice, despite being finished in plenty of time to be there. Coach Martel suspended all five, and St. Agnes played rival Kansas City Pembroke with just 16 players. St. Agnes lost, 28-27.

Gary Kornfeld joined the SLUH football staff as Martel's assistant in 1979, then succeeded him as head coach in 1988. "Paul was a disciplinarian," Kornfeld said. "The kids knew the rules. If you didn't follow them, there were going to be consequences."

Martel believed discipline and conformity were paramount to a successful enterprise.

"I was a strong disciplinarian," he said. "They're going to do it my way, because I'm running this program. If you can't conform, maybe you shouldn't be here."

Anxious to get out of his office, and aware that I did not have grounds for a grievance, since in fact I *had* violated a team rule, I said "Yes, sir" a few times, then finally escaped to the locker room. Composing myself before rejoining my teammates, I stooped to slurp up a drink from the water fountain. Mid-slurp, I was startled when the large, firm paw of Assistant Coach Ebbie Dunn clawed my shoulder.

Coach Dunn leaned in close to me, and said in a low but sure, steady voice, meant for my ears only: "Babe, I just want you to know, that if it had been up to me, you would have played."

"Yes, sir," I mustered. "Thank you, sir."

It was not until much later, many years later, that I realized what a courageous, heroic gesture that was from Ebbie Dunn. At the moment, I was darned near toppled over, crumbled by a mix of conflicting emotions —disappointment, humiliation, anger, loneliness, reconciliation, and then, with Ebbie Dunn's act of sweetness and sensitivity, encouragement and hope. Much later, it occurred to me what Ebbie had done. Convinced that the punishment did not fit the crime, he decided to risk insubordination by second-guessing the head coach, and delivering his verdict to the only person to whom it really mattered, in a most meaningful way.

Many of my contemporaries found it simple and easy to distinguish the good guys from the bad guys in the generational war that was engulfing our country in the late 1960s and early 1970s: anyone older than 30 was the enemy; anyone under 30 a colleague. My interaction with two men on that day, two men in their mid-40s, in the early autumn of 1970, left me with no such conclusion. A man of discipline and integrity, Paul Martel held me accountable, and did it in a stern but respectful way. Ebbie Dunn, a more nuanced man who understood what made us tick and would not hesitate to kick our backside when it was warranted, employed a gentler touch. For each man, and certainly for them both, I was prepared to play harder than ever when I next got the chance. Which, fortunately, was the next Saturday night in Columbia, against the No. 3-ranked team in Missouri, the Columbia Hickman Kewpies.

37// *Thorough and Convincing*

October 1970

HICKMAN HIGH WAS a powerful team from the center of the state, in the city of Columbia, also home to the University of Missouri Tigers. The Kewpies were runners-up to McCluer in the state championship game the prior autumn, and they began the 1970 season by crushing their first three

opponents, holding them to 47 yards and 15 points—combined. Paul Martel
scheduled them because he wanted us to play against the best competition.

"If you are going to beat somebody," he used to say, "beat somebody
that's good. When the playoff system was started, it was doubly important
that you play the top teams, because if you can't beat them, you're not
going to qualify for the playoffs anyway. There's no sense in playing weak
sisters, and end up getting nothing."

Even before this became a sound strategy, given the importance of
"strength of schedule" in the Missouri playoff formula, Martel was noto-
rious for scheduling games against powerhouse teams, usually at their
home fields since SLUH had no field on its campus. Perhaps that is what
one should expect from a man like him—independent, proud, self-confident, disciplined, fearless. For us, the players, it was like a season-long
episode of the "Bull in the Ring" drill. Intense, live or die, no let up. There
were about 500 high school football teams in Missouri in 1970. Of the
12 games we played, six were against teams in the Top 10 in the state's
Class 4A division for large schools. In this game, we were to learn if we
were legitimate contenders for statewide recognition. We dressed in our
game uniforms at St. Louis U. High after our last class, then traveled by
bus two hours west on Interstate 70.

Posted in the *Prep News* the previous Monday was an invitation from
Father Phil Kellett, moderator of athletics, for students to attend the game:

*Fr. Kellett wished to announce that he will begin taking reservations for the
Columbia Hickman bus trip. Bus Reservations will be $5.50 round trip fare
via Greyhound bus lines. Fr. Kellett will also be selling pre-game tickets for
$1.00, of which the school will receive a percentage. Reservations will be
taken until Monday, September 28.*

The buses will leave school at 4:00pm on Friday, October 2, to allow girls from other schools to arrive in time. Fr. Kellett suggests that anyone riding on the bus should bring some food along, as eating facilities are quite meager along the route. The buses will leave immediately following the game and arrive at school at approximately midnight.

Facing our own two-hour return bus trip right after the game, we certainly did not want a somber ride home, and we approached the game with confidence. It did not start well, however. We fumbled the opening kickoff, and Hickman recovered the ball 20 yards from our goal line. The Kewpies seemed hungry to knock us out early, with power runs right into the heart of our defensive line. They ran five yards slightly left, then five more slightly right for a first down near our 10-yard line. After our left defensive end Jim Twombly almost intercepted a pass on first down, Hickman returned with a power run off left tackle for another six yards. On third and goal, four yards from a touchdown, they tried the left side again, but this time defensive end Mike Wiese fought off a blocker to prevent a running lane, and blitzing right inside linebacker Kevin O'Toole moved in to shut down the ball carrier near the line of scrimmage. Hickman lined up for a short field goal, only a couple of yards farther than an extra point, but the placekicker punched the ball to the left of the goal posts.

It was a welcome reprieve. Soon, we would need another.

After we executed three running plays for a first down at our 35-yard line, Hickman intercepted a pass from Doug McDonald at our 44, and went back on the attack. After two running plays yielded 13 yards, defensive tackle Al Fahrenhorst deflected a pass that fell incomplete. On third and 10, Hickman quarterback Lou Onofrio dropped to pass, eluded a sack attempt by Mike Wiese and scrambled to the left, but was tackled by defensive back Tom O'Shaughnessy near the line of scrimmage. From punt formation, Hickman faked a kick and completed a screen pass to the left. Defensive back Tim Leahy read the play and quickly came up to tackle the receiver short of a first down, and it was our turn on offense again.

This time, we acted like champions. After four solidly executed running plays, McDonald took my snap and dropped four steps back to the right, lofted a pass to Leahy, who caught the ball at our 40-yard line, easily eluded his cover man, then sprinted down the right sideline to the goal line for a touchdown. We missed the extra point, but we were on our way to a thorough and convincing 25-13 victory.

One thing that helped us befuddle the Hickman offense was the bizarre innovation Paul Martel had instituted, and we used with great effect in this game and throughout the season. Traditionally, football teams gather in a huddle before each play. In the offense's huddle, the leader, generally the quarterback, calls for the play to be run, either his or the one signaled by the coach. At the same time, across the scrimmage line, the defensive captain tells his huddled teammates which defensive scheme they will run. The idea is that all 11 players will move in synchronization, with every assignment covered.

As the teams approach the ball to launch a play, players size up each other and call out the opponent's formation, usually "even" or "odd," based on where the defensive linemen position themselves. The call is "odd" when there are three or five linemen, one directly across from the offensive center; it is "even" when there were four linemen, positioned across from the offense's guards and tackles. The offense's blocking assignments for a given play will vary, depending on the formation it faces. Unbound by tradition, Coach Martel decided our defense had no obligation to telegraph its alignment, and he trained us to move around like nervous jackrabbits before the snap of the ball ... to ignore the cadence called out by the opponent's quarterback ... and to blast into our assignment the instant the center moved the ball to initiate his snap to the quarterback. The sweet innovation was his introduction of *two* defensive huddles instead of one: five guys on the left in one huddle; five guys on the right in the other. The 11th defender, the free safety, was free to choose either one. When asked which huddle the free safety should choose, Martel winked and said, "Whichever one has the better jokes."

He had designed the defensive schemes so that whatever one half of the defense called, it would mesh with the other. And it made it virtually impossible for the opponents on offense to recognize an "even" or an "odd" formation. The genius of this innovation, I am convinced, was not so much that it gave us a better defense, but that it made us *feel* as if we had an advantage, designed for the smart asses we were. Our confidence was buoyed when the huge Hickman offensive linemen approached the scrimmage line and pointed to which of us they were going to block, which of course we fouled up by jumping into a different position once or twice more before the play began.

Early in Martel's coaching career, because he had played only three years of supervised, organized football, he believed he was at a disadvantage against other coaches. And he compensated by becoming an ardent student of the game.

"When I got into coaching," he said, "the first thing I needed to do was learn all about football. So I went to football clinics. I probably went to 200 clinics during my career, just to learn different things about football."

When Gary Kornfeld joined the SLUH football team as an assistant coach in 1979, he was struck by Martel's devotion to learning and innovating. "He could always change," Kornfeld said. "He seemed to always stay ahead of the game. One time I remember going with him to a college in Illinois, where there was a coach who had a system like the Dallas Cowboys. He would have his offense shift frequently. We spent the day there, having the guy teach us how he did his system. Paul always stayed ahead of the game. He would always change something up. He was on the cutting edge of what was coming out."

Bob Thibaut jokes that Martel's playbook "was one of the hardest courses I ever took. He changed the plays every game. And then he has us running the two-huddle defense. I mean, it was a different type of game than any other high school teams were playing at the time."

Long after retiring from active coaching, Martel maintained a remarkable recall for details of his career, his teams, the games, his players, his coaching philosophy. One afternoon in the autumn of 2015, early in his 10th decade of life, he provided this extemporaneous account of what he did and why:

"A lot of coaches do not adapt," he said. "Let's say they're an 'I formation' coach, they're going to run the 'I formation' come hell or high water. But maybe the kids can't handle it. So then you'd better try something else the kids could handle. That's something I always felt I could do, run something the kids could handle. Whether it be the 'I formation,' or split backs, or wishbone, or 'wing T,' or whatever. If a different team could handle this formation better, then that's the offense we ran. With defense, I thought I was kind of an innovator there, because I drew up my own defense at times. And I had one that I call the Swing Six. But I don't know, if I was coaching right now, with all the wide-open offenses, if I could apply all of that. But it was a defense, that if you could learn what was on two pages, you could learn the whole defense. And a lot of it was stunting, and a lot of it was filling different holes. I hate to say this, to broadcast it, in the 52 years I was involved in football, I think I was smarter than 95 percent of the coaches that were out there. Because of the things that we did, of course realizing I had good kids, because I always felt, the best thing that happens with our ball club is if one guy breaks down, the guy next to him picks him up. Maybe another time, this guy breaks down, and the other guy picks him up. And I think I always felt the players complemented one another out there. And that was pretty much my philosophy."

Worthy of mention from the Hickman game—we had 199 rushing yards, including 63 from Thibaut, 60 from Tim Leahy and five on another touchdown run from Bill Ziegler; and a fumbled Hickman punt snap, which Tom O'Shaughnessy scooped up and carried 20 yards for a touchdown.

Another notable highlight was the debut of Tim Gibbons, the sophomore team quarterback who was brought up to the varsity to kick field goals. The "B" team easily had defeated its first three opponents, so Coach Joe Vitale had been able to sideline Gibbons for portions of those games and hoard quarters that could be used in games for the varsity. He replaced our incumbent placekicker, Thibaut, who was gracious about losing the assignment.

"When I saw Gibbons, I said to Martel, 'There's your kicker,'" Thibaut said. "I mean, come on. You could HEAR the ball pop off his foot."

Against Columbia Hickman, Gibbons put through two field goals, something uncommon in high school football in 1970. In a perverse testament to his status as a lowly sophomore, in the discriminatory, prehistoric, "class-conscious" custom of the day, there was not a seat made available for Gibbons on the bus trip home, and he was exiled to ride home in the back seat of the car driven by Paul Martel's wife Therese. He made the most of it, though, as he became acquainted with the Martels' pretty daughter Mary. Gibbons and Mary Martel were in a serious relationship for five years.

Perhaps the most remarkable story from the game, though, was the performance of Tom Schoeck, the starting outside right linebacker and backup fullback who was emerging as one of the elite players on the team. Probably our most "gung ho" player, the one John Benoist so vociferously challenged with a profane reaction to his call for more sprints that day on the "B" team practice field two seasons prior, Schoeck was relentless, with or without the ball.

On offense, Schoeck tucked the ball under his arm, hunched his head between his shoulders, leaned forward, and motored his long, bony legs in the way piston and connecting rods power the driving wheels of a steam engine locomotive train. To prospective tacklers, he must have *looked* like an approaching train. On defense, he zeroed in on the other team's ball carriers like a heat-seeking antiballistic missile in search of an enemy rocket. On the field before the McCluer game, with both teams stepping through plays during the warm-up session before the opening kickoff, the ever-aware Schoeck was sizing up our opponents at the other end of the field. He noticed an unusual formation and an unusual play. Early in the game, Schoeck recognized that same McCluer offensive formation, anticipated the play he had seen, and interrupted it with a tackle for a loss. "One helluva play," Coach Ebbie Dunn would say later, when we watched film of the game. In a game later in the year, Schoeck read and reacted to an opponent's play so quickly, he burst through the line and got his hand on the football an instant before the running back got it from his quarterback, causing a fumble, which he recovered.

Against Columbia Hickman, Schoeck made 17 tackles. That was remarkable, but not the most remarkable thing about that evening or the following week. He was the younger brother of Jim Schoeck, who had quarterbacked the SLUH team the season before and was spending the autumn of 1970 as a football player and cadet at the U.S. Air Force Academy near Colorado Springs. They were the two oldest of the six children of Gloria Cassell and Dr. Al Schoeck, who had moved the family from Cleveland to St. Louis in 1964 when he took a job as one of the first anesthesiologists hired by St. John's Mercy Hospital, which opened that year. Al Schoeck was tough and demanding, and was not one to entertain excuses. His son Tom played football as if he had something to prove.

On offense, on a running play during his inspired performance against Columbia Hickman, Tom Schoeck took a defender's shot in the lower section of his back, and suffered a ruptured kidney, which was diagnosed two days later. What gave it away, Schoeck recalled, was that in addition to the pain, he urinated a bright red stream after the following Monday's practice. After missing one practice, the gritty Schoeck returned to active duty. He made one concession to his injury: he wore a foam pad for one day.

38// *Dominant*

A MONTH INTO the 1970 season, the *St. Louis Post-Dispatch* began publishing a weekly ranking of teams from the greater St. Louis area, based on the votes of 12 area coaches and two referees who represented the area's conferences and independent teams from both sides of the Mississippi River. The newspaper published a separate ranking of teams from the state of Missouri, based on its sportswriters' consultation with coaches from throughout the state. After defeating Columbia Hickman, we moved up to No. 6 among the metropolitan area's "large-school" teams, and to No. 5 in Missouri.

Prep Top 10

(Published October 9, 1970)

Rankings of area high school football teams by the Post-Dispatch board of coaches, with first-place votes and records in parentheses (points on a basis of 10 for first, 9 for second, 8 for third, etc.).

LARGE SCHOOLS

1.	Alton (4) (2-0)	115
2.	Riverview (7) (3-0)	113
3.	Belleville East (1) (3-0)	97
4.	Lindbergh (3-0)	87
5.	CBC (1) (4-0)	72
6.	St. Louis U. High (3-1)	53
7.	Granite City (3-0)	41
8.	Vianney (4-0)	40
9.	McCluer (2-1)	31
10.	Normandy (3-0)	28

State's Top 15

(Published October 6, 1970)

The Post-Dispatch ranking of the top high school football teams in Missouri, with last week's ratings in parentheses:

1. Riverview Gardens (1)...3-0
2. Jefferson City (2)...4-0
3. Lindbergh (5)..3-0
4. St. Louis CBC (6)...4-0
5. St. Louis U. High (10)...3-1
6. McCluer (7)...2-1
7. Kansas City Center (–).......................................4-0
8. Chillicothe (8)...3-0
9. Kansas City De La Salle (9)............................3-0-1
10. Kansas City Oak Park (4)...............................3-1
11. Columbia Hickman (3).....................................3-1
12. Springfield Hillcrest (–)....................................4-0
13. Cape Girardeau Central (13)..........................3-0
14. Vianney (–)..4-0
15. Cass Midway (15)..4-0

While proud of our standing among the top teams in the area and in the state, we also were mindful that after four games we were NOT in the picture to qualify for the Missouri playoffs. That week, *St. Louis Post-Dispatch* sportswriter Gary Mueller published an explanation of how the state playoff system worked, with this introductory paragraph:

> *Trying to explain the mathematical method by which the qualifiers for the Missouri high school football playoffs will be determined is nearly an impossible task.*

Mueller went on to explain:

- *The point formula, devised by the Missouri State High School Activities Association, awards 20 points for a victory over a team with a winning record, 15 points for a tie with a team with a winning record and 7½ points for a* loss to a team with a winning record.

- Against a team with a .500 record, the points are 15, 10 and 5 for a victory, tie and loss, respectively. Against a team with a losing record, the points are 10, 5 and 2½.

- Adjustments of up to 1½ points are made for playing schools in larger or smaller enrollment classifications.

Accompanying Mueller's explanation was this accounting of where teams stood, almost halfway through the regular season. The standings are for those in the 4A Class, which was for schools with the largest enrollments. St. Louis U. High was among the teams in District Three, and we did not make the first five in that district.

Playoff Standings

CLASS 4A

	Pts.	Avg.
DISTRICT ONE		
Kansas City Center (4-0)	69	17.3
Springfield Glendale (2-1-1)	52.5	13.1
Joplin Parkwood (3-1)	52	13.0
Jefferson City (4-0)	50	12.5
Springfield Hillcrest (4-0)	49	12.3
DISTRICT TWO		
Columbia Hickman (3-1)	52	13.0
Park Hill (2-2)	48.5	12.1
North Kansas City (3-1)	47.5	11.9
Independence Truman (3-1)	47.5	11.9
Lafayette (1-2)	34.3	11.1
DISTRICT THREE		
Ladue (2-0)	30	15.0
Vianney (4-0)	59.5	14.9
St. Mary's (3-0-1)	54.5	13.6
Lindbergh (3-0)	40	13.3
Southwest (3-1)	52	13.0

DISTRICT FOUR

Beaumont (3-1)	52.5	13.1
McCluer (2-1)	37.5	12.5
Berkeley (1-2)	34.5	11.5
DeSmet (3-1)	42	10.5
Riverview Gardens (3-0)	30	10.0

At the same time, the victory over Columbia Hickman left us inspired and confident. We knew the only thing we could do about the state playoff qualification system was to win our remaining games, and we would continue to find out how strong a team we were. We completely dominated over the next three weekends, improving our season record to 6-1 by outscoring the three opponents, 107-7.

In a 30-0 victory against Cahokia (Illinois) High on its home field, we had 394 yards of offense to just 48 for the Comanches, who featured a 6-foot, 205-pound junior named Primus Jones, who would go on to be named to the *St. Louis Post-Dispatch* "All Metro" first team for his play that season. Errol Patterson intercepted two Cahokia passes, and caught two touchdown passes—one each from Doug McDonald and Dan Calacci, who was gradually getting more time at the quarterback position on his way to becoming our starter. "Everything just sort of clicked," Patterson said. "Going into that game, I thought they were the superior team."

Against DeSmet, a school built and opened in West St. Louis County in 1967 by the Society of Jesus, we intercepted five passes and Bill Ziegler displayed his deceptive speed with a 70-yard touchdown run on an option play in a 27-7 victory. DeSmet's seniors were among its first graduating class, having started at the high school the same year our class entered SLUH. One of those seniors was Mike Gibbons, a menacing, 6-foot-1, 205-pound middle linebacker who was the older brother of Tim Gibbons, our placekicker. The elder Gibbons delighted in his assignment on kickoff returns, when he endeavored to punish the younger Gibbons after his kickoff. "I remember that I stayed clear of him," Tim Gibbons said. "But

I also remember him yell 'Get Gibbons!' just before one of the kickoffs." Such was the competitive, brotherly love between the older of the four children of Josephine Ceresia and Hugh Gibbons, who had graduated from St. Louis U. High in 1943. Tim recalls steering clear of his brother at home after the game, too. "I didn't want him to fulfill his need to 'Get Gibbons!' after the fact," Tim said.

Our next opponent was Augustinian Academy. Opened in 1961 and closed just 11 years later, Augustinian drew students from blue-collar families from the neighborhoods near its location in the southeast section of the City of St. Louis.

One of the school's most notable graduates was the Class of 1969's Pat Leahy, who went on to become the all-time leading scorer for the New York Jets as their placekicker from 1974 to 1991. He did not play organized football until he joined the Jets, but he starred on the Augustinian soccer team and helped lead St. Louis University to three National Collegiate Athletic Association soccer championships.

The Augustinian game was a "home" game for us, which we played at O'Fallon Tech High, a mile south of our campus. Errol Patterson's family attended every game, away or home, but this time was late in arriving. Impatiently, the 15-year-old Myrnae already was motoring to get to a seat when the game started, anxious to root for the brother she had nicknamed "Crazy Legs." Dr. Relford and Gloria Patterson were not far behind. At least not until the second play of the game, when quarterback Dan Calacci tossed a pass to their pride and joy, who grabbed it and took off running toward the Augustinian end zone. He was not alone. "I looked over to see Myrnae running along the sideline cheering me on, stride for stride," said Errol, whose 79-yard touchdown catch and run began our most lopsided victory of the season.

Calacci followed the TD pass with a 2-point conversion pass to offensive tackle Al Fahrenhorst. Yeah, a pass to an offensive lineman. Coach

Martel liked doing things like that.

Calacci tried seven passes in the game, completing five for 172 yards and earning his starter's role the rest of the season. We won, 50-0, despite the presence of the gifted Tony Gillick, the Augustinian quarterback who went on to star in the defensive backfield for the University of Missouri Tigers. A running quarterback, Gillick gained zero rushing yards against us that day. He completed just five passes, and threw four interceptions. Our offense produced nearly 400 yards and we improved our Bi-State Conference record to 3-0, with games against Belleville Althoff and CBC yet to play. And we continued to rise in the *St. Louis Post-Dispatch* rankings of teams from the St. Louis area.

Prep Top 10

(*Published October 30, 1970*)

Rankings of area high school football teams by the Post-Dispatch board of coaches, with first-place votes and records in parentheses (points on a basis of 10 for first, 9 for second, 8 for third, etc.).

LARGE SCHOOLS

1. Riverview (6) (6-0) 116
2. Alton (5) (6-0) 115
3. CBC (2) (7-0) 111
4. St. Louis U. High (6-1) 82
5. Vianney (7-0) 77
6. Ladue (5-0) 68
7. Granite City (5-1) 46
8. Belleville East (5-1) 34
9. Beaumont (6-1) 23
10. Roosevelt (5-1-1) 20

One player who did not prosper so well during this dominant three-game sweep was Fred Daues, who missed the Cahokia game after turning an ankle. He returned to action in practice before the DeSmet game, but fell victim to a severe injury during a full-contact drill when a body was slammed into his right knee. "I thought it was sprained," Daues said, "so

I kept playing on it. But it swelled up." The injury was more severe than a sprain, as the cartilage tore, and Daues could barely straighten the leg. Coach Martel kept him out of action, and sent him for ultrasound treatment by Bob "Doc" Bauman, the athletic trainer for the St. Louis Cardinals and St. Louis University sports teams. After treatment and with the benefit of a pain-numbing cortisone shot, Daues would return to play defense later in the season. But his hopes of a football scholarship were diminished. "I was never the same after that," he said.

39// *A Training Table Delicacy*

ONE MID-OCTOBER evening that season, about midway through our football schedule, Del Bannister and I headed home after practice for what I assumed would be a routine mid-week evening. It had been his turn to drive that day, and he dropped me off before pulling his father's mammoth Pontiac Bonneville "boat" around the corner and four houses up to his house. My brother Jim was in Kansas City as a sophomore at Rockhurst College, and Dad was working the 5 p.m. to 1:30 a.m. shift at Jimmy & Andy's Bar. Long after my younger siblings had eaten their supper, I arrived home tired, hungry, and braced for two hours or more of studying. First-quarter exams were approaching, so that hung over my head like the Sword of Damocles.

Mom greeted me with the dinner she had prepared for the third time—first, for Dad before he went to work, then again for my sister JoMarie and brothers Mike and Steve at the regular supper time, then finally for me, when I arrived around 6:30 p.m.

"What's for supper, Mom?" I asked.

"Roast beef and mashed potatoes," Mom said.

My compliments on Mom's cooking were of questionable value to her, as she knew I would eat with gusto anything she put in front of me. Still, we didn't get roast beef that often, so I was pretty enthused about this evening's fare. When she placed it in front of me, however, I observed two peculiar things that sparked my curiosity: (1) the roast beef slices had an assortment of odd bumps on their surface, and (2) my siblings were staring at me with dopey smiles, closely scrutinizing my every move. Hungry as I was, I discounted those observations and proceeded to eat every bite, mildly annoyed by my sister's and brothers' giggles.

"What is so funny?" I said, finally.

"You just ate beef tongue!" said JoMarie, gleefully.

Well, I thought, that explains it. Though two mysteries endure: that JoMarie, a notoriously picky eater, actually consumed her portion earlier in the evening, and why Mom would ever have brought home such a thing. (It was not surprising that Mike and Steve ate the beef tongue, for I believe they would have eaten an automobile tire if Mom had fried it up and served it to them.) I'll have to accept my sister's explanation that she was inspired to eat that meal because Mom had brought her alone in on the secret surprise, promoted it as a "delicacy," and encouraged her to bathe the beef in mashed potatoes before biting into it. And as for why she cooked that offering in the first place, all I can conclude is that either she got a really low price on it at Hippe's Meat Market, or that one of Dad's customers had given it to him at the tavern. That is, after all, how I got my first set of golf clubs.

"Jimmy, I'm so sick and tired of golf," said the forlorn golfer one day. "I'm never going to play again. Give me 35 bucks and you can have these clubs and the bag. And I'll throw in the golf shoes, too."

"Nah," said Dad. "You don't want to do that. In a few days, you'll get over it, and you'll wish you had your clubs back."

"No, Jimmy," he countered. "I'm finished with it. Please, take these off my hands."

"Well," Dad said, "I'll give you 25 bucks for them."

I learned a lot from my father over the years, including the art of negotiation.

40// *Inspiring a Lasting Commitment to Service*

AWAY FROM FOOTBALL, we endeavored to run a functional Student Council, with slightly less than modest success. Our ill-fated idea of re-writing the Student Council constitution plodded along but faltered in the abyss of wordsmithing, and our debate about the merits of awarding "letters" to non-athletes escalated to an absurd level.

One day, President and Principal Father Rich Bailey summoned Phil Schaefer, Whayne Herriford and me to his office. The subject matter was "hair length," a topic that to some had become an odd battleground on which to fight the war of the generations. Presumably forced to confront a topic he most likely would have preferred to avoid, Father Bailey introduced the subject.

"We have to have a policy on hair length," said this brilliant, gifted, very busy man. He wanted our input.

Whayne, Phil and I looked at each other, then at Father Bailey, whose head long ago had shed most of its hair, save for a ring of closely cropped grayish white strands from just over his ears to the back of his head. We came unprepared to litigate the subject, and perhaps Father Bailey sensed that. He looked at Schaefer, who by then had grown his hair to the top of his shirt collar at the neck and to just over the top of his ears, something of an outer limit for students at the time. "That's it," proclaimed Father Bailey. "That's the standard for how long students can wear their hair."

It was a generous concession, I thought, and sat in amazement at how swiftly and surely Father Bailey made this decision.

"Score one for the Student Council!" thought Schaefer.

Our Student Council *did* manage to pull off a successful, more serious social awareness event, one of the first of its kind, thanks to Whayne Herriford. As the local representative of the American Freedom From Hunger Association, Herriford organized a 30-mile "Walk for Development" as a fund-raiser and awareness-raiser to benefit local food banks and other charities devoted to addressing hunger. Herriford introduced the event to the SLUH community with an article in the weekly school newspaper, *The Prep News*. His opening paragraph:

Food for the Walking
By Wayne Herriford

On October 11 the students of SLUH will have a chance to join in a collective venture to awaken this city to the worldwide problems of poverty and hunger. On this date the American Freedom From Hunger Association (AFFH) will sponsor a Walk for Development in which interested and concerned citizens and students participate. The Walk for Development consists of a march for 20 to 30 miles in which the participants solicit sponsors who agree to pay a sum of money for each mile completed. The money collected is divided equally between local and foreign projects.

Beginning at St. Louis U. High, the 30-mile route headed west to Skinker Boulevard, then north beyond the city's border into St. Louis County, then west again to Overland, then south through Vinita Park, University City, Olivette, Clayton, Richmond Heights, Brentwood and Webster Groves, then east through Maplewood and back into the City of St. Louis. It finished where it started, at 4970 Oakland Avenue, the upper field at St. Louis U. High.

More than 2,000 participated in the walk, on the second Sunday in

October, between the Cahokia and DeSmet football games. Warmed by the spectacular weather on a classic St. Louis "Indian Summer" day and the thought of doing something worthwhile for others, we completed the route in less than eight hours. In advance of the event, in what admittedly was a delicious abuse of power, Herriford issued a loaded challenge to the young ladies of Nerinx Hall, the all-girls Catholic college preparatory school in Webster Groves. Would SLUH or Nerinx raise more money for the Walk, through solicitation of sponsors committing money per mile? To the "winner," the "loser" would acknowledge its superiority. Of course, we at SLUH won that challenge, and Herriford extracted signatures of acknowledgement from five of the Nerinx leaders, including Katie Rhoades, my girlfriend; Betsy Sellinger, the Nerinx Student Council President; and Colleen Kellett, a junior and the younger sister of Tim Kellett. Betsy's signed letter read:

> As the president of the Student Council of Nerinx Hall High School I have signed this paper to demonstrate my own personal conviction of the superiority of the students of St. Louis University High School over those of Nerinx Hall, especially those of the classes of nineteen hundred and seventy one.
>
> I especially wish to apologize to the officers of the Student Council at St. Louis University High for having dared to question the integrity and concern of the students at their school.
>
> Sincerely,
>   Miss Betsy Sellinger
>   Accepted: November 10, 1970
>   Wayne Herriford

Many years later, as Herriford and I reminisced about this, and marveled that we could have convinced such intelligent, independent and strong women to sign such a thing, we reassured ourselves that indeed we had "won." But you have to remember, Whayne informed me, "I was the one keeping score." Wicked.

Katie was a good sport about it, for she appreciated what Whayne was trying to do by introducing us to an event like this.

"I had never done anything like that before," she said. "Whayne was making us aware of issues from the outside world, raising our awareness of hunger as an issue. And doing something for somebody else. If he hadn't organized the event, I wouldn't have known anything about that stuff. He was definitely a troublemaker, kind of like he was saying, 'Let's ratchet this up and work on things.' He challenged us, but in a good way."

Easily the most significant achievement of our Student Council was the inauguration of the "Senior Project," a three-week hiatus from our regular academic curriculum so we could spend time on authorized service projects. The concept was introduced by our predecessor class, led by Matt Sciuto, the 1970 Student Council President. Pushed by Whayne Herriford's sense of social justice, a sweet spot for the Society of Jesus, we in the Class of 1971 appealed to the school administration to launch the program during an extended break between the first and second semesters of our senior year.

There was a significant schism within the Jesuit community and lay faculty, we learned later. After all, few Jesuits were institution-upending activists like Daniel Berrigan. Perhaps inspired by the generational mistrust rampant at that time, many in the administration, Jesuit community and faculty distrusted the students and our motivation. Three weeks away from school and our traditional curriculum? Heresy. Scam.

Dick Keefe was a French teacher at the time, early in his 43-year career at SLUH. He recalls a meeting in the school's old library, when Fr. Dave Wayne presented the idea.

"I won't say the faculty erupted, but there was a strong reaction," Keefe recalled. "'What are you talking about?! Taking seniors out of class?!' One faculty member leading the group against the idea said, 'No way, no way. What are we sacrificing?'"

"At first, I thought, 'This is great, three weeks off,'" said Tim Rodgers, the chairman of our Student Council Spirit Committee. As one seemingly unimpressed with those in authority, Rodgers might have been a candidate to prompt skeptics to question how seriously he would take this program. "We were the first class with the Senior Project. Who knew what it was going to be like?"

"It didn't get decided in just that one meeting," Keefe said. "There was a lot of resistance. A lot of questions. A lot of skepticism."

But thanks to the courageous advocacy of Jesuits like Dave Wayne, Rich Bailey, Ed O'Brien, Jack Warner, Tom Jost and Tom Cummings, who were answering the challenge of Father Pedro Arrupe, the Superior General of the Jesuit Order, we pushed through this radical three-week investment in service.

Father Arrupe had served as a missionary in Japan when World War II erupted. Imprisoned by the Japanese who suspected him of espionage, Fr. Arrupe believed he was to be executed. Instead, he gained the respect of his captors and gained release within a month. In 1945, while serving as Jesuit superior and novice master in suburban Hiroshima, he was one of eight Jesuits who lived in the blast zone targeted by the U.S. for one of the two atomic bombs deployed in an effort to accelerate the end of World War II. They survived the blast, and used their residence as a temporary hospital, where they cared for those suffering effects from it.

Upon his election as Father General in 1965, Father Arrupe prioritized service and social justice, as he would later outline in *"Our Mission Today: the Service of Faith and the Promotion of Justice."*[19] In that decree, Father Arrupe wrote: "Our faith in Jesus Christ and our mission to proclaim the

Gospel demand of us a commitment to promote justice and enter into solidarity with the voiceless and the powerless."

And so, the St. Louis U. High "Senior Project" was inaugurated in January of 1971, with three primary objectives: (1) Implement Christian ideals of service advocated by Fr. Arrupe and the Society of Jesus, (2) Expose students to the life and condition of people beyond their life experience and social strata, and (3) Inspire a lasting commitment to service within the students.

Classmates served in the St. Louis State Hospital as caregivers for the mentally ill, in classrooms as tutors for grade school children in the inner city, in St. Louis Children's Hospital to support sick and injured youngsters, in an impoverished community in Spanish Honduras where they helped build infrastructure, and in numerous other service endeavors.

Tim Rodgers and close friend and classmate Jack Enright spent the three weeks in the country of Spanish Honduras, in the town of Progresso, Yoro. They built and painted small, two-room wooden structures to house the indigent there.

"It turned out to be a life-changing event," Rodgers said. "It was one of the most formative things I ever experienced."

To ensure the Senior Project would survive its first year, I spent the 15 "school days" visiting the projects of others, documenting the viability, seriousness, and impact of the efforts and producing a report.

"That was a fairly big risk they took on us," said Phil Schaefer, who spent his three weeks at a Head Start school in University City, which exposed him to inner city children. "We might not have been the best class to try that on. But we didn't screw it up. Everyone I knew embraced it, and took it seriously. It was very powerful."

Today, the Senior Project prospers at SLUH, uninterrupted since 1971, and the concept of student service has been institutionalized at schools throughout St. Louis and the United States. Of course, we understood that the student himself tended to be impacted more by the work than those he served in a mere three weeks.

Through our senior year as Student Council officers, Phil Schaefer, Whayne Herriford and I would get a good taste of the price of public service, and the perils that came from public scrutiny. One memorable *Letter to the Editor* published in our weekly school paper, *The Prep News*:

> Last week's Student Council meeting was a choice example of that organization's ineptness. Any semblance between its meetings and parliamentary procedure is purely coincidental. Wayne Herriford, the secretary, tries to call points of order, but is invariably overruled by the president, who has, of late, not even worn shoes to the proceedings. The total lack of decorum at the meetings is inexcusable.

The anonymous author did not know or likely care that I was shoeless to expedite the transition between our meeting and the football practice I would have to rush to make. He went on to prattle about the fact that we lost some bill that had been introduced six weeks earlier. The letter went on: *The secretary explained this by saying that we should impeach him if we do not like it.*

Whayne and I had a good laugh about that one, many years later. For me, the football practice field increasingly was becoming a place for retreat.

41// *Divine Intervention*

OUR NEXT GAME WOULD take us to Belleville, Illinois, across the Mississippi River from St. Louis. Strong German immigrant families had settled in Belleville, including the Eckert and Schmitz clans from which my mother descended. Althoff High was the Catholic school in Belleville, and the Crusaders had been worthy opponents in football, basketball and baseball during my tenure in high school. Two seasons before, the Althoff sophomore team defeated us, 14-12, so we had reason to anticipate a competitive game now that we and they were seniors.

The game was to be played on October 31, which was Halloween, the evening before what Catholics celebrate as All Saints' Day, which is then followed by All Souls' Day. Those who celebrate All Saints' Day and All Souls' Day do so in the belief that there is a prayerful spiritual bond between those in heaven and those still living. For those who believed in divine intervention in earthly matters, and there were plenty of us on this particular SLUH football team, this game turned out to be one to reinforce such faith. Miraculously, we escaped with a 6-0 victory.

Led by 6-foot-5, 208-pound junior quarterback Mike Abegg, the Althoff offense ran 64 plays to our 45, and accumulated 239 yards of offense, including 179 yards passing, and 14 first downs.

"The Althoff Crusaders have run surprisingly well all over the field against the Junior Bills, but when they get inside the five or the 10 (yard line), the Junior Bills toughen up," said Joe May, who along with Dave Villone broadcast this and most of the Belleville area high school sports events from the town's WIBV radio station. None of the schools from the Missouri side of the Greater St. Louis area were deemed broadcast worthy, so this game was the only one on our schedule with an audio record of it.

Four times, Althoff had possession of the ball within five yards of our goal line. Each time, our defense rallied to stop the Crusaders with a goal-line stand. Tom Schoeck made one touchdown-saving tackle; Errol Patterson saved two scores: once by breaking up a pass, another by tackling an Althoff running back on a fourth-and-goal from our two-yard line. Our defense simply refused to yield the goal line, and forced Althoff to surrender possession of the ball. In addition to the goal-line stands, we intercepted four Althoff passes in the game.

Tim Kellett played an exceptional game, starting as usual at right offensive tackle and substituting at right defensive tackle for the injured Fred Daues. He inspired this praise from the announcer Villone, when he limped off the field to tend to a mild injury midway through the fourth quarter:

> A man injured on the play and coming out of the game for the Junior Bills is Tim Kellett, and that would be a big loss. He is the man who has been in over 70 to 75 percent of the tackles here this evening, if not a lot more than that.

Fortunately, Tim was able to return quickly.

As remarkable as was the timely work of the defense, it was an offensive play early in the game that seemed the special work of the angels, coming with about three minutes left in the first quarter. Capping a nine-play, 85-yard drive down the field, quarterback Dan Calacci took my center snap from the 14-yard line, stepped back and then whirled to his left, holding the football high with his right arm and searching for a target near the Althoff end zone.

Sandwiched between two defenders just a couple steps over the goal line and just inches from the sideline, receiver Tom O'Shaughnessy somehow made himself visible to Calacci, who somehow lofted a pass that somehow O'Shaughnessy caught. The play is memorialized on the grainy eight-millimeter film used to record all our games, but to this day, having watched that play about as often and as carefully as I've seen the Abraham Zapruder film of the Kennedy assassination in Dealey Plaza, I cannot say for sure that O'Shaughnessy came down with the ball safely in the end zone. Fortunately for us, the referee responsible for the call was in perfect position, just several feet from the play, and he immediately thrust his two arms in the air to signal a touchdown. We botched the extra point attempt, then lived the remainder of the game on the edge, desperately trying to protect our narrow margin.

Patterson fumbled the kickoff that opened the second half, and Althoff recovered deep in our territory. The Crusaders made one first down, and began the next series first and goal from our six-yard line. Bill Caputo, Al Fahrenhorst, Jim Twombly and Schoeck made the tackles that stalled Althoff's touchdown push, then it was Patterson's turn on fourth and goal from the two. Lined up behind the center in the Wing T formation, the quarterback Abegg took the snap, faked a handoff to the fullback up the middle, then pitched the ball to the left to running back Robyn Blaha. Patterson charged forward from his right cornerback position to greet the ball carrier, stopping him for a two-yard loss, saving the touchdown, and preserving our lead.

"A beautiful defensive job by Errol Patterson!" called an animated Dave Villone on the WIBV broadcast.

"I knew they were coming," Patterson recalled. "I knew if I was able to tackle the runner, I could not let him push forward because they were so close to the goal line. I was able to push forward and stop him."

Lamented WIBV's Joe May, "(Althoff) just cannot punch it across from inside the five." More than one of us felt the spirit of Ed Hawk. Ed had not been much of a football player, but I felt his presence with us on that field that night.

We entered the game ranked No. 4 in the state of Missouri. Our next two opponents, CBC and Riverview Gardens, were ranked No. 3 and No. 1, respectively, behind and in front of No. 2 Jefferson City. On that same evening, as we were hanging on for victory, both CBC and Riverview Gardens were defeated, which wasn't necessarily wonderful news for us. They did not need further inspiration as they prepared for our coming encounters the next two weekends. After our eighth game, we had climbed to No. 3 in Missouri.

State's Top 15

(Published November 3, 1970)

The Post-Dispatch ranking of the top high school football teams in Missouri, with last week's ratings in parentheses:

1. Jefferson City (2) 7-0
2. Kansas City Center (5) 8-0
3. St. Louis U. High (4) 7-1
4. Vianney (8) 8-0
5. Chillicothe (6) 7-0
6. Riverview Gardens (1) 6-1
7. Kansas City Oak Park (7) 7-1
8. St. Louis CBC (3) 7-1
9. Cape Girardeau (9) 6-1
10. Ladue (10) 6-0
11. Columbia Hickman (11) 6-2
12. Springfield Glendale (12) 6-1-1
13. Beaumont (13) 7-1
14. Cass Midway (14) 8-0
15. North Kansas City (15) 7-1

Jefferson City High, located in the Missouri state capital, had ascended to the No. 1 ranking, which seemed appropriate for the program of legendary coach Pete Adkins, whose Jays teams won 71 consecutive games from 1958-66, then a national record for high school football. Under Adkins, the Jays went on to win nine Missouri playoff championships in his 43-year tenure. We at St. Louis U. High had a much less luminous pedigree, and much more modest aspirations for football success. Importantly, though, in the early autumn of 1970 we had started to show up in the state playoff standings compiled by the *St. Louis Post-Dispatch*. Following is the table that appeared after our victory over Belleville Althoff.

Playoff Standings

CLASS 4A

	Pts.	Avg.
DISTRICT ONE		
Kansas City Center (8-0)	119	14.9
Jefferson City (7-0)	94.5	13.5
Springfield Glendale (6-1-1)	104.5	13.1
Lee's Summit (7-1)	90.5	11.3
Kansas City Southwest (5-2-1)	84.5	10.6
DISTRICT TWO		
Columbia Hickman (6-2)	114	14.3
North Kansas City (7-1)	97.5	12.2
Kansas City Oak Park (7-1)	87.5	10.9
St. Louis Lafayette (5-2)	73	10.4
St. Joe Central (4-3)	71	10.1
DISTRICT THREE		
Ladue (6-0)	90	15.0
Vianney (8-0)	118.5	14.8
St. Louis U. High (7-1)	116	14.5
St. Mary's (6-1-1)	101	12.6
CBC (7-1)	101	12.6
DISTRICT FOUR		
Beaumont (7-1)	97	12.1
Riverview Gardens (7-1)	82.5	11.8
McCluer (4-3)	82.5	11.8
DeSmet (6-2)	88.5	11.1
Ritenour (3-4)	75	10.7

We were starting to believe a playoff qualification was at least possible. Unfortunately for Bob Thibaut, the injury he sustained in the Althoff game was serious.

With the fullback featured in Paul Martel's game plan for Althoff, Thibaut was getting the chance to carry and catch the ball against the Crusaders. Late in the first quarter, we began the drive that would lead to the game's only score. Quarterback Dan Calacci started the drive by narrowly escaping an Althoff defender and completing a long pass to Bill Ziegler along the left sideline. Next, he rolled to the right and connected with Thibaut on a 16-yard pass just inside the other sideline, in front of the Althoff team bench. After an incomplete pass and runs up the middle by Ziegler and Mike Ruggeri, Thibaut took a handoff and raced through a big hole 12 yards straight downfield and into the Althoff secondary. Two defensive backs converged on him just as he planted his foot. One hit him high, the other low, and Thibaut heard a crack.

"That was it," he knew, as he collapsed to the ground in pain. Teammates Errol Patterson and Ruggeri came over, then helped him up and over to the sidelines. He had torn ligaments in his right knee, and his senior season was virtually over. "It was devastating," Thibaut said. An old truism holds that a football team's success is predicated on how well the team copes with the injuries that inevitably befall key players. How true that would turn out to be in the next game, against our arch rival CBC.

42// Homecoming

November 1970

THE CBC VS. SLUH football game never again commanded the level of attention it did the first time it was played in Busch Stadium, in 1966, when the two schools were ranked Nos. 1 and 2 in the St. Louis area and more than 31,000 attended. But it was still a pretty big deal four years later, in the fall of 1970.

"At that time, your entire young life revolved around your local Catholic school parish," Tim Kellett explained. "We knew kids from the neighboring parishes because we had played basketball or soccer or baseball against them. When we played CBC, we knew most of their guys. You went to grade school with them. You played CYC (Catholic Youth Council) against them. You dated some of the girls they wanted to date; they dated some of the girls you wanted to date. Just about everybody I had grown up with or knew, was involved with it, on one side or the other. It was a game you just did not want to lose. It was critical to win. The alumni were really into it. The faculty was really into it. It was a big, big deal."

Now it was our turn as seniors to play in this arena built for men, for professionals. It would be the 44th time the two schools' football teams would meet in a rivalry begun in 1925. In addition to imprinting our place in this historic rivalry, at stake was the Bi-State Conference championship and points critical in the race to qualify for the state playoff tournament.

We in the senior class had lost to CBC as freshmen in 1967, as sophomores in 1968, and as juniors on the junior varsity in 1969. As juniors in 1969, many of us did get to play as the varsity defeated the Cadets, 34-7. It was not simply a coincidence that the 27-point margin of that game matched the one by which CBC had ruined SLUH's 1966 season in the first game at Busch Stadium. Late in the game, Paul Martel called for a two-point conversion after a touchdown, instead of the more reliable one-point kick. He had wearied, it seemed obvious, of CBC Coach Bill Gerdeman crowing about that 1966 game. Paybacks make for a spirited rivalry.

Such a showdown is a worthy endeavor for intrepid 17-year-olds, most of us who were unburdened by the types of thoughts that can tend to freeze up people with more experience, more introspection, more awareness of the effects of failure and humiliation. Though of course tingled with some nervous anticipation, I do not recall feelings of doubt or hesitation. It was our moment, and I liked the attention.

We had the opportunity to practice on Busch Stadium's Astroturf field one day during the week of the game. We exchanged the spikes on our football shoes, unscrewing the traditional 3/4-inch cleats and twisting in rubber, rounded ones designed for friction and better traction on the artificial carpeting. Nowhere near as plush as the versions of synthetic athletic field surfaces in use today, the rug at Busch Stadium in 1970 was little more than a thin, green disguise covering the concrete pad to which it had been adhered. It was like playing tackle football on an asphalt parking lot. A small price to pay, I would say, for the chance to play in that arena.

We did not exactly need a pep rally to generate excitement for this game, but of course we had one anyway. Following tradition, students assembled in the school auditorium during a mid-day break on Friday, November 6. Just a few hours later, we would be in uniform, prepared to play the game. As usual, Tim Rodgers produced the pep rally. Later in the season, before our state playoffs semifinals game, he gave a memorable performance dressed as an ant. Woe to the ant destined to be underfoot as the SLUH marauders ganged up on our opponents. This time, Rodgers introduced Errol Patterson, the only African American player on our team, with the line, "It's about time we added 'a little color' into the program." Patterson thought that was amusing, and he followed with a witty, inspirational address.

Decidedly less inspirational, as was his custom, were the words of Coach Martel in advance of the CBC game.

"Our 1966 team was stronger physically than this current team," he told Gary Mueller of the St. Louis Post-Dispatch. "But this year we're able to get the ball outside and the other people can't bunch up against us inside as they used to.

"This is a good ball club and I don't mean to take anything away from the kids, but I have to go back to my 1959 team. That team was overpowering. I'd just put them out on the field and tell them to go sic 'em and that was that."

That team would be the "Hungry Huns" of 1959, of course. The symbolic older brothers in whose shadows we seemed destined to march but never would match. Del Bannister bristled at that reference to the Huns, just as he would every time he encountered one the rest of his life. In this interview, there was more from our difficult-to-please coach.

"Actually our team a year ago (which finished No. 9 in the state with a 7-2 record) probably was a little stronger than our present team. Through six games, we're about 400 yards short of the 1969 team in rushing yardage and a couple hundreds yards short passing, but we just keep plugging along and somehow manage to squeeze out our touchdowns."

"Squeezing out" a touchdown or two would not be easy against CBC, which had yielded just three in its first eight games, and led the entire St. Louis area in defense scoring average with just 2.5 points per game. The Cadets' four defensive linemen averaged almost 215 pounds per man. At 213 pounds, Fred Daues was our only player who weighed more than 200, and he was diminished by an injured knee.

"Our major problem will be to try and combat their size—there's no doubt about that," Coach Martel told sportswriter Myron Holtzman of the *St. Louis Globe-Democrat*. To sportswriter Jerry Stack of the *St. Louis Post-Dispatch*, he said of CBC's size, "They're going to have a decided edge. Their line averages about 210 pounds a man. We go about 177 on offense and 183 on defense. Whether we're quicker or not is debatable."

By game time at 8 p.m., with the sky clear and the temperature in the low 50s, we were wrapped and ready. As we waited anxiously on the sideline, minutes before kickoff, my heart throbbed as I looked up at the 18,531 people in Busch Stadium, the biggest stage any of us could have dared to dream would feature us. Tim Kellett noticed Bob Thibaut standing off by himself, leaning on crutches, dressed not in his football uniform but in slacks, street shoes and his game jersey over a collared sport shirt. His knee severely injured the previous Friday at Althoff, Thibaut would not be playing tonight.

"How are you doing, Bob?" Tim Kellett asked.

"I'm okay," Thibaut said. "I want you to do something for me."

Thibaut reached into his pocket and took out a holy card. The card had Ed Hawk's picture on it, with the years of Ed's life, and a prayer. It was the card distributed at his funeral in August.

"For every game, I put this holy card in my helmet," said Thibaut. "Tim, I want you to put this in your helmet for tonight's game." Kellett obliged.

About that time, the family of Ed Hawk was introduced on the Busch Stadium field. In a gesture of genuine class, the CBC Student Council had placed an ad in the game program, which read:

C.B.C. Student Council
Dedicates this
Football Game
to the memory of
J. Edward Hawk
Former Vice Pres.
of the SLUH
Student Council.

It was the idea of Carey Prewitt, a two-way starting tackle for the Cadets who also was President of the CBC Student Council. Before the game, James and Mary Hawk and their surviving children sat for a ceremony to honor Ed's memory, flanked by the administration leaders of both schools. In full football uniform, Prewitt presented the Hawk family with a plaque commemorating Ed's young life.

Prewitt had dated Barb Domian, a grade school classmate of Ed Hawk at St. Clement of Rome, and had become friends with him. "I had almost as many friends at SLUH as at CBC," Prewitt recalled. In fact, he had seriously considered attending St. Louis U. High before opting for CBC. Carey's father Lynn Prewitt was in the insurance business, and had come to know Paul Martel when they both worked in Kansas City a decade earlier. Lynn and his wife Mary knew their son wanted to play football, and they encouraged him to become a Junior Billiken.

"Then I watched that game at Busch in 1966," Carey Prewitt said. CBC 33, SLUH 6. "I knew I didn't want to go there. I thought they must have had a bad coach."

Prewitt went to CBC to play for Coach Bill Gerdeman.

It was Gerdeman who wondered what Prewitt was thinking when he brought up the idea of saluting Ed Hawk. "Is your head in the game?" Prewitt recalled Gerdeman asking him. He challenged Prewitt similarly earlier in the season, when Prewitt was occupied with the CBC homecoming and dance. At least Prewitt was clever enough to avoid being caught breaking curfew.

43// Dream Game

HYPE YIELDED TO REALITY as CBC started the game by kicking off. The fluttering I had felt in my limbs, as game time approached, seemed to vanish with that first pop of pads, as we engaged our opponent in full contact. For the first 12-minute quarter, we knocked each other around without scoring, though we had the best chance, advancing to the CBC 10-yard line. Defensive back Tim Cantwell intercepted Dan Calacci's pass in the end zone to kill that drive.

Early in the second quarter, we would strike quickly. After Tim Leahy returned a CBC punt to the 34-yard line, Calacci dropped back on second down. He faked to Tom Schoeck, who leveled the left defensive end, giving Calacci the seconds he needed to find Mike Wiese on a sideline pattern. Wiese caught it at the 37, then powered through three tacklers to move the ball to the 50, near the same sideline his brother Bob had paced on crutches in frustration four years before. On the next play, Calacci again dropped back, again faked to Schoeck as Leahy sprinted from the backfield straight downfield. Calacci lofted a pass to an open Leahy, who grabbed the ball at the 30 and sprinted to the end zone just ahead of CBC defensive backs Tim Cantwell and Rich Coburn. After Gregg Hannibal's perfect snap and Calacci's perfect hold, Tim Gibbons kicked the extra point right through the uprights of the goal post to give us a 7-0 lead.

On our next possession, gaining confidence in our passing game, Calacci took a second-down snap at our 31-yard line, faded back to the 22, and launched a 20-yard pass to Errol Patterson between the left hash marks and the left sideline. Patterson had an opening, and stretched to reach for the slightly overthrown ball with his right arm, tipped it once … twice … then stretched to pull it in but instead was blasted by Bill Donegan, a charging Cadet defensive back, whose full-on hit snapped back the head of the vulnerable receiver. It was a "clean" hit, in football protocol, but Patterson left the game with a concussion.

"I never saw the guy coming," Patterson recalled. "His helmet hit right at my chin. I don't remember anything until Jean Pierre was asking me dumb questions in the locker room." One of our student trainers, Jean Pierre was attempting to see if there was a sign of intelligent life behind Patterson's glazed eyes.

Ironically, Patterson was in the offensive lineup on that play despite Paul Martel's game strategy, a quirky decision to limit his time on offense so he could concentrate on defense. This was surprising, because Patterson entered the game leading our receivers with nine receptions, 294 yards and six touchdowns. "Coach Martel told me I was not going to play offense in the game, because he wanted me to concentrate on defense, stopping their really fast wide receiver, Bob Sheahan. I remember saying,

'I'm not impressed,' or some cocky-assed thing. But he was really fast and quick. Fortunately, on the first play, the quarterback just missed him with a pass, because he had me beat. I got lucky, but learned, and from then on gave him more space." We would find out later, as usual, that Coach Martel's scouting was impeccable.

The next series was notable because Martel called on Gibbons, the sophomore who had not even started the season on the varsity, to attempt a 41-yard field goal. Calacci, the holder, had difficulty handling the center snap, and by the time he had the ball upright for the kick, the 6-foot, 8-inch, 240-pound Mike Holley of CBC had broken through the blocking line, smothered the kick, and then hit the kicker. Gibbons fell hard on the Astroturf-covered ground. Would that shake this young kicker's confidence?

Interestingly, CBC Coach Bill Gerdeman also had promoted a soccer-style kicker to the starting lineup. Andy Gasparovic, a junior who kicked with his left leg, was making his debut in this game. He replaced senior Tom Gallagher, the Cadets' quarterback and co-captain. Prewitt recalls being puzzled by that. "He never wanted a kicker who didn't also play a regular position. If he wanted a soccer kicker, we had Paul Gentile in our class."

Gentile was a star on the CBC soccer team, the younger brother of Carl Gentile, a CBC alumnus who had gone on to an All-America college career at St. Louis University and a career in the National Professional Soccer League. Gerdeman's decision to give the job to Gasparovic would be significant. In retrospect, the decision seems almost incomprehensible, given the amount of pressure focused on placekickers under the most benign of competitive conditions. This was the biggest, most significant game of the year for two archrivals aspiring to qualify for the state playoff tournament.

At halftime, we had reason to feel good. In the first two periods, we had driven for nine first downs and generated more than 200 yards of offense against a CBC defense that had ranked among the leaders in the St. Louis area. Calacci had completed seven passes for 115 yards. We had shut out the potent CBC offense, and held a 7-0 lead.

44// *A Sense of Community*

AMONG HOMECOMING CEREMONIES during halftime was the introduction of the SLUH representatives from the area's private Catholic all-girls schools, each of whom was escorted to a prominent position on the field by a SLUH senior. In most cases, the escort was the girl's SLUH boyfriend. For Katie Rhoades, the beautiful rep from Nerinx Hall who would go on to be voted Homecoming Queen, I was that lucky guy. However, I was with my football teammates and unavailable to escort her, and had to request a substitute. The logical and willing candidate was Whayne Herriford. Whayne, Katie and I liked to think of ourselves as the *Mod Squad*[20], patterned after the popular, counter-culture TV cop series that aired from 1968 to 1973. It starred Clarence Williams III, Gary Cole and Peggy Lipton as three cops with checkered pasts, who used the wisdom they gained as scofflaws to catch bad guys menacing their community. The series was promoted as: *One black. One white. One blonde.* And so, while I was sweaty and hyped up inside my football pads and uniform among my teammates, Whayne and Katie, arm in arm, marched in the halftime ceremony like celebrities: Katie, like a model with her flowing blond hair, natural good looks and ever-present smile, and Whayne resplendent in the black, full-length leather coat he had talked his mother into buying him for the occasion.

Katie relished her involvement with our class, as one of our adopted "Blue Buddies." "I felt like I belonged to something, the way all you guys were willing to accept me," she recalled. Whayne Herriford was one of her favorites. "He was always cheering other people up, teasing them. He had a lot of life in him." It did occur to her, at the last minute before heading off to the game, to inform her parents that she would be escorted in the Homecoming ceremony by an African-American. "They wouldn't have known he was black," she said. "In somebody else's world, it might have bothered them." She was relieved and appreciative that Lois and Roy accepted the information without any visible sign of concern.

Whayne recalls attracting what he perceived as scorn from some who witnessed his friendly one-on-one encounters with Katie and other girls in our social circles. The irony, which was known only to Whayne at the time, was that he had come to accept his homosexuality by the time he was a senior in high school. "I didn't have a name for it then," he recalled many years later. "But I knew I was different. I knew I wasn't interested in girls. I thought there was something wrong with me."

The subject of homosexuality was seldom confronted by the students or faculty at St. Louis U. High in the late 1960s. When it was, it was done clumsily, as I recall, by those ill-informed and uncharitable. "It was horrible, the way we talked about it," Herriford recalled.

Our elders had warned us against our common practice of hitch-hiking. They told us that homosexual predators trolled the roads and highways looking for young men to assault sexually. Homosexuality was closeted then, and considered a perversity by a significant majority. At the time, same-sex marriage was unlawful throughout the United States, and unacceptable in the eyes of the vast majority of Americans. In 1952, the American Psychiatric Association first published a document listing standard criteria for mental disorders. In its inaugural *Diagnostic and Statistical Manual of Mental Disorders (DSM-1)*[21], the APA listed homosexuality as a sociopathic personality disturbance. Reorientation therapy was commonly prescribed, as a "remedy" to "cure" homosexuality.

It is likely that few in the SLUH Class of 1971 were even aware of the

Stonewall Riots, which had occurred in the early summer of 1969 near the Stonewall Inn in New York City's Greenwich Village neighborhood. Weary from a regular pattern of what they regarded as police harassment, members of the gay community in New York reacted spontaneously to a police raid at the Stonewall Inn, and engaged in demonstrations that resulted in violent interaction with police. As accounts of the confrontation were reported by the mainstream news media, pressure and momentum built. Second and third nights of demonstrations ensued over the next six days, with hundreds involved. The riots served to galvanize the gay community in New York City and beyond, leading to an organized effort in pursuit of tolerance, rights, and legislation. A year later, to mark the anniversary of the Stonewall Riots, gay rights organizations organized the first Gay Pride marches, which were staged in New York, Los Angeles and Chicago.

Unlike his personal commitment to racial equality, which was well informed and remarkable for a young man in such a racial minority in our community, Whayne Herriford had not yet enlisted in the battle for gay rights. Like most of us 17-year-olds, he had few discernable skills in the area of emotional or sexual relationships. We were just trying to figure it out. "I knew what I was interested in," Whayne recalled, "but I didn't know how to find it." He invested his time, instead, on doing his part to bring a sense of community to the St. Louis U. High brotherhood. He did his part at Busch Stadium that November evening. He extended his arm as Katie Rhoades's escort during halftime, and he cheered hard for the Junior Billikens football team, which had a tenuous halftime lead over the CBC Cadets.

Two quarters to play. Could we hold on to win this dream game? We did have reason for concern, as we had just one touchdown to show for that hard-fought offensive yardage, and Errol Patterson, our star receiver and defensive back, had been knocked out of the game. Had our good fortune run its course? Fifteen seconds into the second half, we suffered the first serious special-teams lapse of the season.

45// *In Trouble*

BOB SHEAHAN FIELDED the second-half kickoff at the CBC nine-yard line, and sprinted toward the right sideline behind a wall of teammates, untouched, 91 yards for a touchdown. Paul Martel certainly was right about Sheahan's speed. Andy Gasparovic's extra point kick tied the game at 7-7.

Three plays after the ensuing kickoff, we suffered another severe setback.

On third down from our 35-yard line, Calacci took the snap from me and sprinted back to the 25, then shot a 13-yard strike to Mike Wiese. Wiese caught the ball and headed upfield, where he was cracked by CBC defender Tim Cantwell and flipped upside down, short of a first down. Wiese somehow held on to the ball, but twisted his left ankle on the play. While he courageously continued his duties as our defensive right end, Mike was finished catching passes for the night, and we were now without our top two receivers.

Jim Dohr of SLUH was on the field for Sheahan's kickoff return. "I was thanking God it wasn't on my side," he said. An offensive end and a junior, Dohr saw action that season primarily on special teams, and in "mop op" duty when we were clobbering the other team and our lead was secure. "I was a bystander for the first half of the season. In the CBC game, I expected to be a bystander, and have a great seat."

When Wiese injured his ankle, Martel called Dohr's name.

"Uh oh," he said to himself. "I was nervous as could be."

Trying to generate an offensive spark, Martel called the "Flipper Dipper Play"—a pass from quarterback Dan Calacci laterally to halfback Bill Ziegler, who would catch the ball and then quickly launch a long pass downfield to the right end cutting across toward the left. The left end, Dohr was to stay at the line and provide blocking protection for Ziegler as he set up to pass.

"My heart was pounding through my chest," Dohr said. "I took a step and lost my balance. I totally lost my head, and Bill Ziegler got killed. I didn't block my guy, and Bill just got annihilated. He was really vulnerable because he was passing the ball. That was a new experience for me, not to mention it was in front of 18,000 people."

Then CBC's offense began to move, and advanced deep into our territory with its best drive of the game. At one point, the injured Fred Daues took off from our sideline toward our defensive huddle, dramatically limping the entire way. Tim Kellett, who was in at left tackle as Daues's replacement, knew how hurt he was, and confronted him: "What are you doing?! There is no way Martel sent you in!" Fred told him, "No, no, I think I can help." Kellett and others told him to get off the field, and so he hopped all the way back. "It was more than noble," Kellett said. "You could sense the frustration, that it appeared it was inevitable that they were driving in for the winning touchdown, and Fred was determined to do whatever he could to stop them."

Perhaps inspired by Daues's valiance, we did manage to stop the Cadets at our 12-yard line, short of a first down. CBC Coach Bill Gerdeman sent in Gasparovic to attempt a field goal, but he missed it, and we regained possession on our 20. From there, we recovered our own fumble, then had a penalty, then Calacci and I fumbled the snap exchange for the first time all year, and we lost possession. Devastated by that error, I wondered if it would cost us the game. CBC's offense took the field, just less than 20 yards from our end zone. Two running plays later, the Cadets were on our 13-yard line and the third quarter ended, moving the play to the other end of the Busch Stadium turf.

To open the fourth quarter, Bob Jones took a handoff from quarterback Tom Gallagher and charged through the huge hole the Cadets had opened in the center of our defensive line, and powered 11 yards to just inside our 2. Time for another rigid goal-line stand. On the first play, we held firm and stopped the ball carrier. On second and goal, though, Mike Rallo crashed through on the left side and into the end zone for a touchdown to give CBC a 13-7 lead.

"We are in really deep trouble," Tim Kellett thought to himself. "We knew going in that their defense was very, very good. And we hadn't really done that much against them. I started to think we weren't going to pull this one out. They ran it down our throat on that drive, and they hadn't done that before. I was concerned, and thought 'Are we getting tired?'"

Gasparovic trotted onto the field for the extra point kick. What happened next, on what is probably the most dependable and routine play in football, remains hard to believe many years later, particularly for the impact it had on the lives of the boys on that Busch Stadium turf.

On the extra point kick, with Tim Kellett brushing off his block and putting on pressure with a diving attempt to block the kick, Gasparovic pushed the kick wide of the goal post. No good! The score remained 13-7. It is significant to point out that the uprights of the Busch Stadium goal posts were 18.6 feet apart, since that National Football League standard was used by the stadium's primary tenant, the professional St. Louis Cardinals. At that time, the goal post uprights for college and high school fields were set at 23.4 feet apart, more forgiving than the pro standard. But no one from either school was seriously tempted to incur the expense of replacing the goal posts for just this one game. It also is important to point out the cruelty of this fate for a 16-year-old kicker, who gamely had accepted the challenge his coach bestowed on him to play for the varsity.

Would he have to bear that burden, or would his teammates hold on to their lead and make that kick a forgotten footnote? Would this be the opening we needed?

After we failed to make a first down in three tries, CBC partially blocked our punt and took over on its 44-yard line. From there, the Cadets marched steadily, churning up yards and seconds off the game clock. We were in serious trouble. We rallied to stop CBC from making a first down, forcing the Cadets to attempt a 37-yard field goal on fourth down. If successful, the kick would move the score to 16-7, and the way CBC had adjusted in the second half to slow down our offense, with less than five minutes to play, it would have been desperate. If they missed, we would have a chance.

Gasparovic got off a clean kick, and it was on line. But that distance was just beyond his range, and the ball bounced at the base of the goal post. We had our reprieve, and would get a chance from our own 20-yard line, with four and a half minutes to play. Could we cover those 80 yards for a game-tying touchdown and the chance to pull ahead with an extra point? With our two starting wide receivers injured and unavailable to catch passes? Bill Donegan, the talented CBC defensive back whose clean, hard hit had knocked Errol Patterson out of the game, liked his team's chances.

"After knocking out Patterson," Donegan said, "I thought I got it made in the shade."

46// *Driven Hard into History*

CALACCI STARTED THE SERIES with a fullback slant pass to the left toward Tom Schoeck coming out of the backfield. Split 10 yards to the left at the line of scrimmage, Jim Dohr sprinted downfield to try to draw defenders away from the primary receiver. "When in doubt, clear out," Dohr thought at the time. CBC's defenders read the play correctly, however, and zeroed in on Schoeck, who stretched but could not reach

Calacci's pass, and the ball fell to the ground, incomplete. Second down, 10 yards to go for a first down. Time for some history to be made.

"On the first pass, I went downfield on a post pattern and was 10 yards behind the defensive back," Dohr said. As he returned to the huddle for the second-down play, he caught the eye of Ebbie Dunn, our assistant coach standing near Paul Martel in the SLUH sideline area. "I put my hands out, trying to indicate a long pass was open. To my surprise, Ebbie rushed to Paul, grabbed him, and apparently told him, 'Dohr was wide open.'"

Into the huddle rushed the "messenger" with the play call. "Fullback slide out, and look for Dohr long." It was the same play.

Schoeck and Tim Leahy lined up in I formation behind Calacci in the backfield. Ziegler positioned himself to the left of and a yard back from Tim Kellett, the left tackle whose job it was to keep CBC's big, menacing defensive end Mike Holley from spoiling our play. Dohr stood erect and almost casually, hand on his hip awaiting the center snap, as our split receiver wide on the left. Dohr was to run a simple post route. He would sprint 10 to 12 yards straight downfield, hesitate briefly to decoy the defender, then abruptly again turn back downfield. Calacci took the center snap, faked a handoff to Leahy and dropped back eight yards, a bit deeper than normal. Under heavy pressure from CBC defensive tackle Carey Prewitt and both defensive ends—Holley from the left and Tom Sheehan from the right, Calacci launched a desperate throw down the center of the field, then collapsed in a pile of his own blockers and the CBC defenders.

"We were both on the ground," recalled Prewitt. "I thought, 'OK, nothing happened on that one.'"

I was among those on the ground, unable to see what was developing at the other end of the pass.

"Then I heard the crowd cheering," Prewitt said.

Downfield under the arcing pass, CBC defensive back Bill Donegan was just inches from Dohr at our 48-yard line, but Dohr was inches taller than his adversary.

"I gave him some leeway to tease him, so I could get the interception" Donegan recalled. "I thought I was in pretty good position."

"I couldn't believe it was coming to me," Dohr said.

Turning to look over his right shoulder, he glided under Calacci's perfect ball, which floated just over Donegan's outstretched left hand and into Dohr's clutch at the 50.

"I thought I had it intercepted," Donegan said. "But I gave him one too many extra steps, and got burned. It was a perfect pass."

Technically, the ball clunked Dohr on the facemask.

"I didn't catch it cleanly," he said. "I pinned it against my helmet."

Calmly, he rescued the ball securely in his hands.

"You hear pro players saying the action seems to slow down for them, and it was like that for me," Dohr said. "It seemed like it was in slow motion. Up until the time I caught the ball, I didn't hear anything. It was so slow. Then I heard the crowd, and that jolted me back to reality. There was no one ahead of me."

He never broke stride, which allowed him to separate two yards from Donegan, then loped toward the end zone between the hash marks and the left sideline to finish off the improbable 80-yard play. "I really did think I was going to pop a hamstring," Dohr said. "I had never run so fast or so hard."

Touchdown! Game tied, 13-13.

Gibbons jogged on to the field, and lined up for the biggest kick of his life. Normally cool and unaffected by the pressure, an occupational requirement for placekickers, Gibbons acknowledged this was different. "I was freaking out," Gibbons recalled years later. "This was THE game. And that (touchdown pass) was THE play of the season." After a sure snap from Gregg Hannibal and a steady hold by Calacci, Gibbons stepped through and booted the football through those narrow uprights to give us a 14-

13 lead with just a few seconds more than four minutes left in the game.

Thanks in large part to Tim Leahy, CBC would not get past midfield again. First, Leahy forced a fumble after a completed CBC pass at the 48, a fumble Schoeck recovered. On the next series, he intercepted Tom Gallagher's final pass and returned it to the CBC 32-yard line. CBC would not get the ball back as we safely ran out the clock. We were able to savor that most delicious feeling of being on the field of a hard-fought football game, secure with the victory that would be driven hard and unchangeably into history. I was euphoric.

For the second week in a row, we escaped with victory in a most improbable way, and we secured the championship of the Bi-State Conference with a 5-0 record. We were 8-1 overall, with one regular-season game to play. On the losing side that night, Bill Donegan of CBC reflected on the difference a single point was to make in our lives.

"Maybe it was meant to be," he said, many years later. "Maybe Eddie Hawk was looking after you guys that night."

The victory had an uncharacteristic and novel effect on our coach, the stoic Paul Martel. After embracing just about every one of us, he yielded his stern personal defense to an unabashed release of joy.

"Ever seen a grown man cry?" he said to sportswriter Jerry Stack of the *St. Louis Post-Dispatch* after the game. "I don't know. I guess you can express happiness in many ways. But I can't recall crying after a game before."

The next morning, the banner headline of the *St. Louis Globe-Democrat* sports section hollered out,

JUNIOR BILLS' LATE TD NUDGES CBC
18,531 See Pass by Calacci Decide 14-13 Struggle

Unfortunately for Gibbons, that newspaper was an unwitting participant in what was developing into a comical series of indignities for him throughout the season. In his account of the game under that massive front-page *St. Louis Globe-Democrat* headline, sportswriter Myron Holtzman opened with a description of the winning 80-yard touchdown pass from Dan Calacci to Jim Dohr, then added:

Dave Ortmann booted the go-ahead point.

Writing under the pressure of an unyielding deadline, Holtzman noted Number 23 on the placekicker's jersey, looked in the game program he was provided, and saw that number belonged to junior halfback Dave Ortmann. Ortmann was a fine football player and a wonderful young man, but seldom that season was he called off the bench for action. Since Gibbons was not a full-time member of the varsity, he did not have his own jersey. For the CBC game, he wore a second No. 23 jersey. The trouble was, his name and number had not made it into the game program.

With the luxury of the time afforded the afternoon newspaper, which had several more hours before its deadline, *St. Louis Post-Dispatch* sportswriter Jerry Stack was able to spot that mistake. And he used it as his lead.

Tim Gibbons, alias Dave Ortmann, alias No. 23, is the forgotten man on the St. Louis U. High football roster. No. Make that the unknown man.

Stack went on to explain the program snafu, and that it was indeed Tim Gibbons whose two extra points were vital to our victory. The newspaper's headline writer took advantage of Stack's story angle and this is what appeared over the account of the game:

What's-His-Name
Is Jr. Bills' Hero

Perhaps "anonymity" was a fitting theme for our team at that point, as so many different players had been contributing to our success. The victory over CBC was our eighth in nine games. One more to go, the next Friday night against Suburban North Conference powerhouse Riverview Gardens, which before an upset loss to Ritenour had been ranked No. 1 in the St. Louis metropolitan area.

47// *"Whatever You Do, Don't Run the Ball"*

IT IS ALMOST UNFATHOMABLE what happened less than a week later, more than 8,000 miles away in what was then East Pakistan and now is Bangladesh. A devastating tropical cyclone with winds of 115 miles per hour spun north from the Bay of Bengal toward Bhola Island and adjacent land, creating a storm surge that flooded the Ganges Delta. Up to 500,000 people perished, according to some estimates, ranking the cyclone as one of the deadliest natural disasters in history. I have to confess, the news of that tragedy barely registered in my consciousness at the time. Perhaps that's because in November of 1970, we did not have instantaneous satellite coverage and hundreds of news media concerns pumping out information 24 hours per day, as we have now. Blithely, I looked forward to Friday night.

Riverview Gardens High School is located just a little more than 10 miles north of St. Louis U. High, straight up Kingshighway Boulevard through the rough city neighborhoods of North St. Louis, into St. Louis County and a couple miles west of the Mississippi River. To a kid from South St. Louis, it might as well have been a thousand miles away.

I knew the Riverview Gardens football team was loaded with big, strong players who played in the mighty Suburban North Conference. One of its conference rivals, McCluer had won the first two Missouri

Class 4A state football championships. We had already lost to McCluer, and this season Riverview was regarded as better. I knew these public school kids would love to bash the privileged boys from St. Louis U. High.

We had allowed ourselves to think we might be candidates to qualify for the state playoffs at that point, but the qualifying point system was complicated and loaded with too many variables to know for certain. We *did* know that if we lost another game, we would have no chance to qualify. The way we saw it, this was the last game of the season, and for most of us the last organized football game we would ever play. I thought about that as I pulled on my pads, tight pants, and white jersey in the SLUH locker room.

As our bus driver maneuvered his way to the game, we began our ritual recitation of a rosary decade. As had become our custom, Bob Thibaut and I looked to Bill Ziegler, our fellow tri-captain, to lead the rosary prayers and cite the appropriate mysteries. I cannot recall which set of mysteries we prayed that evening, but I'm pretty sure my silent participation was focused and sincere. Many years later, I realized it is silly to pray for *victory*, for a football game outcome is a zero sum. If one team gets its victory prayer answered, it is necessary for other team's to be denied. What were the chances we would ever play a team of avowed atheists? Many years later, I understood we should not have put God in such a tough spot, and instead should have limited my prayer to asking that we not get physically maimed or humiliated.

As we drove into the parking area near the Riverview Gardens field, I experienced for the last time the psychedelic effect of haloing around the stadium's glowing tower lights, the result of abandoning my eyeglasses and yielding to my nearsightedness. Groovy. What I did not learn until much later was that those lights had stood above the original Sportsman's Park, later named Busch Stadium, on Grand Avenue and Dodier Street in north St. Louis. Knowing the new Busch Memorial Stadium would have brand new lights when it opened in 1966, Riverview Gardens Coach Gerry Nordman procured the used lights from Anheuser-Busch, Inc., which owned the old stadium and the Cardinals baseball team at the time. Nordman assigned his players from the classes of 1967 and '68 the job of digging cable trenches and post holes, and they installed the lights themselves.

There was the usual adrenaline rush as we ran onto the plush grass field, and the invigorating gasp of deep breathing the mid-40s November air.

A week from heroically launching two long touchdown passes in our victory over CBC, quarterback Dan Calacci was ready. And we welcomed the news that starting receivers Errol Patterson and Mike Wiese had healed sufficiently, and were ready to catch his passes. "I was ready to come back," Patterson said. "(Jim) Dohr got my pass." Freakishly quick and elusive, Calacci was probably the smartest guy on the team. He was gifted academically and athletically, though he was only 5 feet, 10 inches tall and weighed a mere 156 pounds. What we loved about him, were two much more endearing traits: (1) he was practically impervious to pressure, and (2) he was a maverick. Those who coach football, a fraternity that included Dan's father Dominic Calacci, who was the freshman team coach and an admired history teacher at SLUH, really value the first of those traits. The second, they generally abhor. Football is a game founded on formations, precision, process, and the execution of 11 teammates moving as one unit. Freelancing is generally regarded with disdain.

Coach Paul Martel was a man of much precision and planning. Knowing how valuable his quarterback was and not wanting to see him injured, and knowing he had a blue-chip college prospect in Bill Ziegler at the running back position, Coach Martel had a simple instruction for Dan Calacci before the Riverview Gardens game: "Whatever you do, don't run the ball," Martel had said. "Pitch it to Ziegler."

Early in the game, Coach Martel sent in a play with Fred Daues, who was alternating at offensive tackle with Tim Kellett and serving as a messenger from the sidelines. Dutifully, Daues relayed the play call to Calacci.

"That's not going to work," Calacci said, calmly. "We're not going to run that."

Replaced on the next play by Kellett, Daues returned to the sideline and was confronted by Martel.

"Fred, I told you to tell him to run that play," he said. "Why didn't you?"

"I don't know," said Daues, nobly, covering for his quarterback.

By this time in the season, we were running a lot of option plays, on which the quarterback carries the ball parallel to but just behind the line of scrimmage. In one or two seconds, he assesses how the defense is reacting, and considers his options: (1) pitch the ball to the first runner trailing him, (2) pitch it to the second, or (3) keep the ball himself and try to gain yards upfield.

In the first quarter against the Riverview Gardens Rams, we began our third possession of a scoreless game after a Riverview punt settled in its own territory, on its 47-yard line. We had given up our first possession by fumbling, but Patterson then rescued us by intercepting a pass from Rams' quarterback Steve Knight in our end of the field. We had to abort our second possession with a punt after failing to gain a first down. The third time we got the ball, Dan Calacci's mischievous mind went into overdrive, just a few yards on the opponent's side of midfield.

This time, Calacci crouched above me, surveying the Riverview Gardens defense. "Option left" was the running play called, and certainly, just a few minutes into the game, Coach Martel's amply clear instruction was still available in Calacci's gifted noggin. Behind him were running backs Tom Schoeck on the left and Tim Leahy on the right. Flanked to his left was Ziegler. Dan took my center snap, faked a handoff to Schoeck driving up the middle, and headed left, about two yards behind the scrimmage line. While Ziegler rushed forward to block, Leahy trailed and was prepared for the pitch as Calacci was confronted by two linemen, each outweighing him by 40 pounds. One had a clear shot at him, but wound up grabbing mostly air as Calacci eluded his grasp, spun 360 degrees around, darted between the two defenders, then avoided a third who dived at him. He sidestepped his way to the left sideline, which he followed with a sprint to the end zone for a touchdown. Tim Gibbons made the extra-point kick and we were ahead 7-0. Coach Martel remained calm.

Early in the second quarter, the Rams countered with a bruising six-play, 45-yard drive for a touchdown and tying extra point. Tied 7-7, we spent the last seven and a half minutes of the first half and most of the third quarter pounding each other, with neither side much threatening to score.

48// *Give It To Ziegler*

LATE IN THE THIRD QUARTER, we started a possession on our 20-yard line after a Riverview punt had sailed into our end zone for a touchback. Here was the two-pronged coaching strategy Paul Martel concocted at that point: (1) find an all-state running back, big and strong and fast and sure-handed; (2) give him the ball. In 13 plays bridging the end of the third quarter and start of the fourth, 10 of them running plays between our left and right guards by Bill Ziegler, we moved all the way down the field, capped by Ziegler's two-yard burst for a go-ahead touchdown and a 13-7 lead.

"Yeah, I was tired," Ziegler recalled of that memorable drive. "And surprised. Who gives the ball to a guy that many times? I was as surprised as anybody."

Improbably, Tim Gibbons missed the extra point, and we could not avoid thinking we might pay as dearly for that as CBC had the previous week.

More improbably, we got a reprieve on the ensuing kickoff. Reaching for extra power, perhaps fueled by the emotion of having missed the PAT, Gibbons boomed the kickoff well into the Riverview Gardens end zone, more than 60 yards in the air. It hit the ground as the surprised Rams kick returner backed up and tried to retrieve it. Once, then twice he was unable to pick it off the ground. The third time he got it into his hands, but that was just about the time a streaking Jack Licata arrived from the right kickoff coverage lane. Licata, a junior end who seldom played except on special teams, launched himself full force into the defenseless receiver, tackling him cleanly in the end zone for a two-point safety. Our lead was now 15-7, and we were able to protect that advantage through the remainder of the game.

From our loyal and loud student cheering section, we heard the sweet melody and lyrics from the one-hit wonder Steam song, which our supporters had taken to chanting at the end of our games, when victory was secure: *Na-na-na-na, Na-na-na-na, hey hey hey … good-bye!*[22] It was perhaps ungraceful and a bit unsportsmanlike, but the anthem seemed a fitting embrace for the euphoric taste of victory we had earned. Good-bye Riverview Gardens. Or so we thought.

Fr. David Wayne SJ, special advisor to senior class, 1970-71.

Fr. Ed O'Brien, whom everyone called "Obie," dispensed spiritual comfort to students facing their dark moments.

Fr. Richard Bailey SJ, made swift decision on hair length policy.

Jesuit Jack Warner directing rehearsal for The Fantasticks.

Tim Rodgers, left, and Rick Spurr entertain at pep rally.

Officers Joe Castellano, Phil Schaefer, Whayne Herriford at Student Council meeting.

Excerpt from Pat "Del" Bannister's 5th-grade autobiography.

Whayne Herriford escorts Katie Rhoades in Homecoming ceremony at halftime of CBC game at Busch Stadium.

At Fall Frolics, Whayne Herriford and Pat "Del" Bannister in hippie gear.

The Class of '71

"By merely living our high-school lives with Ed, we have been able to take advantage of the benefits Ed's life has given us. Now that his life has come to an end, it is our duty and privilege to keep the character of Ed Hawk alive by continuing what he himself would be doing right now."

PREP NEWS
September, 1970

J. Edward Hawk, III
Vice-President

Coaches Paul Martel and Ebbie Dunn.

This preseason photo ran in the St. Louis Post-Dispatch with the caption, "Who Gets the Ball?"

Gary Kornfeld, left, became Paul Martel's assistant coach in 1979, succeeded him as head coach in 1988, and retired after the 2016 season. Each coached SLUH 29 years, each is in the Missouri State High School Football Hall of Fame.

Coach Ebbie Dunn at the CBC game at Busch Stadium.

First page of Paul Martel's thick playbook, which the author calls the Manifesto.

Mike Wiese, trying to elude a CBC tackler, played the season with a heavy heart after the death of his brother in Vietnam.

Quarterback Dan Calacci eludes tacklers in state semifinal game against Riverview Gardens.

More than 18,000 watched the SLUH-CBC game at Busch Stadium.

Errol Patterson breaks away for a long gain.

SLUH defense stops CBC at the goal line..

Tom Schoeck gains ground against CBC.

Quarterback Dan Calacci holds, Tim Gibbons kicks.

Bill Ziegler carried the ball 10 times on the winning touchdown drive against Riverview Gardens to end the regular season.

The venerated Fr. Phil Kellett, moderator of athletics, at the 1966 SLUH-CBC game, which drew more than 30,000 spectators to Busch Memorial Stadium.

Billiken mascot at the game in Busch Stadium.

University of Missouri Coach Dan Devine presents the state championship trophy to the captains after the game at Faurot Field in Columbia.

SUMMARY		
SLUH		OPP.
21	Cleveland	0
6	McCluer	14
29	Assumption	0
26	Columbia Hickman	13
30	Cahokia	0
27	DeSmet	7
50	Augustinian	0
6	Althoff	0
14	CBC	13
16	Riverview	7
10	* Riverview	7
28	** KC Center	19

*Class AAAA Semifinals
**Class AAAA Finals

At post-season banquet, Coach Ebbie Dunn gets a laugh with the line: "Coach Martel's reputation grew, since we won it with you guys."

Saturday, November 28, 1970, 1:30 p.m.

M. S. H. S. A. A.
CLASS AAAA
FOOTBALL CHAMPIONSHIP

ST. LOUIS UNIVERSITY HIGH
vs.
KANSAS CITY CENTER

Memorial Stadium
Columbia, Missouri

The author's helmet.

ST. LOUIS U. HIGH
1970 Class 4A - Missouri State Champions

76 BILL DRURY	10 TONY BEHR	68 JOE HIRSCH	83 KEVIN KIPLINGER	87 DANA PROSPERI
75 MARK HOGREBE	42 MIKE AMAD	61 KEVIN O'TOOLE	72 JIM TWOMBLY	88 JACK LICATA
64 BILL CAPUTO	22 BOB THIBAUT (Capt.)	66 JIM DACEY	24 TOM SCHOECK	74 STEVE CRANE
50 JOE CASTELLANO (Capt.)	65 STEVE OHMER	32 JOHN KURUSZ	80 JIM DOHR	81 MIKE WIESE
63 TOM MILFORD	43 TOM WAMSER	23 TIM GIBBONS	12 GREGG HANNIBAL	11 STEVE HINDERBERGER
70 MIKE CHERRE	21 MARK CLARK	44 TONY ZMAILA	30 TIM LEAHY	86 TOM MEHAN
41 MIKE KOENEN	85 TOM UNDERHILL	20 DON BEHAN	33 BILL ZIEGLER (Capt.)	14 DOUG McDONALD
53 MARK HERBERS	23 DAVE ORTMAN	45 ED CADIEUX	71 AL FAHRENHORST	23 FRED DAUES
31 MIKE RUGGERI	13 DAN CALACCI	60 JERRY ROMBACH	52 VIC JOST	77 TIM KELLETT
78 TIM FLEMING	67 TOM MOORE	62 RICH FEDERER	82 ERROL PATTERSON	51 PAT BANNISTER
84 TOM O'SHAUGHNESSY				

COACH PAUL MARTEL   COACH EBBY DUNN   FATHER PHILIP KELLETT   DOCTOR CHARLES R. DOYLE

PART III

TO STATE AND BEYOND

49// *We're Not Finished Yet*

November 1970

WE WERE RELIEVED AND HAPPY to have escaped Riverview Gardens with that victory and a 9-1 regular-season record. In the parking lot after the game, disappointed supporters of the home team were ready to rumble. That is how Phil Schaefer remembers it. "There were fights breaking out in the parking lot," Schaefer said. "Their fans were mad they lost. We knew we'd better get out of there. We weren't fighters."

With the victory, we had leapfrogged Vianney and Ladue in District 3 to qualify for the four-team playoff to determine the state championship among Missouri Class 4A schools, those with the largest enrollments. That was the good news. The bad news? Our semifinals game would be against *Riverview Gardens*, the formidable opponent we just defeated, and felt fortunate to have done so. How in the world would we do that again, just eight days later?

The game would be played in the daylight at Francis Field, the site of competition in the 1904 Summer Olympics, on the campus of Washington University in St. Louis. It was a beautiful day in St. Louis, temperature around 50 degrees. With three narrow victories in a row, could we do it again? Could we continue this fantasy season?

Our indefatigable classmates certainly thought we could do it, or at least that is what Tim Rodgers wanted to convey in the sketch he wrote, produced, directed and starred in during the Pep Rally in our school auditorium on the Friday before the game.

Dressed as an ant, woozy, battered and crushed to near death by the storming St. Louis U. High Junior Billikens on the Riverview Gardens field the week before in our victory over the Rams, Rodgers read a poem. In the voice of Johnny Carson's Carnac, of course. The words of that composition long have been lost to history, but they were inspiring nonetheless. The Pep Rally ran long, as usual, so we were gleefully late for our first classes of the afternoon. Father Wayne jugged Rodgers, of course. Once again, Rodgers had taken one for the team.

The next day, on the historic field at Washington University, the Riverview Gardens players made it clear they believed their loss to us the previous week was merely unfinished business. On their second possession of the game, the Rams scored first with a burst that shook our confidence. Would we be exposed now as imposters, out of our competency level? It seemed that way with three straight plays taking less than a minute. On third down from the Rams' 36-yard line, quarterback Steve Knight dropped back five yards and zipped a pass 20 yards over the middle to end Mark Christian, who caught the ball and completed a 38-yard gain to near our 30-yard line. Then he completed another to end Dave Fowler for 18 more yards, and we were reeling. From the 12-yard line, Knight handed the ball to Devin Arnold, who scooted straight up the middle and into the end zone without anyone touching him. With the extra point, the Rams had a 7-0 lead. Is this where our dreams of a state championship would be crushed, like the defenseless ants of Tim Rodgers's imagination?

We had two promising chances in the fading minutes of the second quarter, but lost them both when Riverview defenders knocked the ball from Dan Calacci's hands and recovered his fumbles. The first time, Calacci was determined to finish a 75-yard march down the field, and he kept the ball on a run up the middle from their six-yard line toward the goal line. He lost the ball just two yards short of a touchdown.

Two plays later, Riverview fumbled and we were given another chance, this time 10 yards from the goal line. However, the Rams sniffed out an option run, hit Calacci before he could find a running back for the pitch, and he fumbled again. The half would end with Riverview Gardens leading, 7-0. And with Dan Calacci uncharacteristically shaken.

50// *It's Up To Us*

IT WAS A SOMBER HALFTIME, for it was the first time all season we were losing at the game's midpoint. I knew one thing. If Dan Calacci's confidence was not restored, we were finished. "Come on, Dan," I told him. "Don't worry about that first half. We need you now. It's up to us." I doubt Calacci needed those words from me or anyone, but I needed them. When faced with the inevitability of an outcome, one way or another with no delay or escape, human beings can retreat, they can face the challenge timidly, or they can face it boldly. In the moment of truth, the opportunity for preparation and planning is over. Either you are trained well or you are not. Either you are good enough or you are not. Either you are lucky enough or you are not. Might as well go in boldly, I thought. So did Dan Calacci.

After Errol Patterson made a touchdown-saving tackle to end a 35-yard breakaway run by Riverview's Bill Eshenroder on the Rams' first series of the second half, our defense tightened and forced a punt. "They had momentum and were moving down the field," Patterson recalled.

"There was a sense of urgency." We got the ball on our 20-yard line, and began with a new focus.

After three Bill Ziegler runs moved the ball to the 40-yard line, Riverview Gardens was penalized for interference on an incomplete pass, and we reached the 50. From there, Calacci passed to Patterson for a 16-yard gain. Tom Schoeck crunched up the middle for a four-yard run that required four defenders to stop him. Two plays later, Schoeck caught a 12-yard pass, advancing the ball to the Rams' 22. After a short run by Ziegler and a scramble to the left sideline by Calacci, we set up at the 12-yard line.

Time for our standard pass play, the 45-4. Tom Schoeck and Bill Ziegler lined up as running backs behind Calacci. Errol Patterson was in tight at the left end; Jim Dohr was just off the line of scrimmage on the right end. Upon receiving the snap, Calacci turns to the left as the two running backs head into the line of scrimmage. To the defense, it looks like a run. Unless they noticed Tim Kellett, our left tackle, and Bill Caputo, our left guard, sprinting to the right, abandoning their running block areas … or they noticed Steve Ohmer, our right guard, spinning off the line of scrimmage, first to his left, then to his right to set up pass blocking. Calacci faked the handoff to our running backs, and spun around to an eight-yard drop to the right. Planting on the 24-yard line, well protected by the pocket his blockers created, he spotted Patterson, who had sprinted from left end on a crossing pattern to the right side. Calacci lofted a pass that landed softly over Patterson's right shoulder and into his outstretched hands at the two-yard line, from where he glided safely into the end zone, two steps ahead of two Riverview defenders.

Patterson was so excited by scoring the touchdown, he "spiked" the football, the act of shooting the ball hard and directly into the ground, an act which many at the time regarded as unacceptably unsportsman-like. "It wasn't too celebratory," said Patterson, "but it was against the rules, and I thought I was going to get a penalty." Relieved that he did not, he trotted to our sideline, where teammate Doug McDonald greeted him sternly. "You can't DO that!" McDonald admonished. Relieved that McDonald finished yelling at him, Patterson did not think much more about it until the next day, when he watched a replay of the touchdown and spike on the local television sports news. "That was great," Patterson recalled several years later. "I think it's proper to get excited. It's a game."

With Tim Gibbons's extra point kick, we had tied the game at 7-7. It was a methodical 80-yard touchdown drive, concluded with a perfectly executed 12-yard pass play. And we had regained our spirit and sense of confidence.

51// *Bring on the Sophomore*

WHAT HAPPENED NEXT was difficult to believe, and remains so, upon reflection decades later. The last time a placekicker in the National Football League used the tip of his toes to kick off or kick for points was in 1986, the year Mark Moseley retired after his career with the Washington Redskins and Cleveland Browns. All kickers now use the "soccer style," which was introduced by Pete Gogolak at Cornell University in 1961, when he used the instep of his foot to launch the ball, in the way a soccer player kicks a long ball. Gogolak went on to a successful NFL career with the Buffalo Bills and New York Giants. In the autumn of 1970, however, the soccer style was rare.

It was not surprising the innovation took off in St. Louis, which had long been considered fertile geography for soccer, especially in the Italian, Irish and German neighborhoods. Five St. Louisans were on the U.S. National Team that upset England, 1-0, in the 1950 World Cup soccer tournament. The St. Louis University soccer team won 10 NCAA championships between 1959 and 1973. Pat Leahy played on three of those title teams before going on to become the all-time leading scorer for the NFL's New York Jets as their placekicker from 1974 to 1991. St. Louis kids, especially those in the Catholic schools, played soccer, not football, in the autumns of their youth. Tim Gibbons was one of those soccer-playing kids, who followed Pat Leahy by four years at the same St. Ann's Catholic School in Normandy. "I had played against him," Gibbons said. "He was one of my heroes." So it was natural for him to try the instep approach to kicking a football, long before he made the SLUH freshman team as a quarterback. "I didn't do a toe kick after the second grade."

The first time I encountered Gibbons, I was heading to practice on the SLUH "lower field" in August of 1970, prior to my senior season. As I approached the concrete steps that descended the steep hill to the practice area, I noticed a football sailing over the fence at the top of the hill that separated the field from the main campus. A team manager retrieved the ball and tossed it back over the fence and down the hill to one of the kickers. Before I reached the apex of the hill, the ball once again sailed over the fence. Once again, the manager tossed it back. I could tell that ball was unusual, old and funky with scuffed leather and a broken lace. Heading down the steps, I saw that kicker among two or three others, who were taking turns booting field goal attempts through a makeshift metal goal post erected on the field's sideline. Since the other kickers were using newer balls, and since none of their kicks were landing anywhere near the top of the hill, I concluded that the old funky ball must have been easier to kick. I was wrong.

"I was blessed with something," said Tim Gibbons, the young man with the old ball. The others made him use that ball, because he was a lowly sophomore among seniors and juniors, clearly an inferior caste in our informal social protocol. "I could kick. My goal was to go over the fence. I don't know why."

Coaches Paul Martel and Ebbie Dunn, the latter who also coached the SLUH varsity soccer team during the winter sports season, had recognized Gibbons's kicking talent. Because he also was a gifted quarterback, the school's quarterback of the future, Martel and "B" team coach Joe Vitale concocted the game-sharing plan whereby Gibbons would pilot the sophomore team offense on Friday afternoons, then kick for points for the varsity later in the weekend. Devised to ensure Gibbons did not exceed the limit of 40 quarters per season set by the Missouri State High School Activities Association, the plan worked very well. Until the final weekend of the regular season.

On the afternoon of Friday, the 13th of November, Joe Vitale's "B" team was engaged in what for that team was a close encounter, a battle with Riverview Gardens. Having won its first eight games by an average of more than three touchdowns, the Junior Billiken sophomores were struggling a bit to put the Rams out of reach. The plan for Gibbons was to have him sit out the second half, to avoid injury risk and to store up a safety stock of extra quarters for which he would be eligible in the varsity contest between the schools that evening at Riverview Gardens. The ultra-competitive Vitale believed he needed Gibbons to secure the victory and a perfect undefeated season, so he sent him in for the fourth quarter of what would turn out to be a 27-13 SLUH victory. The trouble was, while trotting downfield after a kickoff, Gibbons took a shot in the thigh from an opposing team's blocker. "Oh, no," thought Vitale. It was Gibbons's kicking leg, and he suffered a severe contusion.

After the game, his "B" teammates gone for the afternoon, Gibbons was soaking in the whirlpool in the SLUH locker room, desperately hoping the hot, swirling water would coax the pain out of his thigh. Coach Vitale was with him. "How does it feel?" he wanted to know. In walked Paul Martel, who quickly sized up what had happened. The two coaches started to argue.

"What in the world were you thinking?!" said Martel, biting down hard on his pipe.

"Dammit, Paul," said Vitale. "We were trying to win the game."

At that point, Gibbons was more pained by the awkwardness than he was by the contusion in his leg. "It was like watching your parents argue," he recalled. "I was afraid, like I did something wrong. It was pretty incredible."

Fortunately for the rest of us, the competitive coaches put it behind them and Gibbons recovered well enough to kick later that night in our 15-7 victory. And he would be available for the playoff game the following weekend.

To that point in the season, Gibbons had successfully kicked just three field goals, two from short distance in the Columbia Hickman game, the third in our 50-0 rout of Augustinian. Against CBC, Martel sent him in to try a 41-yard field goal, but not only was he unsuccessful, he got knocked on his keister by a charging CBC lineman. At the time, having a talented field goal kicker was thought to be something of luxury, like owning a snowplow in Texas. Nice to have, but not something you were going to use very often. Very few high school teams attempted field goals in the autumn of 1970. Mostly, Gibbons was on the team to kick extra points, then to boot kickoffs toward the other teams' end zones.

In our state semifinal game against Riverview Gardens, after our game-tying touchdown and extra point, the Rams started a series with the ball on their 25-yard line, anxious to regain control of the game and a lead. After three consecutive running plays, Riverview faced fourth down, just inches from its 35-yard line and a first down. The standard play would be a punt, with so much on the line and the Rams so perilously close to their own end zone. But Coach Gerry Nordman did *not* call for a punt. Apparently confident that his offense would gain such a short distance for a first down, and also confident that, in case the offense failed, his defense would stop us, Nordman called for a running play into the left side of our line. Our defense was ready. Tom Milford, our left inside line-backer, blitzed right into the hole for which their running back headed. He stuck his shoulders into the runner's legs, then right inside linebacker Kevin O'Toole bear-hugged the runner's torso, then others joined in to stop him short of the first down. Our ball in Riverview territory, 35 yards from the goal line.

After a 9½-yard pass completion to Tom Schoeck and an incomplete pass, Calacci kept the ball and charged behind me on a quarterback sneak to the 24 for a first down. After we failed to advance on any of the next three pass plays, we were faced with a fourth down and 10 yards to go. Paul Martel did not hesitate. He sent in the sophomore. In the third quarter of the state championship semifinals. With the score tied 7-7. Forty yards from the goal post, which was 10 yards back from the goal line at the back of the end zone. Tim Gibbons was going to try to make a field goal.

"I thought, 'Why not?'" Martel recalled many years later. "I knew he had the leg for it. And he had been getting stronger and stronger. And we weren't moving the ball that well."

Gibbons did not feel the tension he sensed in the CBC game at Busch Stadium, and he was ready. "I wasn't nervous," he said. "If you miss a 40-yard field goal when you're just a sophomore, who cares? Maybe that's one of the benefits of being so young, not getting all the tension. I had a job to do."

Watching from among a group of his Riverview Gardens teammates on the sideline, tackle Rick Bagy thought to himself, "There is no way."

Coach Ebbie Dunn had taught Dan Calacci the proper way to hold the ball for a soccer-style placekicker: place it on the kicking tee straight up and down as you would for a straight-on toe kicker, then pull it slightly back toward you, creating the angle the kicker needs. "I didn't know that," Gibbons said. "Ebbie knew that."

Calacci knelt on his left knee just behind the 30-yard line, his right leg stretched just inside it, his arms up and hands open to receive the ball.

He called the signal for Gregg Hannibal to snap the ball six yards to him. Almost freakishly, a circling wind whipped up, blowing right to left and twisting the small pieces of confetti paper that somehow materialized in the area of holder and placekicker. Creating this distraction is something diabolical an enemy would do, if he were trying to break the concentration of our sophomore kicker. It did not matter. Calacci received the ball, placed it cleanly on the kicking tee, then pulled it slightly toward himself as Coach Dunn had taught. Gibbons strode forward confidently, taking a short step with his right leg, then a full step with his left. He swung his powerful right leg through the ball and sent it off like a rocket toward the goal post, just inches over the outstretched arm of a Riverview Gardens rushing defender. "I knew it was good when I kicked it," Gibbons said. "It's like when you hit a good shot in golf. You don't have to look up." The official near Gibbons carefully watched its flight, pointed his finger at the ball as he took four steps to his left, and then raised both his arms to signal it had gone between the uprights. Most improbably, we had taken a 10-7 lead with just a minute left in the third quarter.

Now it was time to see if Paul Martel's preparation would pay off. In the football manifesto he issued us before the season, he had written:

> Statistics show that most games are won or lost in the last quarter. If a player is not in good shape physically, he cannot be expected to perform up to his capabilities. This affects his mental attitude; his determination to do the job with maximum effort is decreased; and his contribution to the team morale is decreased. There is no easy road to success. Every player must work hard if we are going to meet the measure of success that is desired.

For the entire season, in our 10 games, we had allowed just five touchdowns in the fourth quarter. This fourth quarter, and this game, belonged to us. After sacking Riverview quarterback Steve Knight on both third down and fourth down in the final minute, taking over on offense at the Rams' 30-yard line, we knew it was over. We executed four straight running plays to gain a final first down, then ran two more to run out the clock. After Dan Calacci was tackled on a game-ending quarterback keeper, Tim Kellett turned to the south sideline of Francis Field, facing our teammates there, and started clapping. Errol Patterson raised his arms. Jim Dohr, Bill Ziegler and Tim Leahy each jumped. Then our teammates sprinted from the sideline to join us in celebration. Coaches Martel and Ebbie Dunn simply shook hands and walked toward us. By this time, hundreds of our classmates and supporters had come onto the field from the stands beyond the south sideline, and mixed with us as we shook hands with the Riverview Gardens players. Our opponents congratulated us and wished us well, then headed off the field somberly, their season over. For us, there was one more game.

Too young even to have a driver's license, Tim Gibbons was driven home, justifiably proud of what he had done. As he reached his house, he saw the pretty girl who lived next door, who was a year younger. He told her what he had done: kicked a long field goal to win the state playoff semifinals game for his high school football team. "What's a field goal?" she said innocently.

The world is well served when a St. Louis University High School student gets whacked with a megadose of humility, and Gibbons absorbed that one with grace. We, his teammates, however, knew and appreciated what *THAT* field goal was, and what it meant.

52// *"We Knew They Ran a Lot"*

THERE IS A SCENE in the movie *Friday Night Lights*[23] in which the father of a star running back on the 1988 Permian, Texas, High School team confronts his son with a dramatic truth.

"You just … just ain't gettin' it," said Charles Billingsley, an abusive alcoholic played by Tim McGraw. "You don't understand. This is the only thing you're ever going to have. Forever. It carries you forever. It's a ugly fact of life. Hell. It's the ONLY fact of life. You got one year. One stinkin' year to make yourself some memories, son. That's all. It's gone after that. And I'll be damned if you're going to miss it."

The young running back Don Billingsley, played by actor Garrett Hedlund, stands by and absorbs that emotional lecture, seemingly paralyzed by the compelling, simple truth wrapped in the psycho-dramatic package in which it was delivered. The sobering reality is that we DO only get one shot at most things in life. No "do overs." The message was particularly poignant in *Friday Night Lights*, as the life of the Tim McGraw character seems to have peaked during his own youthful star turn on the high school football fields of West Texas.

Well, our story preceded that of the boys from Permian High, which was chronicled in a book by H.G. (Buzz) Bissinger in 1990, *Friday Night Lights: A Town, a Team, and a Dream.*[24] As described in the book and depicted in the 2004 movie based on that book, the Permian Panthers made it to the 1988 state championship game. And lost.

It is unlikely anyone with our 1970 team was as gung-ho or as desperate as Don Billingsley of Permian about the significance of a football championship. If so, I must acknowledge that I was not one of them. The entire autumn I had allowed an ambivalence about the role of football in society to holster my joy in the game and what we were accomplishing on the field. With the world in turmoil, and so many people in need of something to improve their lives, how could a game command so much time and attention? With all our aspiration about making the world greater, about doing something meaningful, we were spending an awful lot of our time practicing and playing football. Frivolous football. An escape.

A game. Especially a game of such physical aggression, even violence. I cannot actually recall anyone overtly criticizing us for playing this game, and indeed many among my friends, family and acquaintances were enthused about it. But I sensed this negative judgment nonetheless, and felt guilty. Until the week before the championship game.

About that time, I embraced that what we had been doing was important; that this was our opportunity to do something meaningful. Pulling together, providing comfort to each other as we tried to cope with the tragedy and seeming hopelessness of the world. A purpose. A common purpose. Something good. It was inspiring. Do what you're doing, do it authentically, work hard at it, do it over and over until you get it right, support your mates, set a goal, work toward it, achieve it and celebrate the goal or at least the noble pursuit of the goal. For the first time all season, I was guiltless as I thought of how much this game meant to me.

Del Bannister and I talked about it in the motel room we shared the night before the game. "Did you ever think we'd make it this far?" I asked him.

"The chances were so remote," Del replied, "since so few teams even *qualify* for the playoffs. I was just happy we beat CBC. But something special is going on here, the way we've been winning these close games."

We laughed that night, as we reminisced about the fun we had playing sports for the venerable Harry Bresnahan at Epiphany of Our Lord grade school. Mr. Bres was proud of his Irish heritage, and that bonded him with Bannister and our classmate Kevin Cleary, the best athlete among us, who went on to star on the SLUH basketball team. The engaging and eccentric Coach Bresnahan had a decidedly politically incorrect way of engaging the young boys he coached in soccer, basketball and baseball. "Fat Pat," is what he called Pat "Del" Bannister. Usually, I was the "Dumb Dago" who seemed incapable of doing things correctly, especially as I regularly accumulated more fouls than points on the basketball court.

If I did something well, he would upgrade me to "Smart Dago." On the very rare occasion I accomplished something marvelous, like driving in a winning run in baseball, he would praise me as the "Smart Italian." Hard-earned praise, indeed. I didn't mind, for I knew how much this man cared about us. He was the custodian for the school, and his youngest son Dan was a year ahead of us. Dan had attended CBC, as had the coach's most famous alumnus, the iconic Mike Shannon of the St. Louis Cardinals. What would Harry think of us now, Bannister and I wondered, perched as we were on the brink of a state title game?

Having reached the championship game with an average victory margin of less than five points per game, there were two things you could say about our team: (1) We were lucky, and (2) We were probably going to get crushed by Kansas City Center High, which had beaten every opponent and would face us with an 11-0 record. Coach Martel was anxious to review film of the Yellowjackets, so he could conjure up a way to defeat them. He contacted Coach Duane Unruh, but his request was rejected. "I would have exchanged with them, anything they wanted," Martel said. "But they refused. So we had to do everything point blank. The only thing I could do was talk to some coaches who had played them. We knew they ran a lot."

In fact, the Yellowjackets had averaged just eight pass attempts per game. With speedy halfbacks Rolland Fuchs and Ron Umphenour, K.C. Center had dominated opponents with its combination of wishbone and option running game. In the regular season, Umphenour had gained 1,119 rushing yards and Fuchs 792. Fuchs scored four touchdowns in Center's 34-28 semifinals victory over Kansas City Oak Park. And Ted Beckett, a strong and swift tight end, was occasionally called on to carry the ball on the "end around" play. In our final week of practices, we prepared to face that tough running game, though we were a bit in the dark. And certainly "in the cold," as the freezing temperatures plummeted to the low 20s.

53// *Here We Go Again*

FORTUNATELY, lousy weather would be no factor in the game, as we discovered upon awakening in Columbia, Missouri. Bannister, our teammates and I successfully navigated our "bacon and eggs" situation, and headed for the University of Missouri's Faurot Field under a clear blue sky. The temperature had "warmed" to the high 40s, and our hot, adrenaline-boosted blood would keep us limber for as long as it took that day. Errol Patterson, in particular, was relieved about the break in the weather, for he already had made the decision to forego the long underwear that kept him warm the week before. Too restricting, he had concluded. Dressed at our hotel in our simple, clean white jerseys and white pants, we bused the mile or so to the stadium. Busloads of our classmates, friends and families had made the trip, and they were waiting for us in the seats as we jogged onto the lush green grass. Before putting on my helmet, I stared at the *Ed Hawk '71* I had stained over the right ear hole, and thought of my fallen friend. I looked to the hill beyond the northern end zone, and admired the iconic "M" sculpted from huge white rocks, the symbol of Mizzou. This was a worthy spectacle, I thought.

The Yellowjackets won the coin toss and chose to play offense first. They returned the opening kickoff to their 25-yard line, and began their first series in the wishbone offense. Two halfbacks and a fullback lined up behind quarterback Dan Fellhauer. Time for us to see if we could stop their running game.

Tim Rodgers, for one, was acutely concerned by what he saw, from his perch next to classmate and close friend Jack Enright, about eight rows up in the stands.

"I thought, 'holy shit,' they're running a wishbone. We're playing the friggin' Dallas Cowboys," Rodgers said. "They looked professional. It just didn't seem possible that we could beat them."

With three modest gains into the center of our defense, K.C. Center moved 10 yards and were awarded a first down. On the next play, we found out the Yellowjackets could do more than run.

Dropping back seven yards from his 35-yard line, Fellhauer cocked his arm and launched a tight spiral pass 24 yards over the middle to Ted Beckett, the left end. The 6-foot-1, 179-pound Beckett grabbed the ball at his 48, two steps ahead of our pass coverage, spun around and headed upfield, then left to the sideline. He raced to our 24-yard line before our defenders could bring him down. Catching our breath, we stopped the next play, a quarterback option to the right, for no yards. On second down and 10, the quarterback Fellhauer again headed to the right on an option play, and he handed the ball to Beckett, who had started moving from his right end position toward the backfield and the quarterback. He took the ball and continued toward the left, untouched and all the way to our end zone for a shocking 24-yard end around for a touchdown. With the extra point, the Yellowjackets completed a 75-yard, opening-series touchdown drive, and we could not help thinking, here we go again.

"When they threw that first pass and got a long gain, they probably thought, 'Hey, this is going to be a picnic,'" Paul Martel recalled.

How in the world were we going to stop this juggernaut? They just zipped down the field on us as if we weren't there, as if our "bacon and eggs situation" had gone awry and we had failed to get to the game on time. We needed something to change the vibration of this game. It would not take long.

54// *Back in the Game*

PRESUMABLY SATISFIED WITH a touchdown on their first possession, Kansas City Center could not have been prepared for what happened next. Even if the Yellowjackets coach *had* agreed to exchange game films in preparation for facing us. What happened next, had not happened all season.

Deep in our territory, Errol Patterson and Bill Ziegler stood a few yards apart in preparation for fielding the Kansas City Center kickoff. Ziegler looked at his teammate and shouted, "Catch the ball, Errol!" Patterson did not reply, but thought to himself, "Really?"

Patterson felt he didn't deserve that admonition, though he accepted that a fumble or two in his career made some suspicious. One of those concerned, it seems, was the revered Father Philip Kellett, who was the moderator of the athletic department, no relation to Tim Kellett, and an ardent advocate for all Junior Billikens sports teams.

When we were freshmen, Father Kellett entertained us in the Latin language class he taught. Once, exasperated that Fred Daues was struggling with the lessons of arcane Latin conjugations, Father Kellett asked him to come forward.

"Daues," he said, "here's a dime."

"Father," replied a nervous Daues, "what is the dime for?"

"I want you to call your father so he can come and get you, and transfer you to DuBourg High. You're not going to make it here."

One memorable day, as Father Kellett sought to dramatize a point he was making, he struck his desk so forcefully with his ever-present long wood pointer that a crucifix fell from its hook on the wall above him, and struck him on the head. Students looked on in awe. Father Kellett was unharmed, but one had to wonder if the symbolism ever caused him concern.

I came to look forward to Friday afternoons in the late summer and fall of my freshman year, when Father Kellett regularly abandoned his prescribed Latin lesson plans to speak about the football team's chances in its game that weekend. Fr. Kellett confronted a lifetime speech impediment with a booming, confident voice, and he delighted in trying to embarrass students with demands for translation of indecorous Latin phrases, such as the bastardized *semper ubi sub ubi* (*always where under where*).

"Mueth!" he boomed, getting the attention of the brilliant but slightly built Mike Mueth. "Mueth, please translate for me: *I ad infernam.*"

Hesitating, Mueth smiled.

"Mueth, please translate!" Father Kellett implored.

"Go to hell, Father," Mueth replied, eliciting a broad, satisfied smile from Father Phil.

In the fall of 1970, Father Jim Burshek, S.J., lived in a room across the hall from Father Kellett in the Jesuit residence at St. Louis U. High. Late one night he was bolted from his sleep by a booming noise emanating from the room of Father Kellett, who, he surmised, was having a nightmare.

"Catch the ball, Patterson!" Father Kellett bellowed.

Well, there was the kickoff Patterson fumbled in the Althoff game. And there was the Riverview Gardens game the year before, when as a junior, Patterson coughed up the ball after fielding a punt. It was cold and miserable that night, and it was difficult to follow the flight of the ball as it soared above those old, transplanted Busch Stadium lights before descending into his arms just as a Riverview tackler zeroed in on him. "I was never hit so hard," he recalled. "The guy comes and just creams me. I went one way, the ball went another."

As he lined up opposite Ziegler and awaited the Kansas City Center kick, Patterson was thinking positively. The week before, in the semifinals game against Riverview Gardens, he had thought it was about time for a long return on a kickoff.

"On kickoffs, nothing was really happening," he recalled. "I was going to try to change that." He envisioned sprinting toward a scrum of blockers and tacklers, leaping over them, and jetting toward the end zone. And against Riverview, he got the chance. "I fielded a kick, came upon the heap of bodies and was able to leap over the wreckage. But a guy caught me from behind. I felt like I had rocks on my back." What restricted him, he knew, was the long underwear he had worn that day as a concession to the cold weather. "I had an opening, but with all that clothing on I was slowed down, and the guy caught me from behind. I thought, 'I'm never going to do that again. I'd rather be cold.'" That long underwear made its last appearance on our final practice before the championship game, on Thanksgiving Day, when it provided relief during that unbearably cold afternoon. "For the championship game, I dressed differently."

Patterson acknowledged Ziegler's challenge, then turned his eyes and attention upfield. He suspected the Yellowjackets would be kicking to him instead of to Ziegler, who was bigger, almost as fast, and the more accomplished ball carrier. He was right.

Just a step inside our 20-yard line, and between the left hash marks and the sideline, Patterson caught the ball and took off. Five SLUH blockers cleared a hole out of the charging, would-be Yellowjackets tacklers taking aim at him. "I made a move to the outside," Patterson said, "and needed just one more block, from Bill Caputo. And he made that block." He flew right past the crowd and headed toward the left sideline, eluding everyone, including at last the diving Rick Fields, who had kicked the ball to him. Finished with that threat at the K.C. Center 40-yard line, Patterson sprinted toward the end zone for a touchdown. In less than 10 seconds, then with Tim Gibbons's extra point, we had tied the score, 7-7.

It was as if we had just been resuscitated, full charge with the paddles right on the chest.

"Will you be champions?" Paul Martel had written in his football manifesto. "Only you hold the answer!"

Yeah, well, at least we were now back in the game.

55// *A Strange Confidence*

ON ITS SUBSEQUENT SERIES, K.C. Center advanced the ball and generated three first downs, but stalled on its own 44-yard line and punted to us. Starting on our own 22, then benefitting from a defensive pass interference call, we moved out to the 37. From there, we executed our most successful drive of the game, featuring a 10-yard Dan Calacci-to-Jim Dohr pass, a 14-yard Bill Ziegler run, and a 24-yard Ziegler dash up the middle that moved us to the K.C. Center six-yard line. On first-and-goal, Calacci pitched outside to Tom Schoeck, who snatched the ball in the backfield at the nine and charged toward the goal line, lowering his head and crunching his tackler before yielding a yard from the goal line. Ziegler then crashed into the end zone for a touchdown, and with the extra point we had a 14-7 lead, a minute before the end of the first quarter. It was a satisfying drive, 78 yards of versatility and teamwork and execution, and an effective counterpunch in our battle against this formidable opponent. Kansas City Center packed a serious counterpunch of its own, which it was intent on delivering before the end of the first half.

After exchanging punts, K.C. Center began a drive on its 47-yard line, with the goal of tying the score before halftime. Fueled by another end around run from Ted Beckett, this one for 28 yards, and a series of smaller running gains, the Yellowjackets drove to a first down at our nine-yard line, with less than two minutes left in the half. Plenty of time for them to cover the yards and tie the score. With two runs to the left side of our defense, they moved to our two-yard line. And decided to test our right side. Tom Schoeck, our right outside linebacker, saw it coming.

K.C. Center quarterback Dan Fellhauer handed the ball to running back Ron Umphenour, but Schoeck got to the hole first and jammed it up long enough for Tim Kellett and other reinforcements to help stop the run a yard short. On fourth down and one at the goal line, K.C. Center tried

is the kickoff following a touchdown."

Earlier in the game, on our two-yard line with seconds remaining the first half, Kansas City Center ran two consecutive dive plays into the right side of our defense, presumably to avoid the other side, which was patrolled by left linebacker Bill Ziegler, our tri-captain and best player. Twice, Tom Schoeck and friends foiled that plan and kept the Yellowjackets out of the end zone. After its first touchdown, earlier in the first half, Kansas City Center placekicker Rick Fields kicked the ball toward Errol Patterson, presumably aimed away from the other kick returner—Bill Ziegler. Patterson burned them. After its second touchdown, perhaps it seemed time to try something else. Kick it to Ziegler. Indeed, that is what Rick Fields did.

The 6-foot, 183-pound Ziegler caressed the football as it descended near our 15-yard line, between the right sideline and the first set of hash marks, and he headed toward the middle of the field behind kick return teammates eager to clear space for him. As six aspiring Kansas City Center tacklers converged on him near our 35-yard line, Ziegler triggered his after-burner and exploded toward the right sideline. It was as if he was contaminated, for no defender even touched him. His long stride now fully engaged, Ziegler sprinted forward, gobbling up yards and running toward the Yellowjackets' end zone. Touchdown! There is your momentum, right there! We had not returned a kick for a touchdown in our first 11 games, but now we had done it twice. With Tim Gibbons's point-after-touchdown kick, we led, 21-13.

57// *It Was Our Time*

WE WERE STARTING to accept the notion that we could win this game, this championship.

"We seemed to be a team of destiny," Tim Kellett said. "You start *in*

e

u don't get rattled when you are down. Different
.e the play at the right time. You just have a sense
.n the game is close that some way, somehow, we are
way to win."

knew there was plenty of time remaining, and we had to
. way to stop the Kansas City Center offense. The Yellowjackets
.heir next drive at their 27-yard line, and began moving again,
, midfield into our territory, when interrupted by the end of the
.d quarter. Twelve minutes to play.

On a third down with nine to go for a first down, Kansas City Center
lined up with a flanker and wide receiver spread to the right side and
two ball carriers in the backfield behind Dan Fellhauer, the quarterback.
Fellhauer took the center snap and handed off to Rolland Fuchs, who in
turn handed off to the sweeping Ron Umphenour. Mike Wiese and Tom
Schoeck were not fooled, and they tackled him for an eight-yard loss,
forcing the Yellowjackets to punt. The fourth quarter was off to a good
start, and things got better when Errol Patterson returned that punt 32
yards to our 44-yard line.

On our ensuing possession, we moved the ball into Kansas City Center
territory, but turned it over with an interception at the Yellowjackets' 25-
yard line. Fellhauer completed two long passes, and suddenly we found
ourselves in trouble again, this time defending on our own 25. Time for
that cursed end around again, with Ted Beckett heading to the right side.
In something of an upset, we yielded just five yards on the play. Second
down, five to go for K.C. Center on our 20. Our "one-possession" lead
seemed particularly vulnerable. Fellhauer and the Yellowjackets tried a
pass, then another. Each fell incomplete. On fourth down, he tried once
more. And once more, we stopped them from gaining a first down. Our ball,
first and 10 from our 20-yard line, less than nine minutes left in the game.

We led, 21-13, but knew we needed something more. It was clear we needed to try a series of running plays, to grind up enough yards to gain first downs and keep the clock engaged and winding down, to control the ball and keep it away from the menacing Kansas City Center offense. We on the offensive line were not thinking about passively, conservatively protecting our lead. We still had something to prove, and we were ready for the moment.

As it turned out, no one was more ready for his moment than Bill Ziegler, our star linebacker, running back and tri-captain.

Kansas City Center greeted us with nine defenders near the line of scrimmage, and we linemen calmly eyeballed the opponent we intended to move out of the way. With Ziegler and Schoeck lined up behind him, Calacci crouched behind me and called out the play cadence.

"George! Hup One! Hup Two!" On the second number, I hiked the ball up between my legs firmly into Calacci's hands and moved forward and to the right in search of the left defensive guard. Our right guard Steve Ohmer had vacated that space as he pulled behind me to the left to join left tackle Al Fahrenhorst in blasting open a hole for our ball carrier. After clutching the ball from me, Calacci turned right and faked a handoff to the charging Schoeck, who accelerated into the defensive line without the ball. Calacci spun around and softly placed the ball between Ziegler's arms and into his hands. And then Ziegler leaned forward, motoring through the near left side toward the middle of the field. He brushed off one tackler, then sprinted past three others and into an opening. I took off after him, completely extraneous to the play at that point, but determined to be among the first to congratulate him at the conclusion of what I suspected would be a touchdown. As he crossed the goal line, Ziegler exchanged the ball from his right hand to his left, then casually let it drop to the ground in the Kansas City Center end zone. Tim Gibbons kicked the extra point successfully, and we moved our advantage to 28-13 with seven minutes, 53 seconds left in the game.

It was an extraordinary play by an extraordinary player at an extraordinary time.

Kansas City Center's star, Ted Beckett, had one more moment himself, when on the ensuing possession he leaped to catch a Dan Fellhauer pass at our 41-yard line and raced to the end zone for a touchdown. When the Yellowjackets failed in their attempt for a two-point conversion, then failed to recover their onside kick, the score was stuck at 28-19, a nine-point, two-possession deficit. At that time, we knew it was our time.

In the final minutes of the game, we controlled the ball on offense, and Kansas City Center was unable to stop us, the clock, or the advance of the fate they faced. The finals seconds counted down on the Faurot Field game clock, much too quickly for the Yellowjackets yet much too slowly for us. Then, finally, to zero. The game was over. We were champions. Exhausted, physically and emotionally, I tried in vain to freeze the moment. As those final seconds dripped off the stadium clock, I thought of my parents, my siblings, my girl friend Katie. I thought of Ed Hawk, and how much I wished to share our moment with him, with an embrace. Instead, I grabbed Dan Calacci, our quarterback. Tim Kellett and Errol Patterson clutched each other.

Kellett's older brother Tom watched from the stands. One of SLUH's all-time greats, from the Class of 1969, Tom Kellett was then a sophomore on the University of Missouri team. Dick Keefe, the French teacher, spotted him. "Next stop, Super Bowl," he said. Tom Kellett looked at him and smiled, but didn't say anything. "Maybe he had a tinge of regret that it wasn't him down there," Keefe said. "I wouldn't be surprised."

Bob Thibaut's sentiments were similarly mixed. For four years, he was such a presence on the football field and within our class. A leader and a principal player with a certain future in football beyond high school, he was vital to our success. Then his disabling knee injury knocked him out. In his mind, though never in the minds of his teammates, he had become irrelevant. Having watched the championship game from the sideline, he was so happy for his teammates but so disappointed at not being able to play.

"It's difficult, not being a part of it," he said. "It was devastating. Because there is no second chance. There is no next season. It's finite. It's done. It's over. I remember, taking off the shoulder pads for the last time, and saying to myself, 'I'll never put on another pair of shoulder pads.' And I haven't."

The words and gestures of two men, moments after the game, provided Thibaut a lasting comfort. The first was from Joe Vitale.

"Bobby, you were a big part of this, the first half of the season," Vitale said. "You should always remember that."

Next, big Ed Ziegler approached him and put his arm on his shoulder. "Bob," he said, "I know you were a really big part of this."

"That meant so much for me," Thibaut said. "For Bill Ziegler's Dad, who didn't say a whole lot. For him to even say something, that just meant a lot to me."

Bill Ziegler's mind went to a remarkable place for someone who had just completed one of the most spectacular individual big-game performances a player could have. "I was thinking of our teammates, the coaches, the cheerleaders, our classmates," Ziegler recalled. "Our victory belonged to so many who supported us."

Mike Wiese looked up to the sky. "Thank you, Bob," he said to himself, thinking of his older brother. "He was my guardian angel. I believe in that. I thanked him for helping us win. I thanked him for helping me play well."

Our classmates, other friends and family members rushed the field to congratulate us. Katie and a co-conspirator thought the occasion warranted a souvenir, so they pilfered the double-flapped, rubber marker which had stood near the sideline during the game, marking the 50-yard line, and later presented it to me. The spoils of war, I suppose. A minor larceny, my ever adventurous girlfriend rationalized, significant because the number matched the one I wore on my jersey. "I'm sure we thought it was a fabulous idea," she said many years later. She was caught up in the moment.

"It was the most amazing thing in the world," she said. "I'd never been part of something like that. Number One in the state. It was such a big world to me. I related more to SLUH than I did to Nerinx. That championship catapulted SLUH to the top of everyone's list, and I was pretty stoked about it."

Fred Daues, who bravely played on despite having his college football aspirations crushed along with his right knee in practice before the DeSmet game, felt a profound sense of accomplishment.

"It was like we had been on a big journey," he said, "and had gotten it done. We had dedicated the season to Ed Hawk. We had made a contract with each other, to a fallen friend. To be able to take that season to its zenith as we did, it was a tremendous feeling. That's what we did. As friends, to think we would go through the season and do what we did. Not a doubt in my mind. Where do I sign? Absolutely no doubt."

58// *"You're Ziegler, Aren't You?"*

WE HAD DONE IT. Despite yielding 22 first downs and 435 yards from scrimmage, we had upset the Yellowjackets, and forever would hold the title: *1970 Missouri Class 4A State Football Champions*. Ted Beckett, the 6-foot-1, 179-pound flanker, scored all three of his team's touchdowns and accounted for 223 of those yards, 60 rushing on those punishing end-around plays from the "wishbone T" alignment, and another 163 yards on five pass receptions. After the game, Coach Paul Martel told reporter Gary Mueller of the *St. Louis Post-Dispatch:*

"We knew we had to expect their power offense out of the wishbone, but we didn't expect them to start throwing that soon."

Quarterback Dan Fellhour completed just 11 of the 30 passes he attempted, but they covered 281 yards. Even if the teams *had* exchanged film before the game, Martel would not have suspected such a passing attack. In the entire regular season, Fellhour had completed just 22 of 78 passing attempts. Of course, KC Center Coach Duane Unruh would not have uncovered an insight into our kick-returning potential had he examined every frame of the films from our previous games. We had not scored on a kick return all season.

Martel, never one for hyperbole, tried to explain why we were successful on those kickoffs.

"We really didn't feel we had the speed for those long runs," he told reporter Myron Holtzman of the *St. Louis Globe-Democrat*, "but Ziegler does have deceptive speed and once he gets moving, he can go.

"On those runbacks, though, you really have to credit the blocking as well as the runner. They gauged their timing and got good position blocking, and it was a matter of the kid coming along and hitting the hole properly."

As captains, Bill Ziegler, Bob Thibaut and I had the privilege of accepting our championship trophy from University of Missouri Coach Dan Devine in an informal ceremony immediately after the game, on the turf covering Faurot Field.

"There, when Devine was handing out the trophy," Martel said, "I was just so pleased for the kids, because of all the time they put in, to practice and everything. And some of the struggles we had during the season. Some real difficult ball games. And here it all comes to fruition. It's finally the end. And everything turns out. The kids put in a tremendous amount of effort. We just won and won and won. It was a great accomplishment."

As our coaches, teammates and supporters looked on, with the trophy in his left hand, Coach Devine approached us. I thrust my right arm and opened hand toward him. He strided past me, ignoring my hand.

"I grabbed the trophy," Thibaut said. "I wasn't getting the handshake either."

Devine zipped by Thibaut in the center, and extended his right arm toward the fellow on our left.

"You're Ziegler, aren't you?" he said, shaking Bill's hand.

Well, why not? Devine had just witnessed our star score three touchdowns and generate 271 yards with the football in his arms: 150 on running plays, 25 on pass receptions, 85 on the kickoff return, and 11 on an interception return. He also made 11 tackles. Devine wanted that type of talent to play for the Mizzou Tigers, and he wanted to be certain Bill understood that.

59// "We Won It with You Guys"

AFTER THE GAME, in the sanctuary of our locker room, we sat on benches, peeled off the soiled athletic tape that braced various parts of our battered bodies, and sniffed the combination of joy, sweat and analgesic liniment that filled the air.

Father Philip Kellett, the venerable Jesuit priest and athletic department moderator, stood among us and quickly attained our full attention. A brave orator who simply bellowed through the lifetime stutter and speech tic that afflicted him, Father Kellett looked around and pronounced, "You guys … just also … have guts."

The serious and driven Tom Schoeck, nearly skeletal after a season of relentless competition, whose two touchdown-saving tackles at the end of the first half preserved our 14-7 lead, finally was satisfied. "That was a moment to cherish," he said. In hindsight, the poignancy of Father Kellett's extemporaneous salute seems more acute. Less than three years later, in February of 1973, Father Kellett would die suddenly while undergoing emergency heart surgery. A beloved figure, he was just 65 years old. "We did have guts," Schoeck said. "Love and guts for each other, our cheering pals, and our school and our coaches."

State championship in hand, we wondered if Coach Martel finally would yield the compliment we wanted from him. Were we better than the danged "Hungry Huns" of 1959, his very first St. Louis U. High team? Midway through the season, when we were 6-1 and ranked No. 4 in the state, he was not ready for that.

Coach Paul Martel would go on to coach 17 more seasons at St. Louis U. High, where he compiled a record of 200 victories, 79 losses and six ties in a total of 29 years. His teams qualified for the state playoffs six times in the 18 seasons they were held, and won eight of the 12 Bi-State Conference championships contested during his tenure. Including his work as a coach in Kansas, his high school coaching record was 285-105-12. Our 1970 team delivered his only state championship.

To many on our team, he was like the father they wished they had. Most of us desperately coveted his approval.

"I wasn't getting along with my Dad at all back then," was a sentiment a number of my teammates said to me, recalling that time in our lives. "Paul Martel was like a father to me."

Bill Ziegler reflected on what made Paul Martel a great coach.

"It's amazing how good he was," Ziegler said. "Especially since he never really *played* that much football. We didn't have any size. We weren't all that fast. He had to find other ways for us to be competitive. He was innovative. He took big risks at times. He was aggressive on the field, though that never showed in his demeanor. He was not a 'rah rah' guy. The great coach is the coach who is able to get players to play for him, not themselves. I just wanted to play well for him."

Perhaps Paul Martel had been parsimonious with his praise during the season because he wanted to motivate us. Certainly, that is a tool coaches have used throughout the years. We came to understand, however, that Paul Martel did not engage in such tactics. He was a truth teller. We *did* get a compliment from our coach, the best kind of compliment, when we won the championship. His trained eye and devotion to honesty would have precluded him from yielding much praise for our collective team *talent*, but he did say this to Holtzman, the *St. Louis Globe-Democrat* reporter:

"What makes me so darn happy about this group, is that it didn't really have the physical tools as some of our teams in the past. But for sheer grit you can't beat 'em. They just plod along and get the job done."

Complementing that compliment, Coach Ebbie Dunn piled on during our post-season celebration banquet: "Coach Martel was always well thought of, but when we won the state championship, his reputation really grew among the coaches in the area," said Coach Dunn, pausing for effect, "since we won it with *you* guys." Fair enough.

60// *Great Men of Influence*

Reflections from 2017

IF PAUL MARTEL WAS the sort of father some of our players wished they had, Coach Ebbie Dunn was perhaps the type of father we hoped to become. While exuding authority on par with Martel, Coach Dunn had a rounder edge, figuratively as well as literally. Once, upon noticing an impromptu beer belly contest between our world-class entrants Tim Fleming and John Kurusz in the locker room after a practice, Dunn stopped, perused the two surprised finalists, and declared: "I've got both of you beat." Indeed he did.

"If it wasn't for Ebbie," said Bob Thibaut, "I don't think our team would have stayed together. I don't think any team would have stayed together. I really don't. There were so many times he came up to me, and anybody, and put his arm around you, and let you know, that things were all right."

A graduate of CBC, who drove a beer truck in the summers to earn extra money and called each of us "Babe," Dunn could be "crusty," as Tim Kellett put it. One of his common, colorful admonitions: "Babe, if you do that again we are going to have to go to the hospital to get my foot out of your ass." Dunn reminded Kellett of Eddie Burke, his grandfather who died at the beginning our senior season. "They didn't tolerate nonsense, and if you were doing something wrong, they told you about it. But Ebbie had a really good heart. He's one of the greatest men I've ever met."

Dunn was a faithful, unyielding champion of the underdog. Once, during a practice scrimmage, Ebbie noticed a senior lineman grabbing the facemask of a sophomore to give himself an unfair, illegal advantage. He whistled for play to be stopped, walked up to a couple inches in front of that senior, grabbed his facemask, and yanked it sharply to the left.

"How does that feel?" he said. "Knock it off."

During a particularly combative full-contact practice one day during our senior season, Fred Daues pulled the wrong way on a blocking assignment, and crashed into an unprepared Dunn, who was inspecting the play from close range. The coach tumbled, then rolled on the ground for a revolution and a half. His trousers and right arm caked in dirt, he slowly rose to his feet, as we stood in silence. "I was frozen," said Daues, quite concerned about what price he would have to pay for crushing the coach on a blocking mistake.

"Babe," said Ebbie, looking straight into Daues's eyes, "I hope you block that hard when we play the games."

Similarly, in one intra-squad scrimmage, Del Bannister was centering the ball for the second-team offense in drills against the first-team defense. Twice in a row, Bannister hiked the ball to the quarterback on the count of ONE, when the set snap count call had been TWO. Football technicians understand that mistake yields the advantage from the offense to the defense, whose players charge when they see the ball move, regardless of what the quarterback is calling out. The offensive linemen were battered, twice in a row, while they were awaiting another count.

"Bannister," said Coach Dunn after the second mistake.

"Yes, sir," said Bannister, ready for the stern fate he sensed was coming.

"Can you count to two?" asked Dunn, his voice louder but in control.

"Yes, sir," Bannister replied meekly.

"Well, then, let me hear you count to two."

"ONE. TWO."

"Do it again, Bannister."

"ONE. TWO."

Ebbie Dunn left football coaching in 1975, when the Missouri State High School Activities Association moved the soccer season from the winter to the fall. "That really hurt, when soccer came in from the winter months to the fall," Paul Martel said. "It was only natural that Ebbie would stay with soccer, but I missed him. He was the most loyal person I ever had on my football team."

Dunn compiled a record of 592-197-104 as head soccer coach, won Missouri state championships in 1973 and 1990, and was named national Coach of the Year by the National High School Athletic Coaches Association in 1979 and by the National Soccer Coaches Association in 1987. When he retired from coaching in 1992 after 37 seasons, he had more career victories than any high school soccer coach in the entire country. For those of us who played for him, though, we knew that winning games was not his legacy.

"With Ebbie, it wasn't all about the winning," said Dan Flynn, a senior tri-captain on the 1973 team that won the first SLUH state soccer championship. "He saw sports as a platform for college. It was a principle to him, based on his belief in the mission of St. Louis U. High. The U. High meant something to him. Not something arrogant, but something very special. A place of privilege, and we should treat it as such."

Flynn started high school at McBride High, but had to find another school when the Catholic Archdiocese of St. Louis closed McBride after the 1970-71 school year. Flynn and his older brother Neil transferred to SLUH. It was a rough transition for Dan Flynn, who had starred on the McBride soccer team as a freshman and sophomore. He sensed he did not belong among the students and athletes at St. Louis U. High.

"I was in Ebbie's math class," Flynn recalled. "He could see I was struggling. For one thing, I was wearing my McBride letter jacket."

Coach Dunn approached Flynn. "Look, Babe," he said, "what are you doing? I've been here for more than 20 years, and some things just aren't going to change. You have to adjust. We don't do everything right here, but we do many things right."

At the urging of his brother Neil, Dan Flynn yielded to Ebbie Dunn and trusted him. Said Neil, "Mr. Dunn has a plan. You might not like it, but he runs the orchestra, and he has the baton. You should just go out every day and prove you belong in the first chair."

Accustomed to a starting, featured role, Dan Flynn took a while to understand and accept that Ebbie Dunn was going to provide precious playing time to seniors, in order to optimize their exposure to college soccer coaches who had scholarships to offer. Then, as a senior in preseason workouts, Flynn was moved from his favored position on defense to the front line as a striker. "I thought, what is he doing?!" Flynn recalled.

Once again, Dunn called Flynn into his office for a chat. "Shut the door and tell me what's on your mind," the coach said.

"He knew Dad was out of work, and that was weighing on me," Flynn said. "He was very calm. He said, 'Babe, it'll all work out.' It wasn't so much what he said, but the way he said it. I'm not sure if I was in there for five minutes or an hour and five minutes, but when I went in I was very nervous, and when I came out, I just knew it was going to work out, because this guy cares."

Flynn scored two goals in the preseason intra-squad game, was elected tri-captain with Tim Gibbons and Tim Twellman, and went on to lead the Junior Billikens to the state championship. He received a full scholarship at St. Louis University. After college, he landed a job at the Anheuser-Busch brewery, where he rose quickly through the ranks to become President of the company's international subsidiary and a member of the Senior Strategy Committee. After leaving A-B, Flynn became President & CEO of the United States Soccer Federation.

Beloved by so many, Ebbie Dunn died of esophageal cancer in 2002, at the age of 73.

"You just never wanted to lose when you played for him," said Flynn. "He was the single greatest motivator I've ever seen."

I shared Flynn's admiration for Ebbie Dunn, as did most who knew him. For me, Paul Martel was more of an acquired taste. In his position of authority, with sole governance over the St. Louis U. High football program and sole discretion over who made the team and who played, I understood the control he had over me, given my desire to play football. But I thought him to be stern, autocratic and almost bereft of human emotion. When he benched me in the Assumption game for violating curfew, I believed it was because I had accepted the Student Council Presidency and he was making an example of me. He would not tolerate split loyalties on his football team. I resented that and was crushed by the punishment because it cost me 10% of the regular season, 20% of our conference season, and the potential, I thought at the time, to make post-season all-star teams that would enhance my opportunity to gain a college football scholarship.

Once, a few years after our class had graduated, a player's brother stopped in to see him, to advocate for his brother and challenge the coach's rule on haircuts. "I couldn't stand long hair," Martel said. "When the Beatles came along, that drove me nuts. I told our kids, when I put $350 worth of equipment on you, when we go out on the field, we're going to look good." The brother delivered what he must have thought was his payoff line: "Coach, after all, Jesus Christ had long hair." Unmoved, Martel replied, "I tell you what you do. Go up to the Alumni Office, and look at the yearbooks. And you'll find out Jesus Christ didn't play football here either. If your brother wants to play, he's going to cut his hair."

My own father had wielded his authority with a subtler hand. Jimmy Castellano seemed to understand that long hair and beards didn't really matter. In fact, when I returned home from my freshman year at Northwestern University at Thanksgiving break with a scraggly beard, ready for the type of battle many of my friends had been waging with their fathers, Dad looked at me and laughed. "Look at you," he said, simply.

Dad didn't much care about the trivial stuff. Rather, he articulated what he expected from me, trusted me, and held me accountable.

Upon the conclusion of our championship season, no longer beholden to his authority, I came to understand Coach Martel better. A few days after the season ended, I nervously approached him with an unusual offer. I wanted to purchase the helmet I had worn during the season, the battered hat piece that I had defaced by inking *Ed Hawk '71* over the right ear hole. It was a violation of one of his team rules.

"I notice you wrote something on that helmet," Coach Martel responded, the first words he ever expressed about something I had done three months earlier.

"Yes, sir," I said.

"Well, I know how meaningful that is to you," he said. "You don't have to buy the helmet. I want you to have it."

Many years later, Coach Martel told me he knew many players did not like him. He also revealed how much it pained him to have to cut players who did not make the 50-man roster. "Kids would come into my office, beg for a spot on the team, and cry," he said. "People never knew it, but I'd often go home afterward and cry myself."

I have come to realize that Paul Martel was just doing his best, a human being after all, who wasn't really sure he had all the right answers. A wise and talented man who devoted his life to work he loved. A man of strong emotions that he endeavored to hide from others, such as when he mourned the death of his daughter Mary, who succumbed to cancer at age 24 in 1980. "When he lost his daughter, that was a really tough time," said Gary Kornfeld, who succeeded Martel as SLUH head coach in 1988.

Kornfeld joined the SLUH football staff as Martel's assistant in 1979. "Paul was a disciplinarian," Kornfeld said. "The kids knew the rules. If you didn't follow them, there were going to be consequences."

Martel believed discipline and conformity were paramount to a successful enterprise.

"I was a strong disciplinarian," he said. "They're going to do it my way, because I'm running this program. If you can't conform, maybe you shouldn't be here. But I always knew they wanted to be here. And I came to the conclusion that the ballplayers really expected discipline, they really did. I thought one of the problems other schools had, was their coaches had no discipline over their players. It was easy for me at St. Louis U. High, because our kids were there because they wanted to play, to have fun, and to win."

When we were juniors, Tim Kellett felt the crush of Martel's disciplinary hand. In a game at offensive tackle, a game in which we had a comfortable lead, Kellett knocked down his assigned defender and "stayed with the block," as our coaches had preached to us. In other words, he just stayed on top of the guy until the referee blew his whistle signaling the play was over. The defender apparently resented Kellett's stifling takedown, and went after him when they got on their feet. Instead of walking away, Kellett stood his ground. Both players were ejected from the game. Martel called him over as he ran off the field. "You think you're a real tough guy, don't you?" Kellett didn't get very far with his explanation. He didn't play another minute in our final two games of that season.

Still, Kellett appreciated the privilege of playing for him. "I always admired Coach Martel," he said. "I really respected his knowledge and devotion to his craft. He did more with less than anyone."

I came to realize that Paul Martel did not cost me a college football scholarship by keeping me out of a game. (That, it turns out, was attributable to my lack of size, speed, and discernible football talent.) He simply held me accountable, and taught me a valuable lesson.

Over the course of a three-decade career in business, I also came to understand the tinge of envy Martel must have felt for Dunn, who was his assistant coach for 15 years. This, I realized, was the price of leadership. The leader, with ultimate responsibility for the success of the enterprise, has to make the tough decisions, hold people accountable, keep everything together. The feelings and fate of individuals sometimes must be sacrificed for the good of the group. It is almost impossible for a seasoned leader to end up without critics, even enemies.

"Ebbie was a good communicator with the ballplayers," Martel said. "A lot of times, I had the feeling that I was sort of a dictator. I ran the program. And of course Ebbie was always there with me, and we would discuss a lot of things about what we should be doing. Another thing, Ebbie could be a good communicator with the parents. Sometimes I had my problems with parents."

Paul Martel's coaching career at SLUH ended in 1987, after back-to-back losing seasons. He had only four of them in his 29 years as head coach, in which the Junior Billikens were 200-79-8. In 1984 and '85, he coached Henry Jones, who went to the University of Illinois and became a No. 1 draft pick of the Buffalo Bills, for whom he starred as a Pro Bowl safety in the 1990s. Jones and Bill Ziegler are the only two of Martel's SLUH graduates to have earned a pro football paycheck. Martel went on to coach the semipro St. Louis Gamblers for a year, then serve as an assistant coach in St. Louis at Washington University from 1989-94 and at Vianney High School from 1997-2001. He would be inducted into several halls of fame: Greater St. Louis Athletic Association, Rockhurst College Basketball, St. Louis Metro Football Coaches Association, Missouri High School Football Coaches Association, Missouri Sports Hall of Fame, and the St. Louis Sports Hall of Fame. In 2014, Bishop Miege High School honored him by naming its football field, Paul Martel Field.

Gary Kornfeld was 24 years old when Martel hired him as assistant coach. Nine years later, Kornfeld replaced him as head coach. "He took me in, and he taught me the game," said Kornfeld, acknowledging the profound influence Martel had on him. In 2015, he surpassed Martel's career victory total at SLUH. He retired from SLUH after the 2016 season. Like Martel, he was the Junior Billiken head coach for 29 years, and his teams had a 212-105 record. "There is a lot of him in me. Like him, I always try to stay ahead of the game, and make sure we have the latest and greatest stuff we need. Paul was very big on clinics. We always do clinics with my staff. Paul was big on film. He put the time in, and worked it. He scouted. He held players accountable, and they always understood that you're to be a good person first, a good student, and then you earn the right to come onto the field." In 2016, Kornfeld joined Martel in the Missouri State High School Football Hall of Fame.

In March of 2017, SLUH announced Mike Jones would be its next coach, only the third man to hold the job since 1959. An NFL veteran who starred at the University of Missouri, Jones is remembered for making

"The Tackle," when he stopped Tennessee Titans receiver Kevin Dyson at the one-yard line to end Super Bowl XXXIV and preserve victory for the St. Louis Rams.

Even well past his 90th birthday, Martel reflected on his life and acknowledged the pain of tradeoffs he made in pursuit of excellence. Still, he was okay with it.

"One thing I always thought," he reflected, "was I close enough to the ball players? If anything were to be said, I loved every one of them. Because they were there for a purpose, and they did the best thing they could do. And that's all I could ever ask out of a person. But I was not one that would go around and hug everyone. Little be it known, if there were 600 guys who played football during my tenure, I could always say, yes, I loved 600 guys that played for me.

"You know, coaches don't get rich," he said. "Our wealth comes from having a part in so many lives. We're touched by it. I wouldn't have traded it for all the gold in Fort Knox."

After battling the complications from a leg infection for two months, Paul Martel died in January of 2016, just two weeks short of his 92nd birthday. His children Paul Jr. and Pam (P.J.) Croft honored me by asking me to deliver his eulogy. I tried to honor him by saying he was a tough, complex, honest man—a football savant who loved coaching, and the players who played for him.

61// *More Football*

DESPITE OUR Missouri state championship, we did NOT finish the season ranked No. 1 in the St. Louis area. That honor was bestowed on Alton High School, located across the Mississippi River in the state of Illinois. The Redbirds, who won all 10 of their games in 1970 and did not have an opportunity to compete in a state playoff tournament, received 10 of the 13 votes cast in the final *St. Louis Post-Dispatch* poll for large-enrollment schools in the metropolitan area. We received the other three votes for No. 1, and finished second, seven points behind Alton and eight ahead of No. 3 Vianney, which failed to qualify for the Missouri playoffs despite its 10-0 record.

Prep Top 10

(Published December, 1970)

Rankings of area high school football teams by the Post-Dispatch board of coaches, with first-place votes and records in parentheses (points on a basis of 10 for first, 9 for second, 8 for third, etc.).

LARGE SCHOOLS

1.	Alton (10) (10-0)	125
2.	St. Louis U. High (3) (11-1)	118
3.	Vianney (10-0)	100
4	Granite City (8-1)	65
5.	Beaumont (9-1)	62
6.	CBC (8-2)	51
7.	Riverview Gardens (7-3)	48
8.	Webster Groves (7-2)	47
9.	Belleville East (8-2)	37
10.	Mehlville (8-1)	27

OTHERS: 11. Affton (8-1) 15; 12. Roosevelt (7-2-1) 9; 13. East St. Louis (4-4) 5; 14. St. Mary's (7-1-2) 4; 15. (tie) Ladue (6-2) and DuBourg (7-3) 1.

Sure, our team *did* have all-star players. Bill Ziegler and Mike Wiese were selected to the Missouri All-State All-Star first team, and Tim Kellett joined them on the *St. Louis Post-Dispatch* All-Metro first team. However, few played beyond high school, and only Ziegler ever made money from the sport of football.

Ziegler went on to play at the University of Missouri for Al Onofrio, who took over as Tigers coach when Dan Devine left to become head coach of the National Football League's Green Bay Packers, then later at the University of Notre Dame. One of Ziegler's teammates was Ted Beckett, the star of the Kansas City Center team we defeated in the state championship game. In 1971, most college programs fielded a freshman team, as first-year players were ineligible for varsity games, an NCAA rule that was changed the following season for football and basketball. Ziegler led the Tigers' freshman team with 546 rushing yards in four games. He started at wing halfback for the varsity Tigers as a sophomore, but missed much of the season with injuries to an elbow and hamstring. As a junior and senior, Ziegler served as the primary blocker out of the I Formation option offense, blowing open holes for Tommy Reamon in 1973 and Tony Galbreath in 1974. In three seasons on the varsity, Ziegler accumulated 318 yards and two touchdowns rushing and 101 yards receiving.

Undrafted by the National Football League, he wrote letters to all the teams in the Canadian Football League in 1975, with the offer to send game films. The Calgary Stampeders responded, and signed him to their reserve "taxi" squad. In his second season, he made the team and played in the first five games as a slot back, mostly catching passes. However, once the NFL training camps began in the summer of 1976, his prospects dimmed. The players cut from the NFL rosters found their way to Canada, and bumped Ziegler first back to the taxi squad, then off the team. The next season he answered a call from the British Columbia Lions for a tryout, and made it to the last cut before being released.

"That was it," Ziegler said, his dream of professional football over. "I was married. It was time to get on with my life, and quit chasing the dream."

Bill Ziegler married JoAnn Sharamitaro, had four sons, and a long business career in St. Louis, and served as a referee for high school football games.

Errol Patterson, too, had more football in him. Among the fastest and most skilled players on our team, Patterson was a threat to our opponents' defenses with his dramatic touchdown pass receptions, and a menace to their offenses, with his TD-saving tackles. His kickoff return for a touchdown in the championship game against Kansas City Center, probably more than anything, gave us confidence we actually could win that game.

Patterson "walked on" to the football team at Purdue University and earned a scholarship, though he did not play very much. As a senior in 1974, he caught three passes for 45 yards and rushed twice for 23. After earning a degree in engineering, he began a career at Monsanto in St. Louis, then went on to earn a law degree from Georgetown University and to a successful career as an attorney in Washington, D.C., where he and his wife Nancy Pinto raised two children.

In 1976, probably the most enigmatic season in the history of the University of Missouri football team, Tim Gibbons was the Tigers' place-kicker. Mizzou upset the University of Southern California, Ohio State, and Nebraska that season, but lost to unheralded Iowa State and Kansas and finished 6-5. Gibbons scored 62 points with 13 field goals and 23 extra points. Gibbons did not play professionally. Today, he is a successful business executive in Kansas City, Missouri.

Mike Wiese received a scholarship from Southwest Missouri State College (now Missouri State University) in Springfield, but he had exhausted his love for the game in high school, and gave up the game after one season in college. He married Marie Sauer, with whom he raised two daughters, and retired in 2015 after 35 years as a civil servant, the last 25 as a mail carrier for the U.S. Postal Service.

Tom Schoeck received an appointment from U.S. Senator Stuart Symington (D-Missouri) to attend the U.S. Air Force Academy in Colorado Springs, Colorado. His brother Jim had preceded him there the year before, and they were football teammates once again. Tenacious as always but a bit undersized for NCAA Division I competition, Schoeck played as a defensive back on the Falcons' freshman team. A serious concussion that season ended Schoeck's football career, however. Schoeck married Donna Arunski, with whom he raised four sons, and had a successful career as a sales executive.

Al Fahrenhorst went on to play for Southern Illinois in Carbondale. Fahrenhorst had a long, successful career as a beer delivery truck driver in St. Louis.

62// *Beyond Football*

NONE OF THE REST of us from the Class of '71 played organized football again. Fred Daues, whose promising college prospects ended when his left knee was severely damaged mid-season, went on to marry Nancy Lee Elsner, with whom he raised a daughter and two sons, and took over the masonry and construction business his father had started in St. Louis.

In the summer before our senior year in high school, Del Bannister introduced Tim Kellett to Mary Powers, one of our favorite classmates from Epiphany elementary school. Mary and Tim married soon after college, had a son and two daughters, and Tim had a long career as an attorney in St. Louis.

Bob Thibaut went on to a successful career in industrial filmmaking and photography, and had one of his films for McDonnell-Douglas placed in the Library of Congress. After having two children with his first wife, he divorced then married Dennice Kowelman, with whom he lives in St. Louis.

Dan Calacci, our quarterback, went to Princeton University, where his free-spirited goofiness made an instant impression.

Calacci was the first among three randomly assigned freshmen roommates to arrive on campus, and was sound asleep near mid-day, after a night of carousing. He was awakened by a loud knock on his third-floor dorm room. This is how that first meeting was remembered by Brien O'Neill, who stood on the other side of the door with his parents, sister and girlfriend:

I'm not sure what I was expecting, but it certainly wasn't what I encountered. The door was pulled wide open and there on display before us was Dan. He sported a tussled, longish wavy mop of brown hair, and mutton-chop sideburns very much in sync with the fashion of the times. His slits-for-eyes betrayed the fact that our afternoon knocking had roused him from bed after what could only have been one intense night of campus partying. Many more such nights were to follow during the next four years.

But clearly the most noticeable aspect of Dan's appearance was what he was wearing, or, more accurately not wearing. Standing squarely in the center of the doorway, Dan was dressed in only underpants—briefs, as I recall—and nothing else.

O'Neill went on to describe the startled reactions on his side of the doorway, but recalled that Calacci "… merely smiled, introduced himself, and scratched his crotch."

That sounds about right. Carefree and self-confident, Calacci continued to "call his own plays." After Princeton, fluent in Chinese and anxious to gobble up life and the world in large bites and small, he taught English in Taiwan, worked as a photographer in Seattle, then for a railroad in Kansas City, and a bank in New York, and managed to get evicted from Japan. Later, anxious to turn his instinct for deal making into a career in banking and finance, Calacci went on to close deals across the globe, and to marry Debra Rawlins, with whom he had twins Daniel and Helen in 1993. In his mid-50s, he contracted a rare form of cancer. When I played golf with him in April of 2010, Calacci assured me he was pursuing an innovative plan to conquer it. Though he lost his life almost one year later, the disease had not changed him. In hospice care at the end, he cheered up visitors with his big smile and bravely spoke of ambitious plans for the next really big deal he wanted to do.

Two months after his death, a large crowd of family and friends filled the pews in the St. Louis U. High chapel for a service that celebrated Dan Calacci's life. Nearly 41 years earlier, in the same room, we had done the same for Ed Hawk.

St. Louis U. High has helped us carry on the memory and spirit of Ed Hawk with the annual presentation of an award in his name. With wording we crafted to honor him, by a vote of the senior class at the school, the Ed Hawk Award goes to the senior *who through his love and dedication to St. Louis University High School, and through his example of working and giving, was most able to influence his class toward success by cooperation and unity.*

Cancer also ended the life of Del Bannister, the day after Christmas in 2013. His widow Kathy told me his answer to the doctor's question about the President, which triggered my memory of the essay he had written in fifth grade. "I have that essay," Kathy said. "He kept everything." Kathy asked me to deliver his eulogy at a Mass we would celebrate in the remodeled gym at St. Louis U. High. In front of more than 600 mourners, I was able to explain how Del had evolved from his grand, youthful ambition to a more modest, but certainly no less meaningful contribution to his family, friends and community. Until the day I die, I will miss his friendship, his wit, his companionship, and his ability to lift the spirits of others.

Tim Rodgers married Mary Beth McInroy, with whom he raised a daughter and two sons. He believes his role as Chairman of the Student Council Spirit Committee in 1970-71 profoundly influenced his decision to enter advertising, a field in which he has won numerous accolades. He was inducted into the St. Louis Media Hall of Fame in 2015.

Phil Schaefer married Deb Bruemmer, his high school sweetheart, and stuck around in Columbia, Missouri after graduating from the University of Missouri. He started the Christian Fellowship, a nondenominational Christian church for which he has served as Pastor for more than three decades. Pastor Phil and Deb raised three sons.

After we graduated from St. Louis U. High in May of 1971, just about every one of my 209 classmates and I moved on to college and the next phase of our lives. The War in Vietnam, however, continued to lurk over us, like a dark cloud that just would not dissipate or drift away. For the next few months, we were exposed to the U.S. Selective Service and its looming, capricious draft lottery. We had to face the fact that the lives and careers we were planning could abruptly be changed forever by the bounce of a ping pong ball with a number painted on it.

The United States Selective Service System, an independent agency of the U.S. Government, manages the process of enrolling American citizens to serve in its military. In 1969, the Military Selective Service Act of 1967 was amended to enable conscription into the armed services based on a random lottery selection. The first draft lottery was held December 1, 1969. Young men in college were exempted until they earned a four-year degree or reached age 24. In 1971, the Act was amended to make registration compulsory for American males aged 18 to 35, and to end the provision for student deferments.

Remarkably, only one of my close football teammates pulled an unlucky ball, one with a low number that meant certain, immediate conscription into the Armed Services. Tim Fleming's heart sank when he learned his birthday had matched lottery ball Number 3.

The draft lottery reminded the reflective and pensive Fleming of Shirley Jackson's short story *The Lottery*[25]. Fleming observed of that story: "... *the citizens of a small town gathered each June 27 in the public square to draw random names out of a black box. The lottery 'winners' were stoned to death for no apparent reason.*"

"When my number—number 3 ... was chosen, I knew I was going

to be drafted," Fleming recalled. "What made me more agitated was that none of my SLUH brethren had a number that was in a similar position. They drew 'safe' numbers in the 200s or 300s, undraftable numbers. Not that I wished them ill, it's just that I had no one who understood what I was going through. It ravaged my confidence and self-worth, because for the first time in four years I was alone. My brothers could not help me out of this one."

On June 20, 1972, Fleming was drafted by the U.S. Army. He served and survived his military tenure, physically unharmed by the experience but affected by it nonetheless, especially since he had lost faith in the war, the military and his country. Fleming went on to marry, raise a son and daughter, divorce, remarry, and establish himself as an author and voice for those whose vision for America is progressive and liberal.

At Northwestern University, I followed the 1971 lottery with my close friends there. My birthday lottery number came up 357, which meant that for me to get drafted, we pretty much had to be in an intergalactic confrontation with Martians. How different would have been the lives of Tim Fleming and me, if in the less than 20 seconds it took to draw and read our draft lottery numbers, they would have been reversed?

"You lucky mother," was the message I received from my older brother Jim, whose college exemption was grandfathered while he attended Rockhurst University in Kansas City, Missouri. He had drawn lottery number 130 two years earlier, and that was very much in play in 1971. By the time he finished Rockhurst in 1973, the Vietnam War had decelerated and he was not drafted.

Like many other college students and others from our generation, I had come to oppose the Vietnam War and to distrust the narrative of the war advanced by Richard Nixon and our country's leadership. When President Nixon approved placing explosive mines in Haiphong Harbor in May of 1972, near North Vietnam's third most populous city, protests escalated on campuses through the United States. In Evanston, Illinois, I joined a group of fellow Northwestern University students as we gathered on Sheridan Road, the avenue that was the spine of the campus, and spontaneously marched to the home of Evanston resident Lester Crown. The son of iconic industrialist Henry Crown, Lester Crown had become president of the corporation that owned General Dynamics, one of the USA's primary suppliers of wartime hardware. There was a sense of history in the air, walking in solidarity for a cause. As someone opposed to the war, and as an aspiring journalist, I felt I had to be there. In this case, on a temperate May evening, our march ended without incident or apparent impact. Mr. Crown was not at home, we were told at the perimeter of his property. The timber was dry, but there was no spark that night. No "20 seconds of history" to be made.

There would be other gatherings of protest on our campus, other marches, but nothing matching the intensity of those in reaction to the 1970 Kent State tragedy two years before. Northwestern was among those universities closed in May of 1970, when students were dismissed and given "passing grades" for their incomplete classes in that spring quarter. Two years hence, while many sincere antiwar advocates marched to keep alive the momentum of the movement, many of those on Sheridan Road were there, selfishly and cynically, in hopes of another campus shutdown. Early summer vacation. It didn't happen.

Richard Nixon was re-elected President in a landslide in November of that year. In January of 1973, he announced that U.S. involvement in the Southeast Asia war would end. American troops were withdrawn, and in April 1975 the overmatched South Vietnamese Army conceded Saigon to the invading North Vietnamese troops. The peace movement, carried out significantly on the campuses of U.S. colleges, had a profound impact on the disposition of the war. More than 58,000 Americans lost their lives fighting the Vietnam War. And well more than an estimated one million

Vietnamese soldiers and civilians lost their lives during the conflict.

Among approximately 300 St. Louisans killed in Vietnam, eight were St. Louis U. High alumni, six who died before and one after Bob Wiese lost his life in February of 1970. Three were from the Class of 1965: Private Richard Heck, Sergeant Kenneth Watson, and Specialist Four Philip Reither Jr. Two were from the Class of 1962: 2nd Lieutenant Larry Dirnberger and 1st Lieutenant Tim LeClair. John Gates Spindler, Class of 1963, enrolled in the Marines soon after graduating from Washington University in 1967. The young lieutenant won two Purple Hearts for shrapnel wounds, and he survived the North Vietnamese Tet Offensive in 1968. However, he was killed by an enemy mortar shell near the Khe San combat base on April 21 of that year. He was 22 years old. Four years later, in May of 1972, U.S. Air Force First Lieutenant Michael Blassie, SLUH Class of 1966, was shot down while flying his A-37 attack plane on a combat mission during the Easter Offensive. He was 24.

Of course, not all the players on the 1970 St. Louis U. High state football championship team were pacifists or antiwar zealots. We were bonded by something *other* than our political dispositions, and in fact in *spite* of them. In Colorado Springs, Colorado, Tom Schoeck nobly wore the uniform of the United States Air Force as a cadet in the Air Force Academy.

"I recall the local citizens mocking us and calling us 'baby killers,'" said Schoeck, one of a generation of American soldiers who unfairly bore the misdirected brunt of those who had lost faith in the leadership of the country's political and military leadership.

63// *"I Didn't Get the Chance To Say Good-Bye"*

WHAYNE HERRIFORD MIGHT NEVER have dreamed the citizens of the United States would elect an African-American as President, as we did in 2008 and again in 2012. What Herriford finds much more surprising than Barack Obama's Presidency, is the sea change in tolerance for homosexuals in the United States and much of the world. In 1974, in its seventh printing of the *Diagnostic and Statistical Manual of Mental Disorders (DSM-II)*[26], the American Psychiatric Association no longer listed homosexuality as a category of "disorder." In DSM-5[27], published in May of 2013, the APA addresses gender identity differently, with an emphasis on the condition in which someone is intensely uncomfortable with his or her biological gender and strongly identifies with, and wants to be, the opposite gender. This incongruity is referred to as "gender dysphoria," and the focus is on the distress about the incongruity, not the gender identity itself.

Herriford feels fortunate to have witnessed these changes. Whayne decided to "come out" while a student at Antioch College in Yellow Springs, Ohio. He visited me at Northwestern when we were freshmen, and confidently told me the news. Confident, because he knew how I would react. He was my friend, my Blue Buddy, and he knew I would support him without judgment. Over the years, our lives were to take divergent roads, and I did not hear much from or about him, except through his cleverly worded annual Christmas letters. I had no idea how much he suffered, as a single gay man who longed for love, and stepped gingerly through the mine field of the AIDS epidemic that devastated gay communities throughout the country in the 1970s and '80s.

"I lost 30 to 40 close friends" during that period, Whayne said. "I was one of the lucky ones."

Among those who perished were an ex, whose ashes he dispersed in the Pacific Ocean, and another lover whose memorial service he could not attend because his partner's family did not know about them. "I didn't get the chance to say good-bye," Herriford said.

In June of 2015, after 37 states and the District of Columbia had passed legislation affirming the lawfulness of same-sex marriage, the U.S. Supreme Court ruled that acceptance, at least legally, was to prevail across the entire country.

After Antioch College, Herriford earned a Masters in Business Administration from Stanford University, then pursued a many-faceted career in human resources, mostly in California. Later in life, he took an abrupt career turn, when he felt a strong call to service. He earned credentials as a psychotherapist at Northern Kentucky University, and served as a treatment counselor for individuals, couples and families. Along the way, he adopted two teenaged sons in desperate need of a caring, concerned father. Today, he heads Talent Management for a foundation in Cincinnati.

64// *"An Island of Purpose"*

CIVIL RIGHTS AND RACE RELATIONS have progressed substantially in the decades since my classmates and I first became aware of them in the late 1950s. However, while our City of St. Louis avoided rioting that scarred major U.S. cities in racial confrontations in the 1960s, our streets erupted in the hot summer of 2014 in response to the shooting death of an African-American teenaged crime suspect by a white officer of the Ferguson, Missouri Police Department. The locus of the violence was not very far from where we had played football games against McCluer and Riverview Gardens.

More than 50 years after the violence on the Edmund Pettus Bridge in Selma, Alabama, we still struggle with poverty, anger, prejudice, and hate as we try to figure out what to do about millions of disenfranchised, desperate young black men in our country. Certainly, most Americans acknowledge that black lives matter. But sides remain in the pursuit of racial equality, with one side struggling to explain, and the other to understand, how progress is advanced by a campaign labeled "Black Lives Matter." The recommendations from the work of President Lyndon Johnson's Kerner Commission, published in 1968, appear to remain relevant and under-delivered: *investment in housing that would better integrate neighborhoods, creation of new jobs, and hiring more diverse and sensitive police forces.*

Yeah, the world HAS changed a lot in the five decades since I first contemplated the grand and glorious ways I personally would improve it, as I was getting to know my classmates at St. Louis University High School in the late summer of 1967. The American War in Vietnam ended in 1975, and we have made our peace with the Vietnamese people. Despite the fall of Vietnam, there was no "domino" effect, and the influence of communism has diminished in Asia and Europe. Racial relations have progressed, punctuated by our election of Barack Obama as President in 2008 and 2012. The role and influence of women in communities, government, sports and business have grown dramatically. With the advance of science and technology, and the benevolent leadership of talented people, we are living through a remarkable reduction of poverty in the world, and we have found significant ways to reduce polluting our air, land and water.

Yeah, the world still is not fixed. Franz Kafka, the early 20th century fiction author from Prague, who wrote of alienation, absurdity, feelings of senselessness, disorientation, and helplessness in the early part of the 20th century, once said, "In man's struggle against the world, bet on the world."

We still have mortal combat, as battles are waged over territory, resources, ideologies, religion, or causes that are unclear or poorly articulated. People continue to die of starvation and curable diseases, because they do not have access to food, clean water or medicine. People continue to discriminate, bully, hate and perpetrate violence on others. And as Pope Francis, the first Jesuit Pope in history, has emphasized in his pointed 2015 encyclical, *Laudato Si*[28], we are not doing enough to preserve our planet for future generations.

Every year, hundreds of high school state champions are crowned across the United States. In that context, what was so remarkable about our football state championship in 1970? How can I explain the grip that experience has had on me? Certainly, the world offers more serious and more important endeavors to challenge and enrich our lives. Football is just a game. And we were just kids. I'm pretty sure none of my teammates ever sensed the desperation expressed by the alcoholic father challenging his running back son to seize the moment in the movie *Friday Night Lights*, as he warned it would be a final opportunity to accomplish something.

We had greater aspirations for our lives beyond high school, and most of us have achieved successful careers, with the support of loving families. And yet, that season will endure for many of us as a highlight of our lives.

Having spent the early part of my working career as a sportswriter, witnessing and chronicling the accomplishments of athletes under the pressure of competition on much grander stages, I have come to appreciate just how thin can be the difference between winning and losing. How fickle and random can be the bounces of the ball or puck, and thus how serendipitous is the designation of "champion" for history's record books. Heck, our basketball and baseball teams were much better candidates for a state championship in 1970-71 than our football team. And yet we reign and they do not.

Then, too, there is the nature of accepting history's invitation. Of being prepared. Of doing what one can, so that one is ready to act when those dramatic few seconds of history are ignited. There are those who seek out history, attempt to leave a mark of significance, and gain the attention of the public. More typically, I'd say, it happens the other way around, when history seeks its own course, and shoves itself in front of someone who might or might not be ready for it. Most of the time, we are just spectators, going along for the ride. As a 16-year-old junior in high school, Jim Dohr was quite unaware that history would soon tee him up, when he walked to the sideline for the CBC-SLUH game at Busch Stadium in November of 1970. Except for his limited role on special teams, Dohr was not expecting to see any action from the line of scrimmage. Less than two hours later, his 80-yard pass reception and touchdown won the game for us, and saved our season.

"If I dropped the pass, you wouldn't be writing a book about it," Dohr said, many years later. "It's part of the fabric of who I am. It's part of the journey of life that I've carried with me all these years."

Dohr went on to success as chief executive officer of a major real estate firm in St. Louis, with a loving wife and two children. Not someone who dwells on the past, Dohr reflected about the moment's proper place in his life.

"Did it change my life?" he said. "I don't know. So many people have talked to me about it. My mother talked about that moment her whole life after that. It almost got to be a little embarrassing. But no question, it was a very thrilling moment. I was lucky. I was in the right place at the right time. Of all things, catching this pass that led to the only state championship in the school history. Those 10 seconds of my life."

Gary Kornfeld knows how random, and cruel, can be the bounce of the football. In 1991, his Junior Billikens had the opportunity to win the school's *second* state championship, as they were engaged in a close battle with the Jefferson City Jays in the title game. Late in the game with the score tied, SLUH was driving downfield into scoring position. Interference on a SLUH receiver, obvious to most but not flagged, likely would have yielded, at worst, a final score of 7-7 and a co-championship. SLUH attempted but missed a field goal into a strong wind, and Jefferson City got another chance. After a long pass completion into SLUH territory, the Jays kicked the winning field goal.

"It took me six months to get over it," Kornfeld said. I think he's *still* not over it.

After the game, SLUH Athletic Director Dick Wehner visited with his coach. The two understood how difficult it was to get that far. "You don't know if you'll ever get back, will you?" Wehner said. "No," Kornfeld replied, "I don't."

Dick Keefe thought our senior class was special, and the football championship was a fitting accomplishment.

"Your class seemed to have a cohesiveness to it," Keefe said. "It seemed like pretty much everyone was upbeat most of the time, or all of the time, and they got along together. They liked each other. I was there a long time. Some classes stand out in my memory, and were unique. I think the football season contributed to that spirit and cohesiveness. I think that was a big part of it. The tradition. Trying hard. Winning and succeeding. It takes a student body with a strong self-image to pull that off. At the same time, your class had a sensitive side, a thoughtful side. If they weren't on the team, it didn't matter. It was still a big deal."

Like Dick Keefe, Bob Thibaut believes our team had a distinctive character. An inclusiveness, a camaraderie, a touch of sensitivity that maybe other football teams do not have.

"We felt," he said. "We had feeling. You know, we had feelings for each other, and I think it did bring us together as a team. We were never bullies. There wasn't a bully on the team. We respected women. It was more than just the football players. Even guys not on the team were part of the whole experience."

For Tim Fleming, our championship season provided profound significance.

"With upheaval swirling around us in the outside world," he recalled, "I found an island of purpose in that season. I believed not one pronouncement coming from Nixon's White House, not any contrived justification for Vietnam, nor any utterance from my father on the matter, nor any bogus investigation of the assassinations … but I did believe in you and Calacci and Twombly and Bubba and Rojo and Wiese and Ziegler and Errol and Thibaut. In the end faith won out. Corny maxims took the day … 50 guys together cannot be beaten. We did not make many mistakes, we fought like wildcats, and we just knew. I'm still not certain why we were that way, and what made us bond the way we did. Pride? Doggedness? The fear we would let each other down? Maybe it was just faith. Jumping off the cliff and believing the net is there, because 49 others will not let you fall."

Tim Kellett has a similar sentiment.

"While we seemed to be in the middle of chaos around us," he said, "we fell back on football as kind of a respite. Football was old school, and we were vacillating between that and a world of war, drugs, long hair, volatile race relations and other issues. With football, it was one of the few times in life where it's absolute. The definition of 'success' in most endeavors is not black and white, but various shades of grey and subject to one's own interpretation, bordering on manipulation. However, in August 1970, hundreds of young men in Missouri, supported by thousands of friends and family members, started football practice having as their ultimate definition of success, winning the Missouri Class 4A state football championship. At the end of the day on November 28, 1970, there was only one group of young men who could make that claim. It was indisputable. No grey areas. You are the best. The key was the team concept. There was a lot of individual sacrifice, but a feeling of incredible satisfaction that we personally earned the right to be a contributor to the team, with a group of guys that I loved then and love now. I can honestly say there was not one guy on the team that I disliked. I was closer to some than others, but I can go down the roster and remember positive, friendly, and goofy interactions with all of them. I think that is something that was really unique and special to this group. Maybe it sounds trite, but I never wanted to let them down."

65// *A September to December to Remember*

AS I LOOK BACK over the years, I examine my own track record of getting involved to confront social injustice, and must humbly submit a thin resume. I wonder if Elie Wiesel would have judged me harshly for not seeking out a broader stage on which to tangle with the injustice that persists. A survivor of the Nazi concentration camps whose parents and sister perished there, Wiesel spent much of his life imploring citizens to get involved: "... when you witness an injustice, don't stand idly by. When you hear of a person or a group being persecuted, do not stand idly by. When there is something wrong in the community around you—or far away—do not stand idly by. You must intervene. You must interfere."[29]

It is true of me, and I'd say of most of my classmates, that we have done little to bend the grand arc of world history. Del Bannister did *not* become President of the United States, his aspiration as a fifth grader. Like just about everybody in the world, we got sidetracked by our daily lives.

However, long before Del's deathbed reply to his doctor, who had asked him to name the President, I had come to realize it was I who had it all wrong. Del's reply (*"You mean, of the U. High?"*), which he delivered in one of his last moments of earthly consciousness and with one of his last gasps of breath, aptly reflected the change in his focus, made many years earlier, when he realized his effort to "change the world" would be conducted on a very local, very personal, very meaningful stage. No, Del Bannister never became President of the United States. Instead, he became a faithful husband to Kathy Gorla and loving father to his two sons and daughter, and worked his whole career facilitating business and community development in his beloved City of St. Louis. I have come to understand and accept that a youthful ambition to "change the world" was, for me, simply a desire to live a meaningful life.

Contemporary journalist Roger Cohen presented a compelling perspective on heroism and fame, in a column he wrote for the *New York Times*, published October 23, 2014:

> *A core problem with the modern world is that we have heroism all wrong ...*
> *I am less interested in the firefighter-hero and the soldier-hero ... than I am*
> *in the myriad doers of everyday good who would shun the description heroic.*

Born in 1955 to Jewish parents who had emigrated from South Africa to England, Cohen served as *New York Times* European economic correspondent in Paris in the early 1990s, then became the newspaper's bureau chief for the Balkan countries, based in Zagreb, Croatia, from April 1994 to June 1995. He covered the Bosnian War and the Bosnian Genocide. He later was bureau chief in Berlin when the U.S. was attacked by suicidal jihadists on September 11, 2001, and he supervised the paper's coverage of the War in Afghanistan. Cohen has been witness to history and the brave acts of men and women thrust into its crucible moments. And yet he advocates for the less dramatic, much more ordinary contributions of ordinary people. In doing so, he refers to Albert Camus, one of the existentialist authors we studied in Father Rich Bailey's *Philosophy & Religion* course in 1970-71. Cohen continues:

> *In Camus' book, "The Plague[30]," one of the most powerful moments comes in an exchange between the doctor at the center of the novel, Bernard Rieux, and a journalist named Raymond Rambert. Rieux has been battling the pestilence day after day, more often defeated than not. Rambert has been dreaming of, and plotting, escape from the city to be reunited with his loved one. Rieux suddenly speaks his mind:*
>
> *"I have to tell you this: this whole thing is not about heroism. It's about decency. It may seem a ridiculous idea, but the only way to fight the plague*

is with decency."

"'What is decency?' Rambert asked, suddenly serious."

"In general, I can't say, but in my case I know that it consists of doing my job."

Cohen identifies with Camus and his protagonist.

I prefer the approach to life summed up by Camus as active fatalism. The true hero is the unsung one who does his or her daily shift, puts food on the table for the children, gives them an education and a roof over their heads ...

I suppose that by taking solace in the words of Roger Cohen, I am rationalizing the fact that the youth of a Baby Boomer infused by idealized dreams of fixing the world in grand strokes has evolved into the twilight of a life marked by compromise, concessions to what happens when one actually has to play the cards dealt in the hand one holds.

Leo Tolstoy once wrote, "Everyone thinks of changing the world, but no one thinks of changing himself."

I was not very good at mastering Tolstoy's Mother Tongue, despite studying the Russian language for four years at St. Louis U. High (though I'm your man if you need to ask Nina where she is going and to be able to understand if she answers, *"To the post office, to mail a letter"*). I am capable, however, of being guided by the author's admonition about "changing myself." Del Bannister had that one figured out. This ambition is much more in line with what Roger Cohen advocates. Most of us live ordinary lives, it turns out. Also, I have come to believe, the world can be improved but never fixed by its earthly inhabitants.

Catholic Church doctrine acknowledges that an evil devil exists in our world. As Camus' Dr. Rieux did by addressing *The Plague* with the weapon of "decency," we can confront this evil or endeavor to avoid it. Or, as some believe, even exorcise it from one it happens to possess. But it is not within our power to defeat it, any more than we can defeat our physical death. We can live healthier lives, and we can discover cures to the maladies that afflict our bodies. But we will then die from something else. That doesn't mean life is hopeless. Just the opposite.

Rick Warren, the evangelical Christian preacher and pastor who founded Saddleback Church, a "megachurch" in Lake Forest, California, and the author of *A Purpose Driven Life*[31], offered this take on the concept:

> *I used to think that life was hills and valleys—you go through a dark time, then you go to the mountaintop, back and forth. I don't believe that anymore. Rather than life being hills and valleys, I believe that it's kind of like two rails on a railroad track, and at all times you have something good and something bad in your life. No matter how good things are in your life, there is always something bad that needs to be worked on. And no matter how bad things are in your life, there is always something good you can thank God for.*

That is a powerful and insightful perspective, perhaps inevitable for a man who has enjoyed the phenomenal success of his ministry and endured the tragic reality of his wife's cancer and their son's suicide in 2013. Also, it is a testimony to a strong faith in God.

Accepting the inevitability of evil, of loss, of malice, of disappointment, of death, I believe it is possible to appreciate even more the beauty of the world, the kindnesses of others, the good fortune that sometimes falls our way. Certainly, I have been blessed with the good fortune of employers who tolerated, valued and often rewarded my dominant trait of *curiosity*. I find it curious, if not ironic, that I had a long, successful career in the beer business at Anheuser-Busch, whose Budweiser and other brands my father and grandfather sold at their corner taverns one and two generations before. Certainly, I was lucky to have loving and supportive parents and siblings; a daughter Alison and son Adam whose kind spirits draw others to them; more than three decades in the embrace of the wonderfully life-affirming and buoyant Lyn Palecek Castellano; and loyal pals who are always available to listen or laugh. I, too, am blessed to have been the older brother of Steve Castellano, who accepted his fate of a learning disability, bipolar manic depression, diabetes, kidney disease, a chronic cellulitis infection, and a regimen of psych medicine that exacerbated his morbid obesity. He never asked for or expected much, and was content with a good meal, a visit with family or friends, or the opportunity to go fishing. Steve died suddenly in the spring of 2015, when his big heart gave out. More than ever, I can appreciate a simple accomplishment, pursued in earnest, with a disciplined and relentless resolve, in the company of people about whom you care a great deal.

Maybe that, more than anything, explains the grip that a 1970 Missouri state high school football championship has on a group of aging Baby Boomers, many years after they responded to history's invitation with an improbable answer—beating the odds to carve our names into Missouri high school football history.

More aware than ever of the loud clicks of my life clock's second hand, I am confronted with thoughts of fame, purpose, the meaning of life. Winning a high school football state championship is hardly a "change the world" endeavor. It is audacious and self indulgent to believe it deserves even a footnote in history. And yet, there it is, occupying a significant piece of territory in the real estate of my life, and of the lives of many of my classmates who lived that season with me.

Certainly, my classmates and I have done many significant things in our lives. Yet, too, we must acknowledge our failures, our shortcomings, our lost potential. Our humanness. Within my group of close friends, we have had divorces, battles with addiction and severe depression, personal tragedies, career disappointments, and crises of faith. Throughout our lives, we have been running that "Bull in the Ring" drill—staggering to our feet after each blow, readying ourselves for whatever comes next. This is why I wanted to write this book. Not to celebrate the wonderfulness of us, but to offer the perspective that the reward came from the work, not from the title. We were lucky to win a championship.

About 20 of us meet regularly in a Manresan Society group, named for the location in Spain where St. Ignatius deepened his spiritual commitment after his devastating battle injury. Not all played on our football team, but all were a part of our championship season. We mourn our classmates who died, and sometimes wonder why they went first. Our politics stretch from Left to Right, and while that often animates our conversations, it does not threaten the bond we forged nearly a half century earlier. We meet in a room next to the North American Martyrs Chapel at St. Louis U. High, where we went to Mass after football games many years ago, and we continue our spiritual journeys. Rarely, but occasionally, we reminisce.

It is almost as if Father Jack Warner *knew* we would be sitting in such a room at this time in our lives, when he selected and directed *The Fantasticks*[32] at St. Louis U. High, the same autumn we were living through our state championship season. At the conclusion of the musical, our classmate Steve Keller, playing El Gallo, sings wistfully:

> *Deep in December, it's nice to remember,*
> *Although you know the snow will follow.*
> *Deep in December, it's nice to remember:*
> *Without a hurt the heart is hollow.*
> *Deep in December, it's nice to remember*
> *The fire of September that made us mellow*
> *Deep in December, our hearts should remember,*
> *And follow.*

66// *"She Understands"*

ERROL PATTERSON HAS OFTEN WONDERED, "What if we had lost? Would we just have erased that memory? Would we have pushed it into the background?"

As he reflects on his professional career and life as a husband and father, he retains a special place for the championship he won as a teenager.

"Whatever failure I've had in life since, at least we had the championship," he said. "It's always the thing you can come back to, when other things didn't turn out the way I wanted."

That season, that experience, represented goodness in our chaotic world. Most of us had a powerful faith in God, and a powerful faith in each other. Neither, we understood, assured or triggered victory. But they provided a meaningful context, and gave us a quiet confidence. Tim Fleming calls it "an island of purpose." It was our response to the improbable opportunity presented to us, when any one of dozens of slight variances surely would have altered the outcome for the worse. Things tended to go our way during those random "10 to 30 seconds of history" that confronted us. The experience has been an ongoing source of sustenance for many of my teammates and me over the many years that have passed. It stirred something in us, and has lasted for decades, as a place to go for perspective, for reassurance.

In retrospect, Paul Martel seems to have known all this, when as a 45-year-old head coach he understood what a team sport could do for young men. Confident in his authority, undaunted by those in our generation who tended to disrespect and challenge those in his, Coach Martel was steadfast in the beliefs he held and advocated about football, about competition, about life.

In what I have described as his "manifesto," he expressed this insight:

Other important values which are intrinsic to the game of football include: learning the meaning of and developing an appreciation for discipline, sacrifice, courage, work, determination and teamwork; for being able to get up and come back after being knocked down; for fighting to the end when others quit and are forgotten, for having given so much that you cannot give anymore—but you do; and for having the confidence and "heart," so that when the occasion calls for doing the impossible, you will do it.

I know now, as he knew then, that was about much more than football. For me, all that turned out to be true. And it would have been true, even if we had lost that championship game. While hard work and preparation do not guarantee anyone success, I would say it is unusual and unsatisfying for success to come without them. Of course, winning just made it sweeter. Indeed, Paul Martel prepared me well for the life I would confront. Many times I have drawn on that experience for insights into leadership, teamwork, perseverance, faith, and friendship. The result never changes, as we always will have won that championship. Yes, there is something comforting about that. It was an extraordinary accomplishment in our otherwise rather ordinary lives.

I think of Errol Patterson and Tim Kellett embracing after the final whistle of my football career, a moment after we clinched the 1970 Missouri state title. Two 17-year-olds. One, an African-American whose parents had moved him to St. Louis to get him out of the turmoil of central Alabama in the mid-1960s, parents who heard but ignored the racial epithets uttered in the stands while watching our games. The other, a white resident of stereotypical white suburbia Webster Groves, the son of a physician and housewife. Just three months after Ed Hawk, our classmate and friend, was murdered on a street in our hometown, less than three miles from our high school. Two teenage boys, filthy and exhausted, clutched each other in joy.

"It was the best hug I've ever had," Patterson recalled many years later. He said that in the presence of Nancy Pinto, who by that time had been his wife of 29 years. She smiled. "She understands," Errol said.

Endnotes

1 *Palisades Park* Copyright © 1962, 1982 by Claridge Music Company, a division of MPL Communications, Inc.

2 *The Fantasticks: 30th Anniversary Edition* Copyright © 1964, 1990, by Tom Jones and Harvey Schmidt

3 *The Fantasticks: 30th Anniversary Edition* Copyright © 1964, 1990, by Tom Jones and Harvey Schmidt

4 *Witness to the Revolution* Copyright © 2016 by Clara Bingham

5 *My Life with the Saints* Copyright © 2006 by James Martin, SJ

6 Commencement address by Elie Wiesel at Washington University (St. Louis) 2011

7 *Eve of Destruction* by P.F. Sloan, Copyright © 1965 University Music Corporation

8 *Revolution* by John Lennon & Paul McCartney, © Copyright 1968 Northern Songs Limited, 19 Upper Brook St., London W1

9 *For What It's Worth* by Stephen Stills, Copyright © 1966 (renewed) Cotillion Music Inc., Ten East Music, Springaloo Toones and Richie Furay Music

10 *Street Fighting Man* by The Rolling Stones, Copyright © 1968 ABKCO Music Inc.

11 *16 in Webster Groves*, Copyright © 1966 by Columbia Broadcasting System

12 *The Fantasticks: 30th Anniversary Edition* Copyright © 1964, 1990, by Tom Jones and Harvey Schmidt

13 *Abraham, Martin and John* by Dick Holler, Copyright © 1968, Regent Music Corp. (BMI) and Beardsley Tunes

14 *Concussion* Copyright © 2015 Columbia Pictures Industries, Inc., LSC Film Corporation Village Roadshow Films Global, Inc.

15 *McLintock!* © 2006 Paramount Pictures Corporation

16 *The Fantasticks: 30th Anniversary Edition* Copyright © 1964, 1990, by Tom Jones and Harvey Schmidt

17 *No Exit* by Jean Paul Sartre, Copyright © Alfred A. Knopf, Inc., renewed 1976 by Alfred A. Knopf, Inc.

18 *The Exorcist*, Copyright © 1971 by William Peter Blatty

19 *Our Mission Today: the Service of Faith and the Promotion of Justice,* Rev. Pedro Arrupe S.J., 32nd General Congregation of the Society of Jesus in 1975

20 *The Mod Squad*, Thomas-Spelling Productions

21 *Diagnostic and Statistical Manual of Mental Disorders (DSM-1)*, Copyright © 1952 American Psychiatric Association

22 *Na Na Hey Hey Kiss Him Goodbye* by Gary DeCarlo, Paul Leka and Dale Fraushuer, Copyright © 1969 by M.R.C. Music, Inc.

23 *Friday Night Lights*, story by Buzz Bissinger, screenplay by Peter Berg & Aaron Cohen, a Universal Picture, © 2004 Universal Studios

[24] *Friday Night Lights, A Town, a Team, and a Dream* Copyright © 1990 by H.G. Bissinger, Afterword copyright © 2015 by H.G. Bissinger

[25] *The Lottery* by Shirley Jackson, Copyright © 1948, 1949 by Shirley Jackson, Copyright renewed © 1976, 1977 by Laurence Hyman, Copyright © 2016 by Miles Hyman

[26] *Diagnostic and Statistical Manual of Mental Disorders (DSM-II)*, Copyright © 1974 American Psychiatric Association

[27] *Diagnostic and Statistical Manual of Mental Disorders (DSM-5)*, Copyright © 2013 American Psychiatric Association

[28] *Laudato Si* by Pope Francis, Encyclical Letter copyright © 2015 Libreria Editrice Vaticana

[29] Commencement address by Elie Wiesel at Washington University (St. Louis) 2011

[30] *The Plague* by Albert Camus, Copyright © 1948 by Stuart Gilbert, Copyright renewed 1975 by Stuart Gilbert

[31] *A Purpose Driven Life* by Rick Warren, Copyright © 2002 by Rick Warren

[32] *The Fantasticks: 30th Anniversary Edition* Copyright © 1964, 1990, by Tom Jones and Harvey Schmidt

About the Author

Before author Joe Castellano spent the majority of his professional career as a business executive at Anheuser-Busch, the
international beer company, he was an award-winning writer
for the *St. Louis Globe-Democrat* newspaper. Currently, he works
as a business and personal career counselor in St. Louis. He
believes his professional career was greatly influenced by his
experience as a member of the overachieving St. Louis U. High
football team in 1970, which he chronicles in his memoir *Bull
in the Ring*. Castellano and his wife Lyn live in St. Louis, as do
his two married children and his grandson.

Made in the USA
Middletown, DE
17 August 2017